# The
# Angry
# Eye

PERGAMON
PRESS
AUSTRALIA

# THE ANGRY EYE Max Harris

introduced by RUPERT MURDOCH

First published in Australia in 1973
by Pergamon Press (Australia) Pty. Limited
P.O. Box 54 Potts Point NSW 2011
© 1963-1973 Max Harris
Set in 10 point Optima type face leaded 1 point
Printed by Brown Prior Anderson Pty Ltd
National Library of Australia Card Number
and ISBN  0  080  17373  X
Designed by Vane Lindesay
Registered in Australia for transmission by post as a book

**Acknowledgements**   Most of these pieces appeared in *The Australian* and *Nation*. Grateful acknowledgement is made to these journals for having commissioned and published this material during the past ten years.

# Contents

THE OPINION JOURNALIST IN AUSTRALIA

**Introduction** I can be said to have a special interest in the work of Max Harris because I have known him for many years and have been publishing him in *The Australian* for the past ten of those years. He was, in fact, a founder member of *The Australian* team.

In that time I have sometimes had to defend myself against people who found him excessively critical of the Australian political, social, literary and artistic establishment.

But I think every society needs a Max, to identify its successes as well as its failures, its forlorn hopes and its lost causes. And also to shake it out of its smugness and hypocrisy, to act as a catalyst and an irritant. Possibly Australia needs the iconoclast more than most countries, at this stage of its history. But Max's abrasive quality would lose its value if he did not write as wittily and well as he does.

There are few aspects of Australian life which have not at one time or another claimed his attention. Every year he leaves his home base in Adelaide to cast a cold eye over Europe. His interests range widely, and because he is such a prolific writer whatever interests him turns up in print, to interest others. In this collection of articles from *The Australian* he manages to actually relate such an improbable variety of subjects as from punctuation to behavioural psychology.

I have always thought Max to be in some ways the victim of his own fan club; that is, he is admired too much for the ferocious style in which he debunks pretentious people and ideas, and not enough for his creative solutions for the ills he diagnoses.

Let me say finally that although I don't always agree with Max I always enjoy him.

**RUPERT MURDOCH**

# THE OPINION
# JOURNALIST
# IN AUSTRALIA

A writer who works within the medium of the newspaper is a sort of one-armed pugilist. He loses all the contests on points. He endures so many knockouts that he retires from the game with a ga-ga head. Or he develops some pretty fancy footwork, goes with the punches when they can't be avoided, and lives to make an appearance on the feature bill next week.

This is the literary law of life in journalism, and it applies even in the few educated English language newspapers, even if there may be a few honourable exceptions. But I do not know. The reader may be deceived by the speed of their footwork.

I am, of course, referring to that rarely-ventilated subject of freedom *in* the press, as against that dreary bleat about freedom *of* the press.

And by writer I am not referring to the professional working journalist. He knows the ground rules when he takes up employment, and indeed, as he rises in the ranks it becomes his job to apply the most desperately difficult censorship tasks in the whole of that distasteful field.

The whole machinery of a newspaper is fairly largely a censorship apparatus—omission, suppression, alteration, change of stress and emphasis. Even the gathering of material, which would appear to be largely determined by political, physical, or cultural event, is subject to a highly sensitive selectivity. At any given moment there is a vast papal index of subjects which for a weird diversity of reasons a newspaper does not wish to deal with at any given time.

The working journalist comes to live with it. That is '9 to 5' trade.

The writer is another matter. If he is on staff he is in 'features'. If he is not on staff he is a 'contributor'. A newspaper writer, as against a journalist, deals with interpretation and opinion.

He plays the one-armed game in that he enters the ring never quite sure what the Queensberry rules are for that particular day, week, or year. It is not merely that he may have produced a paean of praise for the immortal qualities of a prime minister when editorial policy is to expose the defects of that political gentleman, or any such conflict between editorial policy and personal journalistic opinion. One quickly learns to sniff out these areas of incompatability and avoid them by writing about something else.

There are other, and more subtle shifts in the ground rules which occur constantly and invisibly. At any given moment a newspaper policy may either favour or implacably oppose the use of certain literary skills—satire, irony, mockery, anger, edge, intensity, verbal entertainment, scholarship, distinguished or distinctive writing, vulgar truthfulness, or even simple human sensitivity of response.

My own case is an interesting one in that I have survived for a great length of time in Australia's world of highly constricted opinion journalism. It goes back to the 1940's when, in association with John Reed and the late Jack Bellew, we launched Australia's first modern example of the political opinion newspaper. *Tomorrow* was short-lived, and it was a long time before Harold Levien's *Voices*, Donald Horne's *Observer* and, most memorable of them all, Tom Fitzgerald's *Nation* followed in its wake. With the *Bulletin* updated, Australia suddenly became rich in opinion journalism, and demand tended to exceed the supply in terms of writers who could interpret the social and cultural environment to an ever larger spread of non-specialist readers.

This era of idealistic initiatives in the 1960's provided a vast training ground for writers to develop the appropriate skills in literate and yet public communication.

This was Australia's cultural revolution. This was the source of Gough Whitlam's new and sophisticated nationalism. Except that this was the obverse of Mao's cultural revolution—the Australian Labor Party absorbed the new and liberal intellectualism of the decade through painfully slow osmosis; the Liberal Party preferred to turn a Nelson-eye to the whole phenomenon.

But the spread of this new critical and interpretative process was irresistible and infectious. It spilled over into the publishing industry and the early part of the decade became the Golden Age of Australian publishing.

We are still too close to the events to comprehend that it was a cultural revolution of extraordinary dimensions. The time will come when sociologists will turn their attention to this particular period and establish just how the cultural egg preceded the political hen. How a grass-roots need for a national intellectualism erupted and, like the mills of God, ground away at the petrified modes of political thought.

It is an even more complex process to trace the seeds of this growth back to the 1940's. The ideologies of national imagination and intellectual dissent were the motivating forces behind the Australian modernist painting movement, and the time may come when scholarship will link the Angry Penguins movement in more detail and more sympathetically with Australia's ultimate cultural maturation. That is as may be.

The point is that the coincidence of these forces led to the foundation of *The Australian* just on exactly ten years ago. This was the point at which my own sporadic and occasional involvement with opinion journalism became curious. I commenced writing with the first issue of *The Australian* and have continued to do so every week for ten years. Instead of a slow decrease of commitment through overexposure and an exhaustion of ideas, this field of activity led to a record-breaking stint of opinion work in regional television, and a home-spun page in South Australia's *Sunday Mail*.

These biographical details I trust are not purely egocentric, but lead to an interesting question of some importance to the Australian intellectual future.

I am the oldest living survivor on *The Australian*. My personal survival for 520 weeks is freakish. It has involved fancy footwork, a capacity for humiliation, and a blunted edge of sensibility. The price has seemed worth it, for interpretative journalism, rather than hard news, is what the future of the popular printed word is all about.

Over a decade *The Australian* may have changed character, intention, and direction with bewildering unpredictability. It was possible to be angry, outraged, zestful, enthusiastic, stylish, urbane, or vulgar. And it was all published—the whole conglomerate of energies coming together to make a newspaper unlike anything Australia had experienced before. But these abandoned days of wine and roses could not go on for ever. The ground rules shifted and changed from month to month and year to year. In the days of experimentalism and idealism I found myself writing up football grand finals, and even in retrospect I regard these forays into a literature of sport stylishly and stylistically satisfying.

Over the span of the decade it became necessary for the newspaper to maximise its spread of readership with ruthless editorial precision in order to survive financially. From my point of view the pressures of censorship were more literary than thematic. By Australian standards I was always permitted a maximum range of critical interest—the only intensely frustrating limitation being the principle of dog does not eat dog, and that a critic of the national culture shall never analyse the press itself. The freedom of the press under no circumstances (and I tried many times) extends to the freedom to examine the press. Even so, the freedom to operate critically as a critic did not fall far short of that accorded to a Bernard Levin or a Katherine Whitehorn, in the world-famous 'heavies' of Britain.

But when the editorial blue-pencil is guided by the demands of readership spread, then press censorship is more abjectly directed at the way of writing than by the substance of what is written. Thus polemical literate journalism is not favoured, whereas it is the editorial bread and butter of the sub-literate tabloids. Stylishness and wit, if not transparently clear to readers who scan rather than read, are inclined to encounter a heavy stroke of the blue pencil.

One sympathises with the editors who have to deal with such contributor material. They were not always wrong. Those who were wrong emasculated individualistic style and viewpoint because they were uneducated men. They felt variations from the standard prosaic of journalistic writing were acts of showing off. Those who were right tightened the substance of the discussion or lowered the emotional key because the effectiveness of communication in newspaper terms could thus be improved.

My own chosen task, over the years, has been less fraught with such dangers. I cannot build too much anger or too much pity into what I write for the public press—for the emotions are regarded as not relevant to the kind of communication a reader expects from the daily written word. However, I have always seen my main concern as being the act of cultural diagnosis. I am most interested in trying to define what is happening in the Australian ethos at any given moment, and in establishing what it means. These days there are many such specialists in defining the state of the national culture and the national consciousness. Dozens of writers have essayed books on the subject—some excellent, most atrocious (because the views are instant and impressionistic rather than the result of a long view of the historical process).

My weekly task in *The Australian* has had the advantage of being continuous and geared to both major and minor day-by-day events. I have had the chance to illuminate the macrocosm through the microcosm. Such pieces, of course, have a short atomic half-life. Circumstances change. The cast of characters varies at high speed. Hot issues become dead ducks, to mix a metaphor. It is therefore a matter for the reader to decide if such pieces have a value either as history or as constituting a general cultural value-system in the national context. I am uncertain about this, but the experiment seems worth making.

There is a final generalisation which concerns the reading community. Newspapers were once the gatherers of information and the source of our news of the world. We learned what was happening in the world at our breakfast table or on the afternoon train. This was pre-McLuhan. We are now in the age of instant news. Through television we are enriched by the extra dimension of visualised events. By the time one opens a newspaper in such an age, the events themselves are stale. In many parts of the world the newspaper comes at the end of a long saturation process of news information.

It is now being realised all over the world that the newspaper in its old information role is dying. It can provide extended information certainly—a copy of *The Times* would provide the verbal substance of at least sixty BBC newscasts. Or newspapers can change style and become largely interpretative.

It would therefore seem that my ten years with *The Australian* as an interpretative writer is the beginning of a tradition rather than a quaint aberration of the proprietor.

In such a convulsive shift in the role of the written newspaper world, there will be an increasing place for the general cultural columnist. The offering of moral judgments about society or culture is an important part of communication. Such judgments we all make when we hear of an event or are confronted with a new situation. The columnist's job is to see the wood despite the daily trees. There are very few of this specialist breed—most notably Bernard Levin in *The Times*, Art Buchwald in the *International Herald Tribune*, and not too many more non-specialist specialists.

Whether, as in these selected pieces, I have brought either too little light or too much heat for the taste of critical readers, I still hope that the kind of job I've been doing will proliferate and become increasingly important.

For unless we constantly make judgments on the society we have, we won't have a society worth having.

# SECTION ONE

# Australia

# VULGARISM—
# PRICE
# OF

**AFFLUENCE**   The disfigurement of urban landscapes has been an architectural and public theme for more than a decade.

We have seen it plentifully exemplified in British and American publications, and it has been a cause that has rallied many thousands of people overseas.

Without any perceptible stemming of the overall tide of environmental hideousness.

Now we have a book which portrays the Australian situation. It has the support of the Royal Australian Institute of Architects, the National Trust of Australia (NSW), the editorship of Donald Gazzard, a textual manifesto by John Douglas Pringle, and a selection of exciting and often ravishingly beautiful photographic examples taken by David Potts.

I suppose that the theme needs to be stated belatedly apropos Australia, and therefore this book is intended to serve a modest purpose as a regional conscience-pricker.

Mr John Douglas Pringle certainly has been carried away by ebullient optimism in his foreword when he expressed the hope that this book may be looked back on as a 'revolutionary document'. It may be, but not in the way he thinks.

Most of us are not such simple fellows as this, nor as sanguine as those idealistic architects who hope that one small area of free enterprise culture can be isolated from the whole; its entire natural energies and tendencies reversed while other areas, presumably, plunge merrily on their way to grosser, more primitive, and even more vulgar modes than we know right now.

To me this intense and conscientious book depicts to perfection a number of right-thinking people spitting against a hurricane.

But because their interests are visual and what they complain about is 'the visual assault on the senses', the problem they present is essentially partial and myopic, the special pleadings of a special aesthetic interest.

The text gives no evidence that they are facing up to something bigger than mere bad planning, bad urban commercialism, and crippled aesthetics.

In fact, the preface states quite explicitly that 'our assumption is that it is not too late to see again or to care about our physical environment; that if only enough of us can be made to care enough to attack those who despoil our country, whether through private gain or through official indifference, the lucky country might yet become a civilised one'.

The absurdity of this noble plea is immediately apparent. The idea is that by rallying to the banner of Anna the idealistic architect all can be saved.

But can it?

There still remains the sub-human cultural standards of television material, the delicious horrors of domestic aesthetic, the bastardisation of language by advertising media and social groups.

Does the campaign urged upon us by the promoters of this book include the idea of bulldozing the league clubs and their poker machines in the interests of a civilised class against a lucky country?

Vulgarism is the very life force and dynamic of an affluent urban free enterprise society. The problem is not atomised but total. It cannot be remedied by localised do goodery campaigns from interested parties.

The disfigurement of language is as conspicuous as the disfigurement of the visual environment. The disfigurement of popular cultural values, of music, is just as outrageous.

And above all, and behind all these aesthetic manifestations lies the disfigurement of emotions, sensibility, and character, which is essential to the progressive drive of a consumer-dominated social structure.

Would not Mr Pringle, Mr Gazzard and all the rest of them be more rational by looking at the tree rather than a specific warped branch?

Should they not be looking at a sociological rather than an aesthetic problem? They show no desire to do so in this present text.

Probably because you get back to rather nasty fundamentals. The problem of environmental outrage does not occur as an inevitable part of the economic process in socialist societies. Bad taste, lack of imagination, a certain aesthetic uncouthness, yes! But vulgarisation of sensibility is not fundamental, not integral to socialist societies.

Outrage is not necessarily in economies which are not dominated by the need to develop even more hectic rates of personal consumption.

The crude answer to urban outrage and the vulgarisation of sensibility in the present phase of capitalism, the Galbraithian era, is socialist economics.

But do we want a socialist US, UK or Australia?

If we don't, then we have to accept the inevitability of the emotional and aesthetic disfigurements that are built into the economic process, that are necessary to its stability.

There are compensations in terms of liberty, compensations for the individual who uses the world of conspicuous consumption to creative advantage. But we have to be prepared to pay the price of outraged ears, outraged eyes, outraged lungs, and to see the affluent mass of people developing enfeebled and materialistic motivations.

This is what the pop artists have done—enshrined the excrescences, made the outrage into an aesthetic, valued the cliches at their mass valuation.

Right now the pop artists would appear to be promulgating an incredibly cynical aesthetic revolution, but it's a long way from the negativism of Dada. It's an adjustment of the individual to the environment because such adjustments are historically (and artistically) necessary.

The individuals who sponsored and devised *Australian Outrage* represent in this context of thought an antediluvian conservatism, a sort of intellectual Hans Heysenry.

For, if you look at this book from a fresh and courageous point of view, the very images of Australia depicted as outrageous have about them a fresh, uninhibited, vital vulgarianism that makes them exciting.

How much visually more stirring the tangle of telegraph poles, houses, and hoardings in some of these photographs than the tree-scaped tasteful homes for the emotional pigmies of Canberra (which are put forward in this book as the desirable image).

How dramatic, almost animistically poignant the quarry-scarred face of the Adelaide Hills! How magnificently in the mood of modern sculptured forms the mutilated great tree beside the telephone box.

An ordinary tree is just a tree—but the image on page 100 is man's veritable dream of death.

The book features a study of massed advertising signs at the City of Oakleigh swimming pools. This once again shows what a Milton the official photographer, David Potts, has proved to be; irreparably of the devil's party, and yet not knowing it.

For the mass of signs turns out to be compositionally magnificent, a photographic near-masterpiece. The complex of advertising messages cancels out, and all one is aware of is the urgency and the superb febrility of the scene.

Another illustration depicts a church spire with and without a foreground of telegraph wires. The caption says: 'It all depends on your point of view'. For my money the church spire lacks intrinsic interest.

But set in visual conflict with the convoluted urgencies of wires and poles, the whole thing comes alive. We have in interesting visual form Blake's idea of 'the contraries without which there is no progression'.

It all amounts to this. We can't undermine the basic motivations on which our present form of society is based, unless we turn to controls which are so profound and fundamental as to alter the entire dynamic of our economic system.

It is not a naive matter of breeding a race of sensitive civil servants and civic administrators. It's all much too big and psychologically fundamental for this kind of segmentary approach.

If we don't want the full socialist form of society, then we have to incorporate outrage into our aesthetic. We can't stem the irresistible cultural tide, but we can change our aesthetic.

It has happened before many times in human history. It is certainly happening now. In fact there are as many people who would be as delighted with the visual excitement of *Australian Outrage* as would be horrified.

I don't think this thought for a moment has crossed the architectural minds who put together this enchanting volume.

One realises that with all the goodwill in the world the writers who produced this book genuinely believe in their bygone aesthetic. Let us praise them for spitting against the hurricane.

But also let us temper outrage with acceptance, yes, even appreciation, of the new visual anarchy that is inevitably the heritage of our generation.

*Australian Outrage is published by Ure Smith.*

# LUNCHING
# AT
# SMACKA'S PLACE

I don't know of any book which provides a complete history of Australian jazz over the past thirty years. I haven't heard of any publisher commissioning such a volume for the near future. There may well be a definitive jazz discography buried away somewhere, possibly in mimeographed form. If so, it hasn't found its way effectively into the market place.

Australian jazz remains our national and permanent underground art form, and possibly for this very reason it has remained vital, uncorrupted and stylistically individual for three uninterrupted decades.

It was a rotten, sweaty day in Melbourne. It was not a day to find salt and savor in discussing manuscripts, editing, and Hong Kong printeries. So shortly after midday we publishing tycoons found ourselves at Smacka's Place, somewhere on the outer rim of central Melbourne.

A huge barn of a place, quietly concealed down some drab industrial laneway. But it didn't lack for patrons. Quite a few hundred people were battling away for the barbecued steaks and the indifferent stuffed peppers. The food was plain, the tables large and bare, the beer service seemingly chaotic yet somehow completely efficient.

For all the grimness of the weather and the dimness of spirit one usually finds over in Boltesville, it was a great day for old Smacka Fitzgibbon and his patrons.

They started playing.

The old magic was there, just as richly and unmistakably as it was back in 1945 when Roger and Graham Bell, Lazy Ade Monsborough and the original Bell group used to gather in the Templestowe barn of John Reed to evolve their pioneering style.

One may have heard greater virtuosity and inventiveness in traditional American solo work, but the ensemble playing was, as ever, superbly assured, possessed of that euphoric energy, the instant camaraderie, that characterises the traditional Australian jazz style. And Tony Newstead's musical dialogues, especially with clarinet, displayed the complementarity of feeling and phrase that is the essence of improvised jazz.

Smacka's beer and stuffed peppers began to taste really great.

I looked the audience over with a curious but Brechtean eye. Somehow they largely looked terrifyingly familiar, these balding and paunchy men with their raddled wives and mistresses.

This was not a landscape of languid and lovely youth. Anything but.

And as the atmosphere relaxed and the mingling began, acts of recognition began to occur. These ravaged but lively oldies were my own contemporaries, the impassioned youthful participants in the angry modernist revolution that swept through Melbourne in the 1940s. These were the supporters who rallied to the Contemporary Art Society Exhibition at the Australia Hotel the time the Bells played at the opening and there was a punch-up over Nolan's set of paintings.

Now, in the trendy seventies, it was of some considerable pleasure to see that age had not wearied them although the years had done a bit of relentless condemning. These animated, responding people had continued to love the same music in the same way for thirty years. They had invented faithfulness, as Ern Malley summated the idea of positive human worth in the ultimate line of one of his poems.

This brings me to my present conviction. That the time has come for the qualities of Australian traditional jazz to be analysed and historically recorded. Not changed, nor popularised, but simply recorded. This should be done, and fairly urgently, for any number of reasons.

For one thing, how many people recall that perhaps the first effective impact of Australia on the overseas cultural scene occurred long before the expatriate trek of Nolan, Boyd, Perceval and Tucker. The tour of the Bell group to Poland, Czechoslovakia and Britain in the 1940s caused an excitement and stimulation of the jazz idiom in Europe that no national group outside the Americans had effected before. In one area of the performing arts Australia acquired a mystic and puzzling overseas cultural reputation.

In all the subsequent faithful years have we created a Sir Graham Bell; or a Lazy Ade OBE? The very thought would have the jazz boys falling about in hysterics.

Apart from the fact that Australia has had this indestructible and continuing jazz tradition, whereas countries like Britain and Germany haven't, there remains the job of serious speculation on the individualised quality of the Australian jazz idiom.

There are those who claim you can pick an Australian vintage jazz performance by ear, just from the national style and the musical idiom. I suspect these afficionadoes may well be right.

How did this alien musical form come to bore into the bloodstream of our particularly little country? How did we become recipients of the most difficult of all cultural transplants, as it were? Jazz doesn't take root easily outside America. I don't think any country in Europe would lay claim to a sustained jazz tradition as Australia can do.

My own theories are tentative and will give rise to a modicum of horse-laughter in sophisticated intellectual quarters.

Mingling with the jazz-men and their devotees at Smacka's Place, it struck me that the Australian jazz underground provides the last surviving embodiment of Lawson's mateship imperatives. You won't find the innocent and unforced spirit of mateship back of Bourke; nor at Bob Hawke's pragmatic headquarters. But quite clearly the old musicians, with their sunken chests, projecting pelvises, and bent backs at Smacka's have enjoyed a sustained and reassuring empathy with their now paunchy and raddled audiences. There has been an unchanging human environment in which the tradition has been able to survive and develop. Jazz has built an ethos of mateship around itself.

Then again, Australian jazz has enjoyed only occasional and modest waves of trendy popularity. Nothing to disturb the central musical preoccupations. I don't know of any major group in this country which has been corrupted by the temptations of solo exhibitionism, for example.

Another thought concerns the social origins of our indigenous idiom. It has quite a curious history. Our jazz musicians weren't by-products of Conservatorium training. Nor did they emerge from folkloric grass-roots or honky-tonk entertainment.

They were integral to that whole homogeneous movement over the full spectrum of the arts that mysteriously convulsed the ultra-conservative Melbourne of the 1940s. They were musicians of no identifiable class or educational origin; but they shared passion, purpose, and intense dedication on equal grounds with painters and poets of the time.

They were part of an extraordinary common cultural radicalism.

This was a matter of affinities, not of intellectualism or ideologies. This built-in sense of an authentic and respected cultural role has served the jazz tradition well.

This may be why the jazz at Smacka's Place was as pure and authentic and exciting a fortnight ago as it was when the Bells let rip in John Reed's barn three decades past.

Reverting to the original point. Out of snobbery, trendiness and a plain patronising view of the cultural values, will this aspect of Australian life go unrecorded as the pioneer jazzmen keel over and go to that great drummer in the sky?

I hope not.

# THE
# GROVES
# OF
# EROTICA

No subject projects itself more insistently into the mind than the problem of pornography as distinct from the long and unquestionable cultural validity of erotica.

One doesn't arrive at fixed and didactic answers. One is perpetually adjusting and shifting ground because the social context itself is in a state of quicksilver flux. One tries to work out definitions. What is pornography, and can it either enhance or endanger particular human conditions? How is the erotic distinguished? And assessed as contributing to the proper values of sexual love?

At times I feel some kind of envy of the Moral Activists. The costivity of their thought processes, their arrogant assurance, eliminate any tortuous concern with expressions and manifestations that may possibly be apt to our sad times. They are perfectly content to throw the baby out with the bathwater.

For the fixated moral bigot there is no difference between the erotic truths in such a cinematic sexual masterpiece as The Last Picture Show, and a blue movie filmed for retarded male frustrates. It's a vicious but comfortable psychology.

Nonetheless, the distinctions are becoming clearer. And for the present set of reflections, I must confess to plagiarising freely from the views of the British psychotherapist, Mary Miles.

The definitions are confused, the whole matter is subjective; but erotic art, literature and cinema are expressive of some positive, loving, or serious concern with the human and emotional experiences of sexuality. Thus, to me, Doris Day's bedroom movies are pornographic because they express only an itchy furtive set of innuendoes about the sexual act as an act in itself.

On the other hand, I found the Scandinavian version of Henry Miller's Quiet Days in Clichy perfectly acceptable. Yet the Henry Miller film was prohibited even in London where nauseating 'skin flicks' proliferate at hundreds of little 'cinema clubs'.

Even in liberated London the puritanic tradition is still so strong that it's not easy to accept that sex can be treated as one of the more hilarious episodes in the human comedy. Yet humour can be the warmest possible expression of affection; and affection is at the heart of emotionally adult sexuality. Henry Miller is one of the garrulous button-holing bores in modern literature, but his writings are comic erotica, not pornography.

And to the extent that erotic communication can enhance our adult human experience of sex, I am and always shall be anti-censorship and anti-repressionist.

But I do confess that there is a dire problem of pornography; that the young are threatened by it; that it is being crudely and ruthlessly promoted. I believe that there is an answer to it, but the answer doesn't lie in covering the external symptoms with a moral salve, but in fundamental emotional education. Pornography must be made to die a natural death. This won't be achieved through legal or social censoriousness.

What exactly is the problem of pornography? What are its justifications? When and how is its influence baleful?

Fundamentally pornography depersonalises sex. Its obsession is with bodily activity in and for itself. It identifies with the functional obsessions of the small child, which Freud discovered and analysed as infantile sexuality. As Mary Miles puts it:

> '. . . the real danger of pornography is that it exerts a pull-back from the development of adult sexual love to forms of infantile sexuality. Under normal conditions this phase gradually gives way to adult sexuality. What is dangerous about some current trends is that they make this more difficult and prolonged.'

The pornography problem is really a matter of democratic rights for a particular sort of individual. And an urgent issue of emotional and cultural education for the post-pubescent young.

There are millions of adult individuals who have never outgrown the inward, self- and function-obsessed conditions of infantile sexuality. The sexually impotent, the maladjusted, the masturbators, the isolates—these are also human beings with private rights in the community. They are not to be blamed, as the Christians tend to do, for emotional and sexual retardations that they couldn't help.

And I don't think they pose a problem. If voyeurism, fantasy, onanism, lie at the heart of their human experience instead of normalised adult sexual relationships, then they should have their pornography.

And they do in London. The porn shops in London do not need police supervision. The shops are patronised only by such deprived and solitary human beings. The young don't buy pornography. They tend to live it.

Now here's the real problem. Society is building the pornographic or infantile psychology into the framework of accepted values and behaviour patterns. The young are educating themselves into the idea of sex as a personal appetite —to be evaluated and indulged in as such.

The young will still accept the social value that the person who eats grossly for the sake of eating, without regard for the qualities of the food, or the cultural restraints involved, is properly a victim of gluttony.

And clever as she is, would Germaine Greer recognise that dehumanised appetitic sex can involve retardation if the sexual act is constantly being divorced from mutual emotional self-realisation?

This is the modern agony of the young. This is the most radically destructive force that has happened to the Western human psyche over the past two revolutionary decades.

Here we have the reason for the weird traumatic contradictions of the young (especially women). They accept the present degradation of sexual potential by viewing it as a physical appetite of no great significance. Yet they sentimentalise it imaginatively, aware somehow of a deprivation through retardation—and they read Elizabeth Barrett Browning, Leonard Cohen, Rod McKuen in gigantic numbers. They seek out fantasy sexual idealisations in a way that wasn't even matched by the Swinburnian dreaming of the late Victorians. Ah the pity and sadness of it all!

It is no answer, although it's the easiest way to crawl away from the truth, to deplore the commercialisation of an egocentric and purely physical philosophy of sex. The seduction of the young is being carried out by the young, vide the film industry and the youthful dominance of production and direction.

The extension of the sexual self-centredness of the bodily-obsessed child into adulthood is the illness to be cured, and this can be achieved only by building emotional values back into both sex education and general education.

The old-fashioned sex education text books may well have been correct in laying emphasis on relationship as against the supposedly avant garde principle of extrapolating the physical processes from the experience of love that should accompany the routine physical procedures.

The teaching of conventional English literature may well instil some idea of the quality and value of such massive emotions as love.

But is not more emphasis placed these days on subjective 'expression' than on absorbing the potentials or the emotional experience of others? I think so. Perhaps the pedagogues weren't so fuddy-duddy when they required reluctant youngsters to learn a Keats poem by heart back in the bad old days.

Linguistics provide the exact reflection of the devaluation of sexual experience. While words such as interflora, inter-city, etc., are exploited as trendy and meaningful, the emotionally-loaded word 'intercourse' has fallen into unfashionable disrepute.

The young university talk of having sex (subjective), having it off (subjective) or f--ing (depersonalised). Intercourse is out of favour because it suggests emotional mutuality.

This linguistic degradation of sex is pervasive. In the *London Observer* on April 9 the word f--- occurred three times. In a weekend family newspaper with a circulation of millions. This was not a matter of journalistic boldness. The word was required to describe the psychological quality of certain film and theatre scenes. The word occurred four times in Elizabeth Taylor's film X Y and Zee, and six times in the academy award winning The French Connection.

This cold detached biological word, exactly as it is, will be absorbed by filmgoers in Australia, and it will reinforce the growing youthful belief that this is fundamentally what sex is about—just coitus. A biological pleasure-function.

One fights this sad enfeebling of the potential richness of human relationships not by banning the film use of the word. One fights it by requiring that emotional values be injected back into the total educative process, from five-year-olds to post-graduate students to adult education in the community at large.

Pornography is the raw material that feeds infantile values that have sadly survived into adulthood. It is the consumer product for a particular state of mind.

It is time for Moral Activists, so often emotionally retarded themselves, to cease making moral judgments about their fellow human beings who are afflicted with this mental condition, or even about the product that brings them release from psychological tensions.

It is possible (once the real problems are clarified), for permissives such as myself and people with what I believe to be misdirected and destructive concern, to get together on the positive task. To counteract the seduction of the young by the young.

If the present social mores tend to take the humanity out of sex, then it is surely the central and essential task to crusade for the revaluation of human experience between men and women. These days there's a dirtier word in the English language than f----—it's love. Let's be devils and use it. And talk about it. Right out loud.

# A
# LOVE AFFAIR
# WITH

**SYDNEY**  It has been customary to be anthropomorphic about conceiving Sydney as female and blowsy, Melbourne as male and dishevelled.

This time-honoured practice seems fair enough. Even after 25 years of comings and goings one continues to be surprised and delighted by the urban omnipresence of females who are slightly ratty, atrociously dolled-up, heartily self-assured, doing their own thing in their own town with a disarming if noisome vulgarity. Sydney has a female climate about it.

And as gaudy females are more entertaining than beefy males, Sydney is clearly the pride and joy of all Australian cities.

I love the place.

But urban vitality is not the stuff that endures, particularly in a decade of vast structural change. The blowsy females are being driven out to concealment in the supermarkets of the suburbs. The age of people-pollution has hit Sydney hard, and possibly fatally.

Urban strangulation is the greatest environmental problem of them all—when there is too great a concentration of people for the urban geographical resources to cope with. Sydney is not the full Calcutta catastrophe, but it is approaching the human asphyxiation of New York or Istanbul, or even London on a bad day.

People are mobile creatures, equipped with legs and wheels. When they can't move, or mobility becomes an anxious ulcer-creating stop-start process of endless frustration—then people become the product of their frustrations.

I can endure the sewage in the sea and the carcinogens in the Sydney atmosphere, because a technological cause can be eliminated by a technological cure.

But what government can act, and how can any government act, to cure the creeping transition from living city to dead anonymous megalopolis?

The day of reckoning is not far off for Sydney, but while it has not fully arrived we can still celebrate its quaint and unmistakable identity.

Sydney's vices are as interesting as its virtues, and, peace to the shade of the obsessive Germaine, the vices are those generally attributed to the unliberated female. Incestuous egocentricity is the endemic psychological disorder. Sydney sees itself as its own total universe, and consequently it is warm-hearted, alive, but about as stupid as any great city could hope to be.

The shallow atmospherics of the place guarantee that its role in the total cultural configuration of Australia will be as minimal as it always has been.

When Angry Penguins launched the modern Australian movement in art and literature, Sydney summoned up its competitive muscles and produced what Robert Hughes historically designated as the Charm School, a splendid coterie of insignificant visual decorators. It would be discourteous to nominate them now, but a quiet waddle around the NSW Art Gallery will show you this artistic flowering pathetically memorialised.

The trouble is that when horizons are limited by instant intellectual self-satisfaction, you can have the free play of imagination. But the imagination that is untempered by the hard critical processes of the intellect becomes a bit of a plaything. Historically Sydney's cultural life is as superficial and momentary as its hedonistic weekend recreations. Sydney is really no richer than its sensory surfaces.

Imagination, goodwill, enthusiasm—yes. Cultural drive and critical acumen—alas, no.

What one requires of an urban environment, full of colour and stimulus, is that it should also be a focal point for critical and cultural standards. But Sydney would wet its metaphoric pants if this arduous responsibility devolved upon it.

It is a fine place to reside, but not to achieve.

In consequence Australia's painters and playwrights and poets come from all over.

Sydney chalks up a disproportionately modest percentage as the nation's hub. It is not like this in London, New York, or Paris.

The young men of the media in Sydney prematurely suck toothless geriatric gums and reminisce like old gaffers about the grand old days. They are now fillers of air-time, or servants of the great god, Trend.

Imagination they don't lack. Creativity is there waiting to be used up. But Sydney doesn't want human resources challengingly and uncomfortably employed. You don't tell a woman her make-up is lousy and her clothing hilarious.

In consequence even down where the Freds are browsing in their nocturnal pastures, the herd heroes are largely wasted. The John Laws and Brian Hendersons of Fredsville could well be their own men, real individuals down in the jungle of the sub-culture. Instead they work their little fingers to the knuckle ingeniously becoming cardboard copies of prototypes inferior to their own originals.

In terms of Australia's more serious cultural identity in the modern sense, Sydney is less important than it ought to be in comparative world terms. Even so, a cultivated hedonism is ineradicably part and parcel of the national image we present to the world. Personally I don't apologise for it, and I wouldn't want it otherwise. This coloration derives dominantly from Sydney (and, these days, to a lesser extent, from Perth).

# MOOMBARBARISM
# IN
# ACTION
I was greatly moved to read some small tribute to the reflections in this column in the posthumous book by Robin Boyd, 'The Great, Great Australian Dream'.

One so often feels the need to apologise for constantly reverting to the theme of the distant and undistinguished identity of Australia. Particularly since the mythic qualities we have lived with have lost all reality and relevance in the growth of a series of high-stress urban entities over the past twenty-five years.

Robin Boyd's life and work showed that there is no dismal and incestuous self-consciousness in a constant thinking about the Australian ugliness and the Australian redemption. It is as some kind of tribute to Robin Boyd that I turn once again to reflecting on the identity of Australian cities. It is the cities we have to think about. That is where the people are. That is where most of the living goes on.

The cities provide the heart of the future's environmental problems. We have to know right now how they are lived in, and how long they can be lived in before their unique characteristics are engulfed or destroyed by growth or change.

It is regarded as old-hat stuff to compare the attributes of Melbourne and Sydney with or without malice afore-thought; to ponder on the mystery of how Adelaide and Perth at a given size symbolise something of civilised urbanism while Brisbane, roughly the same size, embodies the nightmare of Australian cultural grossness. Yet these are the things that have to be considered despite the susurrations of the semi-sophisticated.

Melbourne obsesses me more than any other Australian city. I continue to be amazed that a city of such a size and yet with such an individualised colonial history can remain so implacably monstrous. The place is gross, ugly and un-redeemed even by accidental aesthetics. It reflects with appalling precision the materialistic egotism and philistine arrogance of its chosen political leader. And I am not in-dulging in one more side-swipe at the Boltes of Victoria.

Yet Melbourne produces a vital breed, not of dissenters but of cultural aberrants. It is this consistent history of high and productive individualism which makes Melbourne so problematical. For the life of me I can't understand the bloody place.

c

In cultural terms, as both Robert Hughes and I have consistently pointed out, there's something epicene and episodic about the creative drive of Sydney. But Melbourne has produced Nolan, Boyd, Perceval, in fact the entire corporate identity of the classic modern Australian school of painting.

The painters, along with the satirists like Barrie Humphries and Phillip Adams, are conjoined in a distraught love-hate relationship with its charmless streets and faces. Writers like Morris Lurie, Barry Oakley, Peter Mathers, erupt from its suburbs with new languages and new angers. It is rich in speculative minds like Stephen Murray-Smith, the late Robin Boyd, Germaine Greer, Jean Battersby. Such a cataloguing is invidious because it tends to isolate this peculiar subterranean Melbourne energy as individual and incidental.

The fact is that a generous preoccupation with the qualities of non-materialism is widespread within Melbourne. It's a genuine underground movement, and it involves a large spread of the ordinary non-famous urban population.

You only have to record the number of galleries that advertise in *The Age* each Saturday, and the mind boggles at the scale of the art industry within the metropolis. It is easy to attribute the art industry to the status-hunting of a vulgar nouveau riche. It can't be written off as easily as that. At his Cultural Centre, Eric Westbrook finds himself surrounded by cohorts of friends and supporters who will work like maniacs for the arts with anonymous and selfless zeal.

The hub of Melbourne's mystery is that it is distinguished by a vigorously humane and liberal component despite the charmless, faceless, physical characteristics of the city.

Yet this great force of people of cultivation is sociologically totally ineffectual. The barbarians rule the whole shebang. Melbourne is Barrassi-land, and that's that.

It has to do perhaps with David Riesman's convenient psychological categories of the inner-directed and outer-directed man. Whereas Sydney conducts a running love affair with itself, uninfluenced by anything or anyone in the outside world, Melbourne perpetually asserts and justifies itself. The self-assertive process is dominated by the mass of the intellectually unwashed. The vulgarians can't be subdued by any subtle civilising process gradually coming to the surface within the urban structure.

This is noteworthy within the activities of the mass media. The power struggle between the civilised and uncivilised forces usually shows up in a sneaky penetration of the media by the cohorts of liberal and cultural enlightenment. It works that way in Sydney. Other voices and other minds manage to be heard through the stuttering tabloid illiteracy of media communication.

Melbourne is where they make Bellbird, and, what's more, everyone is assumed to think the way they do in Bellbird. Graham Kennedy is King still in Melbourne's nostalgic memory. It's the land of doting mumhood while the boys are out at footy practice. It's the capital of commercial pop.

The virtuosity of this impenetrable arrogant vulgarity was manifest in a documentary two-hour film made about the climax of Moomba's cultural manifestation—a street procession of totally incredible cardboard floats. Whereas any major city in the world would have been shamefaced about the financial waste, the aesthetic pollution, and the comical atavism of this appalling cornball event, the media commentator showed a far more pop-eyed innocent amazement about the wonder of it all than the sullen citizenry in the streets.

Under the official surface of his allotted task one might expect that a relatively educated commentator would recognise that in this sophisticated age a flurry of funny floats is more apt to the needs of the Back to Birdsville Committee. Yet the television spectacular culminated in the breathless observation, *Well, after all the fun of the Moomba parade, people at the Adelaide Festival must find it pretty dreary.* Viva Barrassi! And Adelaide hooted with disbelieving laughter.

Thus it is that Melbourne provides the great national urban dilemma. The hangman still has a job. The restaurants don't need to understand the principles of charm or mannerliness. The young languish for a vote. The cultivated voices can't be heard for the raucous uproar of the crowd. Nothing can be done. Even so, Melbourne is part of Australia. The Bertie Russell of the town is Bertie Newton.

And unless there is a miracle of cultural loaves and fishes, the Australia of tomorrow will still be the sum total of its parts, as it is now. And Melbourne will continue to provide the grotesquerie which the visiting European mind contemplates with a mixture of fascination and disbelief.

# THREE CHEERS
# FOR
# ADELAIDE AND PERTH

If Australia is ever to produce two recognisably different urban cultures, it will probably be a matter of Perth and Adelaide establishing a different atmosphere from the high-pressure razzmataz of the eastern seaboard.

Already my critical colleagues from the writing game diagnostically sniff a profound difference.

Perth and Adelaide they tend to like enormously as holiday cities, where the lighter attitude towards materialistic pressures invigorates them more than the relatively unpolluted air and the clear light. These two cities are felt to be cultivated, hospitable, of a population size compatible with a civilised human ecology. And, if anything, they tend to be more outward looking than the manic self-obsessiveness of metropolitan Sydney or Melbourne.

Perth is the jewel of Australian cities. Sydney's geographical glory is a lost historic relic—one experiences occasional unexpected moments of ravishment when one comes upon water, light, and perspectives at the right time. Perth is Australia's finest city as an entity. So far, praise be, the urban planning has not been a disastrous destruction of the visual sightlines. The freeways contribute to the general sense of space and freedom.

At one time Perth possessed the environmental attributes, but one had to accept an embarrassing degree of small-town psychology and paranoia as a sociological concommitant. The isolation syndrome was very real and somewhat boring.

Industrial growth and subsequent affluence can often be considered as the great destroyer. For Perth it has been the appropriate therapy. God bless the mineral boom. The city now carries its own form of assurance and pride and self-containment.

It is a land of lotus-eaters, but what is wrong with that dietetically? The passions are not as intense as the pleasures, the hedonism may seem pretty empty after a while, but at least the medical profession doesn't wax fat on the ulcer industry.

And no longer is Perth culturally starved in terms of the national perspective as once it thought itself to be. These days the culture circuit, both within and outside the summer arts festival season, begins or ends in Perth. God bless the flight routing of Qantas and BOAC.

I once asked the film producer, Sidney Box, why he had left the frenetic pleasures of the British industry he so notably featured in, to become a denizen of such a city as Perth. He replied: *Name a better one*, and didn't wait for an answer.

Adelaide has to rely on its peculiarity to maintain its typical identity in the Australian social climate. It is environmentally acceptable, but that's about all.

You would have to be wacky to think of it as a beautiful city. But it does seem to both please and fascinate the visitor. It is full of sharp contradictions. The social conflicts of our time appear in clear relief rather than obfuscated. It is a place for talking and diagnosing rather than doing. This is because Adelaide has no other visible virtues except its curiously clear integrity, and the rest of Australia tends to look towards Adelaide when it is in a mood to see the wood from the trees.

The political crystallisation is, for example, a thoroughly well-observed phenomenon. In South Australia, politics is not a power version of snakes and ladders played by calculating, devious or ambitious men. It is all terrifyingly high-principled.

It is an unsullied area of social experimentation for the ALP. If there is to be any renaissance of liberalism as a modern and relevant ideology, then the concept work is being carried out very painfully by Steele Hall and his associates right now.

Even the philosophy of right-wing autocracy, as exemplified by Mr Renfrey de Garis in the celebrated all-powerful Legislative Council, is presented as a genuinely held set of principles. No one doubts the integrity of Mr de Garis. He truly believes that the well-being of the peasantry should derive from the autocratic paternalism of a vanished landed gentry.

So the confused, disguised, and ill-understood forces in Australian society as a whole are personalised in Adelaide. Like some medieval allegorical morality play.

It is, in short, a national area which is fascinated by principles rather than tactics. And this is not limited to the political shop-window.

This stubborn individual integrity has to deal with a large number of different sorts of pressures. The most famous battle of principles centres with boring regularity on the Adelaide Festival of Arts.

Since Perth and Adelaide initiated the cultural festival concept in Australia, the whole nation has been devising ways and means of horning in on the act in some form or other. The big operators and promoters have seen the festival system as a mighty opportunity to move in for a quick killing. Regional community effort creates the atmosphere and the audiences. The operators surge in and rake in the dollars.

But Adelaide has stubbornly insisted on remaining a festival of the arts. Emphasis on the word arts.

The Adelaide-Perth philosophy has been that no one in sophisticated Europe launches into onslaughts on Edinburgh, Salzburg, Glyndebourne. No New Yorker insists that the jazz at Newport would be improved by the inclusion of Buddy Greco, Vera Lynn, and Rod McKuen, plus Victor Silvester. There's no thought that Salzburg would be much nicer if it introduced a Rio de Janeiro street parade as the prime activity.

Adelaide and Perth are in a state of war with the eastern seaboard, because that different and Americanised segment of Australia can't leave it alone. They can't believe, or tolerate the unaccommodating notion that the arts festival concept is not adaptable to the purposes of the quick dollar.

The director of Moomba has launched his down-grading campaign against the two festivals which are what they are intended to be. Good luck to him. The more that cultural buffoonery confines itself to Melbourne the better for serious creative standards in the rest of the country.

The problem is that pressures arise in Adelaide and Perth calling on those cities to compete with the street orgy concept of cultural occasion. Both cities will have to fight bitterly to retain the integrity of their long-sustained concept work for 1974. The battle could well be lost, particularly in Adelaide which has had a fair old punishment from ignorant media idiots.

Harry M. Miller left Adelaide roaring as if he had been gored in the pocket. *Where was the fantastic mardi gras parade, the dancing in the streets and the parks, the open air concerts, the barges on the beautiful Torrens drifting up and down serving drinks, or even coffee or tea?*

Because of these deficiencies, in the future, Harry M. won't be bringing another show to any Adelaide Festival of Arts.

Well, that's some relief for Mafeking, although I am rather enamored of the anthropomorphic barges that serve you drinks. That would be quite a technological spectacular!

Be that as it may, the arts festival microcosm does reveal the conflict of values and purposes that exists between the thinking of the eastern seaboard and the besieged entities of Adelaide and Perth.

It is important to Australia's diversity and identity as a whole that the regional cities survive on their own more educated terms into the future. It is possible that the larger metropolitan cities of Australia are entering the American era of forty years ago—the public ballyhoo, the idiot manipulation of mobs, the drum majorette dawn of vulgarism triumphant.

Should the omens be as gloomy as all that, then let's all pray together for Adelaide and Perth. It would be quite a drag to have to export one's self to Edinburgh to experience the cultivated life and enjoy the cultivated pleasures.

# THE
# AESTHETICS
# OF
# ANXIETY

One day I believe people will be writing about the art of the past decade in terms of the aesthetics of anxiety.

It is not without significance that the artist, Edvard Munch, has been hauled from a minor and obscure position in the modern hierarchy and is now commanding passionate dedication and attention. The virtuosity of Picasso, the technological abstractions of Leger, the lyricism of Chagall are being seen as increasingly irrelevant to the state of our aesthetic responses.

Munch is the artist of the primal scream, the painter who did not depict an anxious and distorted passing world as such, but who projected his own sense of vast insecurity on to everything he looked at. His distortions spring from a much more disturbed sensibility than that of, say, Francis Bacon.

Thus, while Munch may not come to be critically regarded as the top of the modernist hierarchy, he is in the process of being assessed as the painter who worked closest to our contemporary sensibility.

We are only at the very beginnings of this process of recognition. We are only now fully resolving the problem of why affluence and material security should breed a pathology of anxiety.

We can glibly throw off the cult phrases—the loneliness of the atomic family, the breakdown of the kinfolk system, the personal desolation that follows the philosophy of sex as appetitic rather than a means of securing lasting contact between human identities.

We know all about anxiety all right as the most potent common human emotion.

We can discuss it in all its diagnostic detail and contradictoriness. The booziness of the jaundiced journalist, the claret-quaffing self-bolstering of the young executive, the spurious camaraderie of the kids puffing pot, the grim sense of lost potential in the pill-swallowing housewife, the nervousness of her teenage daughter insulating her genitalia with the protective complexity of panty-hose and briefs against the social expectations of sexual casualness that surround her (who would ever believe women once wore scanties?).

There is little one can add to the present sum of almost neurotic self-knowledge.

But literature and drama and painting, which interpret the human condition, have not flourished over the past decade. And I think this is because anxiety is a negative and colourless condition of the psyche. As aesthetic nourishment it is short on essential proteins.

# TO
# DEFINE
# TRUE
# MATESHIP

Australia has been too concerned with problems of physical survival and economic development to make any contribution so far to the world's interchange of ideas or intellectual movements. Ideas come into the realm of the settled refinements of life, and 'battling', the Australian *modus vivendi*, is conducive to athletic greatness only. Yet Australian social history has been rich in special forms of group experience, unusual relationships of man and environment. One would expect that a long history of unusual and indigenous human relationships would in the end crystallise into a set of local ideas about the human condition.

The only national idea that emerged from the formative century of our history was that of 'mateship'; and this idea was treated instinctively and ethically, without systematic efforts to clarify it as a concept, by its protagonists, Henry Lawson and the bush balladists.

In consequence it has never been apparent what is the precise and special connotation of 'mateship' in terms of the Australian background.

Lawson completely lost sight of the very definite historical origins of mateship by giving the word a plural and quite different meaning. For Lawson a man had a certain number of mates, united by community of work or interest, and the human loyalties that bound them constituted 'mateship'. This was not the idea that operated so powerfully and mysteriously throughout the greater part of the nineteenth century. In Australia a man had a mate, and mateship was the special form of relationship that existed between two men, usually men who worked in physical isolation, deprived of the company of women, doing without sexual intercourse, and yet not remotely inclined towards homosexual affections. In our early history mateship was a shy synonym for love, describing a condition different from friendship yet largely devoid of sexual undertones. The difference between this kind of mateship and that which Lawson erroneously adopted is quite prodigious.

To clarify the point it is necessary to look at the social conditions which brought into being the odd Australian idea of having a 'mate'.

From 1826 onwards, thousands upon thousands of flocks of sheep began their occupation of Australian pastoral land, irresistibly, from all directions, from Sydney, Moreton Bay,

Van Diemen's Land over to Portland and Port Phillip, over the ranges from the Swan River. A shepherd, a hut-keeper, a flock, and a fortnight's supply of rations were deposited in an untamed expanse of bush, and a further out-station had been created, a further strongpoint had been taken. In the late 1840's the aboriginals pressed back to the deserts, launched a kind of instinctive counter-attack in New South Wales along a vast front. But they were powerless to stem the tide. Shepherds and settlers replied to the spearings and sheep-stealing with guns, quiet massacres, and poisoned flour, and the sheep grazed out to the boundaries of desert.

The deployment of people to occupy the pastoral lands was peculiar. The men almost invariably worked in pairs. Every flock of approximately 500 sheep was the province of a shepherd, who had the job of taking them out daily, grazing them, and returning them safely each night to hand over to his mate, the hut-keeper.

In the hut-keeper's hands lay all the domestic arrangements, plus the guarding of the sheep at night against the omnipresent dingo. There were usually many out-stations of the kind to every home-station, the single squatter-owner often having runs in a number of widely separated districts. The shepherd and hut-keeper would have outside human contact at the most for a few hours once a fortnight. A large proportion of the rural population were involved in shepherding, their way of living organised as a gross caricature of marital domesticity.

Sometimes a solitary shepherd was sent with a flock to camp over a range where good new temporary pasture had been found, or something of that kind, but total solitude almost invariably wouldn't work. The shepherd would go soft in the head . . . not driven crazy in the ordinary sense, but overwhelmed by a great mental torpor from which he could not be aroused. The insanity that so frequently accompanied lone shepherding was quite an economic problem for squatters who wished to take advantage of good grass in relatively remote parts of their run. Unless they sent a number of men and a number of flocks the sheep had to remain lean. This phenomenon was most acutely observed in the 1840's by Edward Curr, the most literate of all the squatter-authors of the period.

Not only the sheep industry was based on the working principle of a man-and-his-mate. It existed pervasively through all forms of rural labour. Alexander Harris, the emigrant mechanic, who roamed the Australian backwoods for sixteen years from the mid-1820's and wrote the classic *Settlers and Convicts*, gave a fascinating account of the lives of the army of timber-fellers in the giant cedar forests of

New South Wales. Again the basis of work is the team of two men living completely as a unit, and often isolated from human contact for as long as a year, sleeping in a single tent, or a crude slab hut. This principle extended to that whole labour force which went out contracting with squatters and settlers for timber splitting, felling, fencing. Most rural work was done by a man and his mate, and, what is extraordinary, rarely, if ever, were larger groups required. Bush carpentry, for example, the building of the homestead or slab hut for the settler about to establish himself up the country, was the work of a contracting team of two men. Even bullock drivers, the most hardbitten and sodden of old lags, usually teamed up with a mate, though their work did not strictly call for two-man operation.

Here we have a quite extraordinary phenomenon, not to be found elsewhere on such a scale at any time during the modern historical period . . . a quite large population of men, living together in pairs, geographically dispersed over a vast landscape, and enjoying only very sporadic and inter-mittent contact with larger social groups.

The question arises what kinds of relationship developed out of this man-and-his-mate pattern of conjugality. The re-lationship was expressed in a concept and a word unique to Australia . . . 'mateship'. Obviously the term hasn't the same meaning as 'friendship'. Friendship implies a positive affec-tion or regard for another person. But it by no means implies a high degree of human interdependence. If one loses a friend, one loses a friend. It is not to say that a loss of one's own personal identity has taken place. Mateship goes be-yond friendship to a form of sexless male marriage, the word marriage providing the only helpful analogous term.

Nor is mateship to be confused with the well-known phenomenon of collective identity that human beings ex-perience within a highly cohesive group enjoying communal interests . . . as, for instance, the blind mutual loyalties of groups of soldiers, or shearers on the wallaby, or Jewish pioneers in kibbutzim, and so on. It was, however, to this kind of group devotion that Lawson applied the word mate-ship, at a period of Australian social history when rural workers, the shearers particularly, were beginning to coalesce into a distinct proletarian class.

The real phenomenon of a man-and-his-mate did not go unrecorded and unobserved. It was a constant source of wonder and interest to writers of the pre-1850's era, ob-served by such disparate minds as Therry, Cunningham, Surgeon Wilson, chronicler of the Port Essington settlement, the wild Joseph Holt, and any number of other occasional authors.

As usual it was only the invaluable Alexander Harris who attempted anything like a psychological analysis of mateship. At one stage he became the mate of an old Irish convict hurdle-maker, a ferocious alcoholic, but gentle and conscientious in other respects:

> 'Although I was now only second in command, and one does not very easily fall into the whims and put up with the blunders of an inferior workman, I must say I liked the old man very much. There was a natural conscientiousness about him which commanded my confidence. There is a great deal of this mutual regard and trust engendered by two men working thus together in the otherwise solitary bush; habits of mutual helpfulness arise, and these elicit gratitude, and that leads on to regard. Men under these circumstances often stand by one another through thick and thin; in fact it is a universal feeling that a man ought to be able to trust his own mate in anything.'

Our emigrant mechanic's most significant observation is that mateship is 'a universal feeling' in the bush and it has plenty of documentary substantiation. An intimacy of two men, closer, more constant, more self-contained than even that of husband and wife, does not seem to have led to what one might expect; that is, desperate irritation, explosive incompatibilities or a developing animus barely held beneath the surface of the mind. The opposite seems to have been the general rule. In the Australian conditions of life mates experienced an emotional interdependence of a kind one usually associates with remote and unreal ideas of platonic love.

You worked in isolation and your mate was the only other human being you saw. He came to represent the whole of humanity. There was no human to hand apart from your mate! and every individual has need of other human beings, for one goes mad in total isolation. You *had* to like your mate and be bound to him. It seemed your mate was part of yourself and yet miraculously 'other' than yourself. You became lost and absorbed in his way of being as well as your own. In order to exist in these conditions a man had to have a pretty deep understanding of his own humanness, and its link with that of his mate. This sense of a common core, as it were, was more powerful than surface differences of character and personality.

It is a subtle and quasi-mystical conception of relationship, by no means as easily analysed as friendship, group loyalty or even sexual love. It has attracted the attention of contemporary thinkers however. It was classically stated in the famous 'lifeboat image' in Herbert Read's *Poetry and Anarchy* and many of the modern theologians have taken over the idea from Martin Buber's *I and Thou* philosophy. The analogy between mateship and the humanism of Buber, Heidegger, Sartre, and Tillich would be worth considering, but it is enough now to establish the very special category of experience implied in the term 'mateship', an indigenous Australian curiosity, no less astonishing than the platypus.

# A
# CONTINENT
# WITHOUT
# WOMEN  *Our sexual mores before the American invasion.*

The Australian has never had a very clear image of himself. It is doubtful if the idea of an Australian character came to be seriously considered until P. R. Stephenson's energetic but confused *Foundations of Culture in Australia* was published in 1936. For one thing, Australia had no real pretensions to nationhood apart from her English associations; and, for another, few Australians had experienced direct contact with the sexual and social mores of other cultures.

The Australian was clannish, loyal in a mates-together kind of way, and devoid of any impulse towards self-analysis. 'The old Aussie . . . she'll do me'; but there was no reasoning as to *why* the Australian life would do.

There was no self-analysis, but there was a trace of self-consciousness. The much-publicised Australian inferiority complex did exist fairly pervasively. Australian social mores and institutions were crude measured against the maturity and sophistication of foreign cultures, and against them the Australian set his aggressiveness, lack of curiosity, and the moral idea of being a 'good bloke'.

The event which stirred the Australian into analytic thinking about his national character was the flooding of USA troops into Australia. This vast influx of foreign yet English-speaking peoples at a time of tension was traumatic in an important way which has been overlooked. It was a shattering interaction of cultures, revealing unexpected differences of value and human behaviour. It stimulated that awareness of national character which finds practical expression in any Australian pub any evening. Establishing a national character is, these days, basic conversational material . . . Australians don't go for this picking-up sheilahs in the street like the Eyetalians . . . Poms winge, Australians get stuck into a problem and deal with it . . . we are establishing the image of ourselves as a Weird (but wonderful) Mob. We do not realise how relatively new all this is.

It is conventional to explain this emergent consciousness in terms of windy political generalisations . . . that Australia reached something like national maturity in the war years because of her major contributions in the military arena and her role in the councils of world leadership. The explanation is far more rudimentary, because attitudes are not imposed exogenously from above, but occur from below, through an evolution in the consciousness of *individuals*.

The American pattern, particularly their sexual mores, differed overtly from the Australian. The Americans were sexually avid, many were quite honestly predatory in their pursuit of women; they appeared habituated to easy talking and rapid sexual conquest, with a lack of any *'ayenbite d'inwit,'* backbiting-of-conscience as the medievals called it. We may have erected a sexual myth about the Americans (just as they do about Negroes), but the reality of the situation is not altogether the important thing. The important thing is that Australians, of either urban or rural background, became equally aware that their sexual and moral mores were differently formed from the American, or, for all they knew, from the European or the English.

It was highly important that the Americans brought our sexual pattern into question, for this is a fundamental element in national character, an element from which other characteristics are derived; for example, our social pattern of drinking, obsession with sport, patterns of domestic behaviour, etc. The Australians discovered from the Americans, after not a little dollar-envy and sexual jealousy, that they embodied some problematical attitudes that they had never worried about before; that had never previously appeared either praiseworthy or blameworthy, or anything other than in the natural order of such things.

His sexual pattern he found to be compounded of shyness verging on indifference, perhaps redeemed by a crude delicacy, a sexual decency, honesty of erotic intention, a lack of the showiness which could have concealed integrity and simple morality; or which could have indicated a lazy monogamy of approach to sexual relations.

He was not sure whether this pattern was crude and hillbilly or had some justification in terms of an Australian philosophy of living. With the European migration of the post-war years, and a constant scurry of distinguished overseas visitors criticising the vulgar maleness of Australian life, he has been placed in a position that has been hard to defend. At best Australians have only been able to put forward the suggestion that although they are sexually ill-bred, yet this may perhaps be better than the smooth and treacherous hand-kissing of the Continental or the 'quick line' of the Yank.

Fortunately or not, the movement of modern history is rapidly ironing out the interesting differences of cultural and moral mores that are to be found between one national group and another. Mass-communication media meant the spread of a conformism not only in economic behaviour and materialistic living, but in cultural habits. The sexual archetypes for Americans, English, Germans, Italians, or Australians are Monroe and Presley . . . the same image is being imposed on a variety of cultural patterns. The traditional forms of human relationship in the old and established communities—Italy and Japan, for example—are breaking down under the process of 'modernisation'. In Australia, a generation formed by Brando, James Dean, and a sex ideal of aggressiveness may produce different patterns of life from those which prevailed when Australia was a clannish isolated community of Currency lads and lasses, unchanged for almost a century. Too late the cult-figure of Chad Morgan, the Sheik of Scrubby Creek, has appeared to grace our musical life with an indigenous hillbilly balladry. His Australian erotic fantasies . . . 'You Can Have Your Women, I'll Stick to the Booze', 'Chasing Sorts in Childers', etc. . . . are already atavistic. Even way out in Chudinwilla his language would strike the rural youth as olde-worlde where jokers and sheilahs have been replaced by cats and squares.

It is thus an academic task to enquire into the origins of those ways of behaving that are now stigmatised as 'Australian'. But it is still a necessary exercise in self-understanding.

In one way our habits stemmed quite clearly from convictism. In another sense, the obvious origins lie in a history of population unbalance, of social relations necessarily of an all-male character leading to stiltedness and feigned casualness in heterosexual matters.

The first consideration is the more interesting. The effect of our convict origins has been consistently underwritten by our historians because it was rapidly bred out of the nation during the goldfields era. But if implanted attitudes are not changed by an influx of population but rather absorbed by the newcomers, then convictism is the prime source of Australian character.

The 'pure merinos', the handful of landed gentry and the officer-settlers clung to their Englishness. The emancipees, on the other hand, had lost their English roots, and were confronted with the task of evolving a 'way of life' from scratch. This was effected vigorously but casually. The Bank of New South Wales was created by ex-convicts, a symbol of their fiscal power. But as late as the end of the 1820's the institution of marriage gave them no concern . . . concubinage was the rule rather than the exception.

In 1826 we have this distinct 'Australian' way of life being reported by Cunningham in his *Two Years in New South Wales*, a Mayhew-like study of colonial behaviour patterns. He was particularly fascinated by the first generation of native-born Australians, the product of the convict concubinage system, and it is astonishing how little his impressions of 130 years ago differ from those of students of contemporary Australia.

'They are generally remarkable for that Gothic peculiarity of fair hair and blue eyes which has been noted by other writers. Their complexions when young are reddish sallow . . . The young females generally lose their teeth early, this calamity always commencing about the period of puberty . . . They do not commonly appear to class chastity as the very first of virtues, which circumstance arises partly from their never being tutored by their parents so to consider it, but more especially from never perceiving its violation to retard marriage . . . Currency youths marry early and do not seem to relish the system of concubinage so popular among their Sterling brethren here . . . I cannot find that they indulge in exchange of love tokens, mementoes of roses, shreds of ribbons, broken sixpences, and the like tender reminiscences . . . They display spirit and courage as well as great clannishness . . . They are all fond of frolicking in the water, and those living near the sea can usually swim and dive like dabchicks . . .'

The pattern here reveals itself in the process of formation. Marriage and sex are casual by-products of the business of colonial life. The native-born Australian attaches little other than a practical value to the rite. For one thing, the Australian was under none of the moral pressures of religion, as a result of which the importance of sex and family life are stressed. The Church in Australia was but a shadowy affair under the exceedingly remote control of the Bishop of Calcutta. While concubinage was good enough for emancipees and those citizens who could still remember the 'hundred hungry days', regularisation was necessary for their children at the period when the conflict between the emancipees and the 'pure merinos' was about to break out in unbridled animus. But that was all.

Apart from the casual acceptance of the sacrament of marriage, the Currency lads had no awareness that sex life could be attended by a savage moral code; that back amongst the English working classes 'sin' was attended by ruin and disgrace—as evidence by the songs and street ballads of the period. The new colonial moral code was an easy-going one. It had to be, since the new generation was largely illegitimate, and the mothers of the blue-eyed toothless young Australians were largely culled from the transported whores of England. With courtship stripped of its sentiment and rituals, marriage unattended by shibboleths or fanciful rituals, lack of sexual obsession became an un-mistakable Australian characteristic.

Later, with population growing apace, and with the dis-balance between male and female population still acute, sexual casualness became a virtue of necessity, a kind of character-fixation. The newcomer, to be accepted, had to conform rapidly to this manly sexual indifference. Nothing demonstrates how quickly and firmly this attitude was im-bedded than the social history of the goldfields, a few decades later.

The goldfields were lawless and uninhibited, peopled by a mixture of nationalities, and one would think that this vast army of occupation would have altered the existent mores. But the evidence does not point that way.

Whereas a hard-headed historian such as S. H. Roberts could describe the Sydney of 1830 as 'a miserable little growth of putrefying ulcers—a mess of social infection . . . a place of convicts and prostitutes, clerks and grumbling labourers', the goldfields of the 1850's seemed tame by comparison.

If anything is needed as final evidence, we can turn to Australian literature. Geoffrey Dutton has examined the almost complete absence of amatory themes in Australian writing. As far as Australian writers are concerned, right up to modern times, male-female relationships have no poten-tial literary substance. There are no Australian love-poems. There are few detailed studies of women in the Australian novel.

A national characteristic which discounts the significance of sexual life is bound to be subject to certain pressures, unless psychoanalytic thinking is to be altogether rejected. These pressures were met by our peculiar all-male drinking habits. Drinking habits were fairly clearly a substitute form of sexual release in the Australian environment. Drinking became ritualised here more than in any other country—a fact which has escaped the attention of social historians.

Two great motives contributed to Australia's all-male ritualistic drinking. Drinking becomes a social force where there is great suffering and despair. The rum-sodden char-acter of early Australia differed little from the gin-mad lanes of Hogarthian London. The convict population was too depraved in the first instance, or too brutalised by the System, to find any hope of regeneration in New South Wales. Drink was the only value left in existence.

The other form of drinking was of a cathartic kind, and was characterised by the drinking 'session' or the shearer's 'blueing of his cheque', and it extended to the town classes as well as to the rural isolates.

The daily land auction of Port Phillip was also an alcoholic free-for-all, and there was no charge for the drinks whatsoever. The free and unmarried mechanics of early Adelaide drank with such unrestrained zest that a horseman could not ride down Hindley Street for the empty bottles.

It is clear that alcoholic addiction pervaded all social classes in colonial Australia, that it was as prevalent in the free as in the convict colonies, and that gregarious drinking provided sexual release. It seems more than likely that the Australian national characteristic of the male separating his social existence from his domestic and family life stems from these colonial causes.

It might sound somewhat forced to suggest that the Newcastle miner or the Collingwood factory worker or the Riverina grazier still reflects attitudes which originated with the progeny of convicts a century and a half ago. But solidified attitudes provide the basis of all national characters, and it is amazing how resilient they are to even convulsive changes of economic life or population structure. A New England mentality still survives in the USA, the character of the British proletariat still reflects attitudes that emerged during the Industrial Revolution. It is not impossible that Australians should still show signs of the major moral trauma in their history.

# ONE WORLD? YOU'RE JOKING

We arty-crafties thought the great adventure of the age would be some sort of global coming-together. By the 1970s we would have seen the end of provincial literatures, nationalist painting idioms, insular creative reputations. That's what we thought back in the 1950s.

In a world characterised by rapid communications, a free flow of ideas, there would cease to be English writers, American writers, Australian writers. There would just be good writers, assessed and esteemed in relation to their achievements, irrespective of their geographical domiciles.

The British were growing up, and would abandon their attitudes of arrogant self-esteem. The Americans would abandon their chip-on-the-shoulder defensive claims for the output of their creative people. Australians would invade the European community from their remote outpost, and in the new pure era of a cultural meritocracy the occasional Australian individual of genius would find a place in a large and all-embracing international evaluation of the arts.

It was all a dream; a dream less prophetic than that of Martin Luther King.

In the days of glorious optimism we foresaw that Britain would renounce imperial power with dignity and reason, but we did not anticipate that there would be a cultural turning-inwards, a resolute determination to do and praise the English thing. As the British drag themselves into the EEC, and brush up their French, one supposes that there will be even less of an urge to envisage English literature as that literature which is written in English. Wherever it chances to be written. Or for what we deem to be the common cultural tradition of England, America, Canada, Australia to actually become a single interacting, rational tradition.

Let me be more precise.

I had always imagined that if one day there were to be a fresh version of that most stately authority on poetry, Quiller-Couch's 'Oxford Book of English Verse', then it would essay a more realistic coverage of the great poetry written in the English language. This would be a step forward from old Quiller-Couch's limited response to the writing of the American nation.

The event has come to pass, under the editorship of Dr Helen Gardner. And through her the British have marched doggedly backwards. Dr Gardner has eliminated the poetry of America, except that she allows Ezra Pound a special dispensation because 'he was at the centre of a modern movement in England'. So we turn to the great Oxford repository and find that Whitman never lived, breathed or contributed to the idiom of poetry. Nothing-poets, like Stevie Smith, Henry Reed, Keith Douglas, have achieved their Oxford immortality for decades to come. But Robert Frost apparently does not measure up to the minor squawking of these nonentities.

What hope, in these circumstances, that any Australian poet will ever find a place outside the idiot limitations of nationalism. None. In my lifetime none at all.

Ah hah, you will say. Wait a minute. What about Patrick White. He has achieved an international stature appropriate to his achievements—and he is an Australian, writing in Australia.

I beg to differ. The case of Patrick White exemplifies the proposition that we live in a world that stubbornly insists on the inward insular book. Patrick White has an accepted international name—but as a maverick, a remote geographical freak. Not, however, as a dominant giant in the contemporary literature of the English language.

In this I am supported by the most vital of all living literary critics, Mr George Steiner, no less, author of *Language and Silence* and *The Death of Tragedy*.

In a recent issue of the New York Review of Books, George Steiner was deploring the enfeebled condition of what he calls 'English english'. That is, those segments of English language literature being produced by the British. And George Steiner declared quite blankly that there is not a single writer in England who could anywhere near approach the stature of the Australian, Patrick White. I quote Steiner precisely.

If this is true, or anywhere near being true, I have yet to find the fact simply and pervasively integrated into British critical writings. Oxbridge undergraduates read E. M. Forster endlessly. Good home-town stuff. I doubt if they are ever obliged to study a Patrick White novel. In the international context all Patrick White receives is the patronising and episodic pat on the head as a meritorious but irrelevant outsider.

More than any other group the Australian modern painter has attempted to be accepted as a normal component in the internationalism of art.

The artists commute fretfully and endlessly between Australia and overseas. Sid Nolan has been the most determined of all in his view that art is of a piece. The themes of painting may be environmental, nationalist if you like, but the painting itself is an act of universal communication.

In the long run Nolan still finds himself 'placed'. And that place is a sort of schizophrenic no-man's land with Nolan wandering around picking the Flanders poppies. The influential critic, Nigel Gosling, responded to Nolan's recent showings at the Tate and the Marlborough by expressing surprise that Nolan has been a London resident for only fifteen years. Even so, his work, according to Gosling, falls into the classification of the 'English eccentric'.

I don't find this forcible incorporation of an artist into a national class as surprising. If you purchase one of the Tate Gallery's guide booklets you will find Nolan featured as a 'modern English artist'.

While he is being forcibly anglicised in one area, Nolan is being detribalised and devalued as an Australian artist. In the American magazine *Newsweek* (11/12/72), Nolan is summated as 'a superior book illustrator and little else'. The Kelly works it finds plain 'laboured'.

The point is that Patrick White loses out by staying here. Nolan loses in all directions by going some place else. The point of Nolan's exile is, and always has been, that he can recall and keep intact his formative Australian imagery by living outside the politics and pressures of the local art environment.

And one supposes the euphoric self-importance of a New York critical celebrity hasn't helped that dream of two decades ago. He came to Australia frenetically insisting that New York is where it is all at—because New York is where he was at. But in the visual arts the world itself is where it's at. Or at least, this is the way it should be. This is the way we dreamed it would be in the 1970s.

The incestuous sickness of national self-centredness is, alas, more in evidence in these days of trade blocs, and obsessive national self-interest than ever it was back in the bad old days. The French are more chauvinistically French; the English more exclusively English—and so on.

And lest it be thought that we have escaped this cultural narcissism because of a desire to be accepted as tiny contributors to a creative international community, let me leave you with a parting thought.

In our part of the world the greatest poet of the past few decades lived a couple of hours away across the Tasman.

Time, one hopes, will establish him as of unmistakably superior stature to our local familiars—A. D. Hope, Judith Wright, McAuley. As far as you are concerned has James K. Baxter been a familiar household word? Has your kid ever come home with a Baxter poem to study for Matric? If this is so, you'll surprise me.

# STATELY
# HOMES
# AND CEREBRAL
# GNOMES

At Launceston the Commonwealth architects have produced the most graceful panoramic airport terminal in Australia. It's a building which permits the eye a large and sweeping appreciation of both the visual drama and serenity of the Tasmanian landscape.

But for some reason best known to themselves, the Tasmanians are natural nest-cackers.

The culinary resources of the airport are limited to execrable versions of the pie, the pasty, the sausage roll, the sandwich—and cups of tea in which a bloatedly ineffectual teabag is half-submerged like a long-drowned corpse. When asked what one is to do with the teabag the Taswegian waitress indicated an enchanting set of alternatives. Either haul out the bag and let it dribble away in your saucer, or heave it into the glass ashtray. Neither alternative seemed to offer a prospect of graceful living.

Tasmanians seem to relish contradictions of this kind within an environment which exists as the most perfect still surviving in Australia. Potentially the tourists surge into Tasmania to experience a non-pollutional ecological balance between human activity and natural environment. They pour into Tasmania to dream dreams of vanished life-styles, to fantasise the brief history of Australia itself.

Tasmania is a bit like Greece in that it will grow richer from its past than from insisting on the possession of an industrial present.

If there has to be a balance between these two incentives, no Tasmanian government of recent vintage seems to have achieved it. The hydro-electric present seems to have rampaged out of hand like the creation of a political Frankenstein, while the historic resources are handled in a quaintly disordered fashion.

Government agencies and the Tourist Board operate autonomously and seemingly in competition with the National Trust. The Government doesn't seem to have latched on to the idea that the National Trust is the expert body with a trained understanding of sequential priorities, and that finance should be channelled to and through the Trust.

For instance, the contiguity of Entally House, Franklin House, and Clarendon, and even the White House at Westbury, constitutes a stately home circuit, a one-day pattern of visits, which could prove eminently profitable. Eminently profitable only if those delightful restorations are jointly promoted and developed. Alas, the Government view is that Entally is a Government site to be sold in isolation to the gigantic tourist trade. For the rest, the National Trust and private individuals finance their projects, and sell their attractions as best they can.

In fact, if the exquisitely dim breed of politician that Tasmania produces were able to see the economic potential of the island as we urbanised and envious mainlanders view it, then they'd be far less silly in the skull with the excessive hydro-electrics and consider the whole historic conspectus as uniquely part of their responsibility.

Dr C. Craig, in association with E. Graeme Robertson and other specialists, has produced a series of brilliantly beautiful and influential books which have captured the archtectural imagination of the nation. Currently the team of Dr Craig, E. Graeme Robertson, and Kevin Fahy has published the first book to my knowledge on Early Colonial Furniture. It's a most exciting revelation as an account of how early craftsmen in Australia recalled, varied, and adapted the great styles of English furniture-making to their own Colonial purposes.

To date the researchers, scholars, and enthusiasts of Tasmania have found commercial publishers willing to undertake such lavish and prestigious projects. But I can assert with a modest degree of expertise that cultural contributions of this original and valuable kind are increasingly costly and uneconomic in the present context of commercial publishing.

Since the historic resources of Tasmania have not yet been fully researched, let alone published, is this not a situation which calls for the Tasmanian Government to become involved? After all, the Tasmanian community, as denizens of Australia's touristic Greece, has the most to gain from an ever-increasing awareness of the past as a country we all need to revisit from time to time.

For instance, when the hydro-electric dreams are forgotten nightmares, millions of Australians will spend their future money around the little town of Ross just to see an astonishing bridge carved with Gothic symbols and grotesqueries by a forgotten artisan who had mad cathedral dreams. Yet the fine published work on Ross Bridge was financed by a quixotic and pathetically optimistic Hobart bookseller.

As I see it, the people who love and present Tasmania to the world do it as a lonely minority, and they will bring a basic prosperity to the island in spite of and not because of governmental philosophies.

It is not as if the work were completed by front-line publicists and the dedicated grass-roots workers in historical evaluation. A magnificent stimulus to our languishing sense of pioneering recall will come when we have a book on the common domestic artifacts of the colonial era. Although folk museums are springing up all over Australia, Tasmania still provides the finest and most extensive repository. Convict copper utensils are a subject in themselves; the pioneer kitchen provides a field of aesthetics as well as quaint fascination for the holidaying mum.

An intellectually enlightened Tasmanian Government would have its own publishing and printing division to ensure that the island remains the focal point of such national interest. Or, alternatively, it would provide a subsidisation system for publication as the mainland commercial entrepreneurs opt out of this difficult field.

It could do any number of other things.

Don Dunstan, for example, has provided a catering adviser for restaurants in South Australia to advise individual enterprises on the economics and advantages of regional gastronomic specialisation.

The idea sounds wacky, but you only have to eat and drink around Tasmania to realise how astute the Dunstan notion is: Tasmania services the tourist carriage trade of Australia, yet it can't rise above the dismal proletarian conventions of Melbourne's football epicureanism, the greasy spoon short-order culture.

Tasmania fills me with joy and wonder. Its people delight me. Yet as I mentioned at the beginning, its corridors of power must surely be peopled by pinheads who cack in their own nest, presumably because they don't recognise a nest when they cack in it.

# A
# NON-PHILOSOPHY
# OF

**LEISURE**   We are now entering that phase when the thirty-five-hour working week is going to be the big industrial issue.

Given Australia's curiously disadvantaged situation in terms of costs and markets, I have misgivings about its effect on our economic collective well-being.

The less-discussed aspect of the thirty-five-hour week is the whole philosophy of leisure in Australia. The unions are setting out with blind conviction that a man realises his identity best when he is left to consume the hours of his life at his own discretion. By and large work is held to be bad, leisure good.

This pervasive philosophy doesn't say much either for the job satisfactions to be found within the economic framework of Australia, or for the human commitments that have become so conspicuously absent from the Australian life-style. Italians and Greeks visibly seem to enjoy their work. They seem to possess an inbuilt capacity to realise themselves in carting bricks or, in general, selling fish and chips. Australians don't.

I must confess that I have always tended to support the philosophy of national slobdom against all-comers, particularly itinerant overseas critics. I have propounded the early Herbert Read thesis that work, ideally, should be the necessary interruption of a day's leisure.

Alas, and likewise alack, the Herbert Read theory doesn't really work in our sun-bronzed environment, for the elementary reason that our leisure satisfactions are as pitiful, dulled, and desperate as our work satisfactions.

Leisure is a good only in that it does do something positive in realising our human identity during the short span of a lifetime.

In this context I have to desert Gough Whitlam and Bob Hawke in favour of Donald Horne, the late Robin Boyd, and all those supercilious foreign observers of Australia's mores who deplore the utter mindlessness of the Australian at play.

It seems to me a great pity that Mr Whitlam and Mr Hawke have declared in favour of non-work as if it were dogmatically an absolute good in itself. In the absence of any philosophic rationale from these intellectual gents, the concept has the blinded air of any fundamentalist religious doctrine. The thesis is true by virtue of revelation rather than rational evidence.

Yet we cannot witlessly discard the monumental mountain of accrued criticism that Australians in the leisure situation present a gross and vacuous image of poker machines, pubs, booze and betting. To the rest of the world we appear possessed of a considerable amount of free time which we consume as mindlessly and with all the conformism one would expect of Hitler's well-trained hordes.

In short, leisure creates a sort of vacuum which is filled by a surge of dim activities which do not at all bear the stamp of man in process of creative self-realisation.

The critics are not altogether wrong.

I find this vacuum principle strangely exemplified whenever I am in Melbourne. The worship of football as a primitive religion fills the gaps in what I imagine would be relatively educated conversation. Although I am a stranger in the midst, for some inexplicable reason any lapse in any group exchange is filled with a great rush of air by someone dragging in the state of football affairs as the upcoming topic. This is a cerebral refuge not only for taxi-drivers but for university graduates and business executives.

The Whitlam-Hawke answer to the pervasively satirical and contemptuous view of Australian leisure traditions no doubt will be that critics and cultural do-gooders should mind their own business.

If Australians like to work for only twenty hours a week and spend the rest of life on the poker machines or in front of the idiot box, then it's their own business. Who is to lay down any rules as to how their lives should be lived?

I don't think we can escape the thirty-five-hour-a-week article of faith as simply as that. For one thing I don't think Australians are all that happy in their vacuous traditions of recreation between work, bed, fornication, and death.

I think there are dreams and longings, aspirations and frustrations which are not self-evident in the Leagues Clubs or at the Sunday morning barbecue. There are in most of us occasions of realisation that we ought to be more than the sum total of our materialist pleasures and consumptions. And I am not thinking of any sort of religious ratbaggery.

When I launched recently the first Antiquities and Ethnographic Society in Australia I was dumbfounded to find that 2000 plain untutored folk out of 12,000 circularised all proved eager to investigate the survivals of ancient or primitive civilisations.

I am continually astounded at the fervent desire of people to make or do things out of their own personal resources. Doll-making, pottery, woodworking, dog-breeding, chess-playing—you name it, and any reputable bookseller will tell you that there's more shy demand for guides to simple creative realisation than there is for the entire conglomerate of sex literature.

People do instinctively sense the malaise of both materialist work situations and materialist leisure consumption. This unease, in my experience, is more profoundly present in housewives, mums, suburbia generally, than it is in the affectedly whole-earth youth brigade. And I find it more touching, and more exciting.

Yet I suspect that Australian industrial life is not the essential villain in the piece. Nor is the education system blandly to be blamed in the usual cliche fashion. Trade union economic materialism is also ingrained as a sort of fingernail grime into the Australian way of life from the 1890s to the present.

In terms of human justice, the obsession has been justified and still is.

But now Mr Whitlam and Mr Hawke are crusading for leisure as a general human demand. If they continue to do so without any practical plan or defined philosophy for the purposes of leisure in an affluent Australia, their zeal may do more harm than good.

# THE LONELINESS
# OF THE
# LONG-DISTANCE

**LIBERAL**  Of course I'm terrorised. I've been losing a mint on the gramophone record section, selling about eleven LPs a week. I'll have to get out from under as best I can. If I can.

Above all else I'm terrified of receiving one of those telegrams from Bob Hawke. And I suppose the Gramophone Record Hole-Punchers Union, the Label Lickers Union, the LP Delivery Transport Union, the musicians and sundry other members of the brood are all involved. In the bad old days of running-dog capitalism I'd just have discontinued the record section of my little establishment and found a more profitable product to sell.

But I've never incurred the wrath of my mates the workers before, and I don't propose to now. I'm asking Bob Hawke to race over for a conference of all parties concerned to see if I can't wrangle an ecumenical blessing for the switch from a less to a more solvent operation.

Terrorised yes. But it's no real problem.

Alienation is. Increasingly I find socio-political alienation to be not a heady academic abstraction, but a significant and distressing emotion. As real as pity, unhappiness, anger, worry, and all the rest of them.

There is nothing abstract about the nightmarish pursuit in one's mind of the kind of language that will set up lines of communication with a student generation that is stiff-necked and brutally uncompromising in its belief that it and the 'old progressives' have no points of contact.

This theme will recur largely as a productive result of clashing recent judgments over issues at Queensland University. Some few versatile students are willing to talk in the language of the Russell-Orwell-Sartre generation, and they will have the chance to put their views to a larger public.

Right now, alienation from the values and morality of the working class movement provides the greatest distress of all, especially since one has spent a lifetime vigorously holding to the view that the national economic cake should be more fairly divided, and that world resources should be shared out to better the total international human condition.

One has had no mercy on the acquisitiveness of the corporate organisation, the anti-social behaviour of the giant monopoly, the cold-blooded exploitation rather than employment of human resources. I've always felt myself to be a true child of the Depression.

Yet, as I learned it over the years, there is a sort of base morality that informs economic struggle. This basic social morality is what differentiates the human day-by-day aspirations of the working people from the depersonalised financial calculations of the corporations.

Now I'm in doubt whether the trade union movement is becoming as morally corrupt as their capitalist counterparts are deemed to be.

My question, flung into the darkness and silence that seem to surround problems when they become moral rather than pragmatic, is whether morally noxious and anti-social industrial actions are justified in a class situation as viable and malleable as we have developed in lucky Australia?

Let me cite situations from my own backyard.

At Port Pirie there was a strike against BHP. It seems that the workers struck a wages and conditions contractual agreement on their own initiative. Apparently they chose the American form of collective bargaining as the best way to secure justice. But later they didn't like the agreement they themselves had made, and struck because they were expected to keep it.

Question: Can Australia remain a high-income, high-productivity nation if contracts are of the Hitler-Chamberlain variety, binding on one party only, the other party at liberty to tear up the scrap of paper when it ceases to suit its purposes? Is there here a breakdown of honour in the working-class movement?

I've seen a shop steward on television boasting and gloating that he'll give a car manufacturer hell with wildcat walkouts come the period when the new model cars are about to be launched and the company is at its most vulnerable. I may have heard it wrong, but it sounded awfully like industrial blackmail to me.

I'd have gone white with fury if a company spokesman, by the same token, had declared there'd be layoffs when cheap seasonal labour became available over the Christmas period, or some such threat. Is organised disruption a legitimate method of industrial struggle in a country with such advanced machinery for civilised negotiation as Australia?

Question: When the first cut price petrol station opened in South Australia the Miscellaneous Workers' Union fronted up and, according to the Press, threatened that if certain union employment conditions weren't met, they'd immediately barricade the entry and exit of the service station to prevent motorists physically from buying the petrol, was the union misrepresented? If not, is violent and presumably illegal interference with the civil rights of the citizenry an accepted technique of the contemporary trade union struggle?

I know more or less in advance the sort of answers I'll get.

First. I've only come up with a garbled and unjust amateur version of each of these events.

If so, then isn't it a matter of supreme urgency that the trade unions should develop sophisticated informational systems so that men of goodwill should understand industrial situations in the round? It's no longer any use to blame the media as capitalist running dogs. My feeling is that the trade union movement doesn't care one teensy scrap one way or the other if the citizenry at large are alienated or won over.

The movement is anti-modern in that it remains inward-looking, incestuous, isolationist. Yet it is important, terribly important, that there should be a rounded understanding of our troubled industrial areas.

There is a substance in the statistical reality that countries like West Germany and Japan are surging ahead in terms of material well-being for all classes through rational and ethical industrial procedures. Britain, and perhaps Australia with it, may be falling behind into a second-rate situation because wildcatting and anarchic situations have built up.

Why? Why?

I'd surely like the trade union movement to bring the light of public relations information into my fuzzed field of view.

Second, I'll surely be side-tracked with the argument that the working man is losing financial ground while profit levels, and the ability to pay better, are balance-sheet facts of life.

This is relevant to other discussions, but not to this one.

It is not even the controversial question whether low-level developments in productivity, produced by constant industrial instability, will destroy the potential for greater material well-being for all people in Australia.

My soggy point was one made by Orwell years ago when he found that the less well-off community possessed a virtual monopoly of an all-important quality. Dignity, human morality, integrity.

These days it sounds sanctimonious and conservative. Old-fashioned I may be, but I still see no reason to admire a cunningly short-sighted shop steward any more or less than a cunningly short-sighted company director.

Ho hum. After this I guess Bob Hawke will make me go on stocking those rotten gramophone records. Foolish lad, Harris.

# THE
# FRAGILE RIGHT
# OF
# PERSONAL PRIVACY
Two newspaper editors were called
before the Senate Committee of Privileges and severely re-
primanded by that parliamentary institution for publishing
news about the impending Drug Report. The editors were
unable to speak in their own defence at any stage of the
Senate's procedure.

This led one of the newspapers to produce a thundering
front-page editorial attacking this pompous and rather ludicrous exercise in political high dudgeon.

'The offence was manifestly trivial,' the editorial said.

No person who followed the events closely could really
disagree.

The editorial continued:

'But the issues it has raised are not trivial. They go to the
heart of the rights of newspapers to seek information and
publish it in the public interest. Unlike the rules of parliamentary privileges, the rights of newspapers are not en-
acted or defined. They depend on tradition and consent.
They are therefore vulnerable, and whenever a newspaper
concedes some restraint on its freedom it abridges its
rights by some degree.'

Again, no person of contemporary sensibility could really
disagree with this. The erosion of public freedoms by
gestures of government autocracy has to be resisted as one
of the growing social horrors that have developed within
modern democracies.

I suppose I have read this particular editorial in variant
forms about fifty times over the past few decades. Such
editorials were common during the censorship of the war
years, and the occasions are recorded by Sir Paul Hasluck in
his *Government And The People*. Such editorials pop up
with alarming frequency in relation to television, radio and
Press in that most news-conscious of all nations, Britain.

It always seems that authority by its nature tends to use
all available power systems to resist proper public survey.
Therefore it is in our individual interest to support the media
in their occasional fights to subject the world of affairs to
the widest possible scrutiny.

Without indulging in too gross an exaggeration, the media
are also in the front line in defending the private rights of
the citizenry against violation by an increasingly impersonal
juggernaut of government and administration.

This said, let us proceed to the next editorial observation:

E

'Save for the normal embargoes on matter that is libellous, obscene, seditious, or prejudicial to justice or national security, no newspaper in a democracy recognises any restriction on its right to seek out and publish the news.'

Here is where I shudder with something approaching sociological panic.

That most appallingly subjective of words 'news' is used as if it identified something objective, recognisable, palpably self-evident. What is news of the utmost import to a Fleet Street sex tabloid is anathema to *The Times*. What is 'news' to *The Times* is an unpublishable nothing to the sex tabloid. What is news is in fact what verbal or visual products you happen to be selling to whom.

And I shudder at the quoted paragraph, because even though it is directed against those who would govern by secrecy, its effect is also to trample in an elephantine way over any fragile rights I thought I possessed as a powerless and humble citizen to some sort of inalienable personal privacy.

At any moment any one of a hundred media blokes for any one of a hundred different reasons could subjectively decide I am 'news'. Then the citizen and the media are at war.

The media recognise no restriction, no moral or humanistic restraints, on their right to seek out and publish me as 'news'.

By Christ, by the same token I recognise no restriction, no restraint on my right to seek out, define, and retain any supposedly inalienable rights to personal privacy. I will have a little say whether my sex life, bank book, or social life constitute news or not. If some telly or radio bod thinks he has the right to define what part of my life falls into the news category, then he's going to have a bloody nose. I reckon my rights have priority over what he claims are his unquestionable rights.

It's the great modern predicament.

It's a vast issue, appallingly important, and too little ventilated as perhaps one of the most terrible issues of our times.

The tendency of corporate capitalism has been to invade and destroy the whole basic concept of personal privacy and personal dignity.

The Orwellian processes of this age of computerised depersonalisation are spearheaded by governmental agencies, from the security services to the Bureau of Census and Statistics; by the practices of the corporate business institution; and by the mass media in response to ever more outrageous and capriciously subjective definitions of what they loftily and unsupportedly declare to be 'news' and matters of public interest.

The mass media are in a desperately schizophrenic situation.

In fairness to the media one has to point out that they've led the fight against snooping, against bugging, against the endless new limitations placed on personal freedoms, against the insidious invasions of privacy by all the various forces of public bureaucracy.

If we finish up in the situation envisaged by the late lamented Ern Malley, that man's only inalienable right to privacy in the end will be at his own funeral—then it won't be for lack of media courage In spotlighting the creepy invaders.

But it's hard for the media to see themselves advancing pari passu with the invading forces.

They oppose the process as they see it, but they are themselves a central part of it.

It is possible for us impotent Freds to discuss the monstrosity of our private lives becoming governmental dossiers, but how can we ventilate the role of the media except through the media, as is my rare and relatively unique privilege in this context?

The media aren't going to launch a massive campaign to limit their own profitability by imposing a rigid system of controls over intrusions on the rights of the individual to protection from media scrutiny in non-public areas.

Our editorialist recognises no restriction on seeking out news, definitional or otherwise.

The fact that the conflicting issue of personal privacy didn't even spring to mind when the editor let rip with his declaration indicates that the role of the media as an intrusive agency in a Packard age of shrinking private individual rights doesn't even loom large in the thinking of people in the media biz. By the same token one wonders how large it looms in the thinking of people in Cabinet, ASIO or even Census and Statistics.

I am aware that highly defined reporting codes exist in what we called the quality Press. But this is the Age of Information.

You just think of the daily output of words by talking heads on radio throughout Australia! And if some worthy statistician were to add up the amount of material forthcoming each day dealing with unquestionable public issues as against the amount of material dealing with provincial, individual, time passing non-issues that aim to provide listener or reader titillation, then I think we'd find non-news represents ninety per cent of the total output of the Tabloid Society we inhabit. The editorialist I have quoted is thinking only of the ten per cent of material that is genuinely of proper and unquestionable public moment.

How does the media work as the enemy of privacy? It works by huff and puff and bluff. The media obey the laws of the land, but the laws of the land rarely concern themselves with notions of privacy or dignity. In Australia there are, in effect, no laws on the statute books devised to safeguard the privacy of personal information, according to an eminent jurist of my acquaintance.

Once I had a small fire at my home. The fire brigade quickly put it out. A TV film unit turned up with their grubby paraphenalia and marched in the front gate. I decided that the distress of myself and my family in the early hours was not definable as 'news' and in any real public interest. So I told them they could film whatever they liked off my property and out in the street. The umbrage at this restriction of their inalienable right to seek out news was remarkable.

I was told I might come to regret my lack of co-operation in the future. Technique: moral blackmail. And, incidentally, they kept their word.

When I took part later in an ABC documentary, I was asked after the filming to sign a standard disclaimer form in which I consented, among other things, to permit the ABC to use any words they chose over my filmed image.

They could distort, send-up, misrepresent my presence, make me look a yob and an idiot. Yet not to sign the disclaimer would have made me look a proper pompous nark. Technique: the invidious situation.

Such personal experiences with the media are of minimal import. I'm a battle-scarred old pro and if I don't know how to look after myself now, I never will.

One thinks more of the perpetually invaded dignity of simple, ignorant, confused, panicky, inexperienced ordinary people. Caught with their intellectual pants down in one of those execrable street interviews, or suddenly and confusedly involved for the first time in human events that take on the colouration of 'news'.

Simple people possess fragile and legally invisible rights to dignity and privacy. But to me they are rights. All-important rights.

Let us suppose that as editor of the Wagga-Wagga Pigeon Breeders' Gazette, I conned the housekeeper of a distinguished metropolitan editor into letting me take a peek at the bank account of her employer. Nothing libellous, obscene or seditious in publishing the financial facts about the mass media bloke. I've decided his personal bank balance is news and in the public interest. I've decided there shall be no restriction on my rights to seek out and publish the facts. Would my fellow media workers support me in my claim to be exercising the legitimate traditional freedoms of the Press?

Of course not.

Freedom from the Press, from the media, is an issue in this eroded, corrosive and vulgarised era just as important as freedom of the media to subject public life to scrutiny.

Both rights have to be reconciled. In Britain they have made considerable progress towards both acknowledging and resolving the problems.

In Australia we haven't even begun to discuss the matter. It's about time we did.

# GOOD ON YOU, SPORT

'Harris, a neat little rover with a strong left-foot kick, gave a most courageous exhibition' (*The Advertiser*, year dot).

I can quote the reference verbatim because it's the only Press clipping I ever kept. You forget a lot of things, but you don't forget receiving the umpire's vote for the annual inter-collegiate footy match.

And thus, instead of becoming the saintly Schweitzerian figure of my acknowledged prime, I could well have slithered down the path of ruthless egotism and mean self-aggrandisement so characteristic of competitive sports.

I never quite overcame the addiction to sport and even now suffer withdrawal symptoms if deprived of an occasional fixture of interest. Fortunately booze, cigarettes and high living caught up with me at a blessedly early age and I was saved from the moral corruption of competitive sporting activity.

We have reached a period in our population and social development in Australia where the morality of competitive sports is worth debating seriously—as it has been debated with bitter cynicism and unsavoury facts in the United States.

One can even hinge the debate on the present series of test cricket matches. There must be thousands who share my doubt as to whether these six weary battles of humourless sporting attrition do honour to either British tenacity or Australian phlegm. It's the dour and cheerless solemnity of it all that basically turns one off other than the baying and yelping of the over-agitated journalistic morticians who dutifully bury each day's play for their lugubrious readers.

Where's the colour, the personality, the ebullient joy of the game itself, eh?

Where are the wayward ones, the individualists, the game-players, the ones blissfully unaware of their national responsibilities—gone, all gone, alas.

And does this grisly periodic cricketing saga cement the bonds of friendship between us and the dear old Mother Country? It creates about as much general bonhomie as exists between warring generals. The purpose of the activity, at the level of real public psychology, is for the Poms to finish up feeling superior to the colonials, or the Aussies to cock a superior snook at the toffy-nosed masters of Empire. Very inspiring!

When you get down to the basic moral issues, there isn't much of an argument, even at the most cunning level of Christian rationalisation. The doctrine of Jesus and the ethics of Christianity have never uncovered much virtue in the notion of proving yourself superior to the next bloke. In fact there's something rather morally despicable about wanting to show the other bloke your legs will go faster than his, or whatever.

By the same token, the old Etonian codswallop about character-building and self-discipline has taken a fair sort of contemporary hammering from liberated head-shrinkers.

Excessive pre-occupation with winning against the other bloke, either through individual or team performance, is scarcely conducive to producing a stable, relaxed personality. Transfer the motivation to the character in your own suburban street or in the office hierarchy, and surely you've identified the number-one twirp in your immediate vicinity?

The justification for competitive sport has to come, not from Christian ethical rationalisation, but from Darwinian natural selection, the survival of the fittest, and all that stuff. It's in the nature of men to strive and to compete against each other. That's how the race progresses to bigger and boomier and more modern wars, etc.

This Hitlerian theory of primal instinct may be sustainable once again. Indeed, Robert Ardrey is leading in that direction in his new book *The Social Contract*. And no one will question that the competitive drive exists outside sport. In theatre there's the chronic upstager, in art there's the mercenary self-publicist, and in the world of business there's the creepy class classified by Vance Packard as the pyramid climbers.

The competitive instinct is not restricted to sport, there's no question about that. But no one in his right senses would consider the instinct ennobling or inspiring or psychologically valuable. We rate it as an inevitable but distasteful contemporary evil—yet howl in pain when the perceptive young choose to drop out from the whole team system of sport.

We can't very well deplore the psychology of the competitive drive when it exists nakedly in human affairs and laud it on the playing field. Yet this is precisely the insane prevailing mode of public thought.

I'll leave you to punch holes through this simplistic argumentation while I proceed to consider the rather special nature of the Australian situation.

It has always struck me that one of Australia's virtues is that our preoccupation has been fairly heavily centred on non-competitive recreations, largely because we've got a lot of space and surrounding water. Swimming, surfing, camping, bush walking, fishing (I've no objection to a bloke competing with a succulent snook as against fellow human beings). The loner sports have been our thing.

With the odd exception of Melbourne, a curiously atypical Australian town in many ways, we've been lackadaisical and lazily amateurish about organised competitive sport. This tradition is the source of some of our urban virtues.

One of the grim cultural adjuncts of post-war British and European migration has been to intensify a needless shift to the claustrophobic and gladiatorial spectator sports that provide partisan emotional release in cramped and under-privileged urban societies overseas.

Should we consider this change of recreational pattern progress or regression?

Before making a snap judgment we could well contemplate the angry crisis now dominant in the highly regimented area of American competitive sport. Sport has become both impersonal and degrading for the sportsman, the moral effects debilitating, the competitive instinct blind and obedient.

In this context the evangelical religions have swooped in, under the notable leadership of the inevitable Billy Graham, and to devastating effect. St Paul was a terrific sports addict, claims Billy, wisely omitting to give Jesus a team guernsey; and the gum-chewing heroes of the arena sit around and believe it.

For competitive sport achieved an atmosphere akin to religious fervour, with the same sexual overtones.

And evangelism is, of course, another competitive sport that is bound to appeal to individuals with an appropriate build-up of the contesting reflexes. It's the competitive soul rather than goal-scoring game that Christians play to the bewilderment of older and more civilised religious faiths and philosophies.

So sport and Christ are mixed up in a raddle of morally dishonest distortions of values. The American establishment uses the 100,000 members of the Fellowship of Christian Athletes as a primitive bastion while the dissident young opt out of the whole sporting situation in a mood of cold rational hostility.

Like it or not, competitive sport US-style stinks.

Reason tells me we'll retain traces of the sane society in Australia while soccer struggles vainly to establish itself; athletics remain an underfinanced parklands activity while we spawn casual swimming champions out of nowhere,

**62/63**   while the Rod Lavers pick up their volleys on mum's back lawn, and Aussie Rules remains in its condition of benign stagnation.

And we'll all try not to feel really venomous if the Poms win the Ashes again.

# THE
# BLACK AND WHITE
**WART SHOW** Wartsmanship! It's the new skill, the game of the moment, the national hobby.

It's become such a cult that they even know about it overseas—the British Race Relations Board have been helping us draw in one particular moral excrescence quite recently.

If the Australian propensity was at one time to exude a roseate complacence, the late 'sixties and the early 'seventies are seeing a swift end to the age of narcissistic innocence.

It's a rambling story which I propose to tell with an improper measure of intellectual leap-frogging.

We always knew that the dark side of the Australian lunar landscape concerned race and colour—the White Australia policy and the social history of white settlement in this continent in relation to the original Aboriginal peoples. This has always been the gigantic wart on the leanly handsome Australian proboscis. We're as racialist a mob as any in the world, and with the additional ugliness of being blandly hypocritical about it.

We've always known there have been some unpretty aspects of our social history—poisoned flour as a means of exterminating Aboriginals, as recorded by Edmund John Eyre; Aboriginal hunts in Queensland as substitutes for the country fox hunts; the good old-fashioned Eumerella massacre in Victoria so enthusiastically reported by the novelist, Rolfe Boldrewood.

The Tasmanian Black War has been analysed in depth by both Travers and Clive Turnbull. Writers from Kylie Tennant to Hector Holthouse in his new book *Up Rode the Squatter* have never avoided the issue of the genocidal components in Australian history.

But it's taken until now for all these facts to be analysed, unified, and interpreted in the factual academic style. The series on Aboriginals in Australian Society sponsored by the Social Science Research Council of Australia and emanating from the Australian National University Press has not been largely publicised. Yet I would imagine it's the most serious and thoroughgoing library of expert monographs ever attempted to give the nation an insight into Aboriginal problems, both as currently existing and historically causated.

The most dramatic and radical of the volumes is Professor C. D. Rowley's, *The Destruction of Aboriginal Society*.

Despite the scholarly detachment with which the theme is analysed on a national scale, one senses an important new theory—that the Aboriginal presence affected the nature and quality of the European settler who moved into the rural environment.

Our invasion destroyed Aboriginal society. It also gave us a hard-core rural population of rapacious, ruthless, and racialist temperament. For these were the kind of settlers attracted to and capable of economic success in taking over Aboriginal tribal lands.

Dr Rowley's study is probably as revealing on the theme of the cold lethal racial bastardry of our pioneering ancestors as it is on the tragedy it involved for the Aboriginal society.

It is not merely a theme of killer squatters. The romantic and peripatetic rural proletariat enshrined by Dr Russell Ward at the heart of the Australian myth was no better. They shared the ruthless colonialist temperament of their employers.

And if we turn now to McQueen's *The New Britannia*, the radical new bible of the iconoclastic young, we see the trade union movement emerged from the social context of Australia as reactionary, self-centred, backward, and totally devoid of generalised humaneness or national vision.

The corollary of this new hard look at our warty history is a Jungian suggestion. The modern Australian does not invent policies; he inherits ancestral bigotries.

It is not as far-fetched as it might seem to relate the history of our great grand-parents to the recent Australian government fiasco over assistance to coloured British migrants.

Our political pastors involved in telling the British to keep their noses out of Australia's sovereign affairs, genuinely believe that our European-only immigration policy is the product of an intellectual decision backed by social consensus.

Perhaps it is. But the ugly ham-fisted handling of the situation is straight from William Faulkner country. Or from the ancestral reflexes of Australian history.

Most of us these days believe human rights, and racial issues, rightly or wrongly interpreted, transcend national sovereignty and that it is the duty of civilised nations to give a proper explanation when such matters are raised.

National sovereignty, 'interfering with the domestic internal affairs', is the inevitable refuge of the South Africans; thundered out by the Russians when they storm into Hungary or Czechoslovakia; piously proclaimed by the Greek colonels in their more extremist days. Used by Australia to foist off a racial question, it reflects ancestral bigotry and ruthlessness. 'Bugger you, get off my property or I shoot.'

As an echo of the ancient past living in the present, Mr Arthur Calwell's response that Australia 'doesn't want a multi-racial society' is indicative of the fixated idiot processes the trade union movement has inherited.

'Race', for poor old Arthur, is skin colour, not culture. Coloured scientists, engineers, doctors, and teachers from Britain may well be educated and cultivated beyond the moral crudities of the Alf Garnetts, or those in Australia on behalf of whom Mr Calwell is speaking. Skins of such a colour, culturally advanced beyond the Australian norm, tend to solve our problems, not create them.

The problem in fact most in need of solving is accentuated by our governmental high-horse psychology. Australia is becoming the paradise garden of the American and European bigot, the dream country for frustrated racialists.

This is no fantasy. My Australian identity has brought wet delight to the eyes of muscle-brained uniformed officials in places like Miami where I'm told 'Australia is the place to migrate to. You Aussies know how to handle the nigger problem all right.'

Meanwhile, if we must have a racialist migration policy, let us not, in the name of the half-civilised condition, have a ministerial high-horse psychology to go with it.

# VULGARLAND'S CULTURAL POLLUTION

It has been my wont on occasion to be whimsical about Surfers Paradise. It was amusing to observe naive Australian vulgarity attempting to ape naive American vulgarity.

In my present mood the time for whimsicality is past. It is the season of anger and of home truths plainly spoken.

The catalyst for this change of disposition lies in my devotion to an aspect of conservation. I am a people-conservationist. I think people are just fine to have about the place: that they are happier alive than dead; that they look nicer in one piece than senselessly mutilated.

Therefore, along with many millions of fellow Australians, I subscribe to that commonly accepted road theory that speed kills. The intelligent section of the national community, the responsible authorities in every State government and every safety organisation, are putting a great deal of effort and a not inconsiderable volume of public finance into the task of educating people that speed is not glamorous, or socially desirable, not remarkable, or acceptable in law.

From the happy Gold Coast has come an expensive, spectacular, and nation-wide counter-attack against this educational campaign—in the form, God help us all, of a Speed Week!

This is literally and unequivocally true. The telly set does not lie for ninety minutes non-stop.

From the tasteful environs of Surfers Paradise an unbelievable mechanico-sexual extravaganza was mounted for showing all over the nation on the magic box. Speed Week, it appears, was climaxed by a catwalk fashion parade of thirty cars that can go very fast, and this entertainment bore the bewilderingly jet-setting title of 'Concours D'Elegance 1971'. By some nasty act of sexual association, the thirty automobiles were attended by model females displaying the very latest in Queensland fashion gear.

It is not my intention to expatiate on the aesthetic horrors of this visual occasion. I will omit the word-count of 'fabulous' as the basic adjectival equipment of the lady commentator. I won't attempt to convey phonetically the pseudo-American inflections of the homely young gentleman commentator. As an admirer of high fashion, its disciplines, restraints, and sense of excellence, one forgets the Queensland habiliments displayed by the young ladies. They symbolised in their gaucheries and sloppy workmanship the sort of couturistic nightmare Givenchy or Yves St Laurent might experience on a particularly appalling LSD trip.

It is worth recording that the national televiewing public was informed that one particular car has only three speeds—fast, very fast, and 'hello judge' (Gold Coast audience rolling around in comic uproar). There were clucks of family approbation when it was proudly reported that a famous mini-car is capable of belting along at 105 miles an hour.

One mustn't be too outraged. The enemy is legal and within his rights.

Big Brother, who knows what's good for us Freds, wants the purveyors of one form of speed incarcerated mercilessly while the purveyors of the speed that really kills on a grand scale are subject to no governmental legislation on the matter of engine power. One can scarcely blame the Gold Coast for getting high on a psychologically and socially disastrous drug.

Speed Week is over. But the Gold Coast remains. And so does an attitude hardened from a previous condition of satiric tolerance.

The Gold Coast is, or is rapidly becoming, an organic excrescence carcinogenically formed on the Australian cultural organic pattern. It is natural that it should be the venue for a pro-speed week. It has to be considered not in terms of environmental pollution. It can look as vulgar and garish as Queenslanders would wish it to be. It's their eyesore.

Rather it has to be considered as integral to processes within Australia of cultural pollution.

The Gold Coast is quite desperately and quite self-consciously attempting to superimpose on the Australian recreational pattern a combination of the tasteless vulgarity of Miami with the loud uncouthness of Dallas, Texas. It's an unnatural innovation imported from America and imposed on the present pattern of leisure by one of the most monumental hardsells in Australian commercial history.

It is not known to us island isolates how rare such Vulgarland concepts are in the big wide world. There's Miami, Las Vegas, Honolulu, and perhaps Blackpool if you want to be unjust to a remarkably innocent British seaside tradition. The fashionable watering places of Europe, indeed of the world, may be popular and crowded, but they don't market garishness and vulgarity as products in themselves. It is indeed remarkable how people have largely insisted that grace, taste, and tradition remain central to their notions of what personal recreation is all about.

The Miami-Las Vegas-Gold Coast pathology is, in fact, a malformation on the cultural body politic. There are few

American exports that we Australians have resisted. This cultural environmental hazard is perhaps one that we should.

To possess a Vulgarland-capital is not natural to our national hedonistic instincts. Our recreational tradition is a rich one. There is no reason on earth we should be compliant and tolerant towards the predators and destroyers of a creative recreational tradition.

We have exploited our snow country and the Barrier Reef in recent years, as we are jolly well entitled to. In so doing there has been an enlargement of our environmental pleasures without debasement.

Tasmania is the loveliest touristic pleasure of all available to us mainlanders. Tasmania has absorbed the flood of pleasure-seekers with no visible signs whatsoever of a wholesale vulgarisation.

Add it all up, and one supposes that Australians are outdoor hedonists because we have such a largesse of things to be hedonistic and outdoorish about. It is all natural and organic to our culture and I get a bit hackled when the Donald Hornes and Ronald Conways tend to define it as a predisposition towards the stupefied, sensual, and brainless.

What we do have to remember is that a passion for recreation is capable of being thought of and exploited in terms of consumer economics. And if a salesman talks hard enough we'll usually buy.

Therefore the time has come to depart from soft satire.

We must tell of Queensland's Miami exactly as it is in the pattern of cultural environment. It is a genuine pollution issue in terms of Australian creative recreational values and traditions. If we can successfully be sold one Gold Coast on the American model, then we can be sold a dozen more. Then, comrades, we've had it!

## IT'S TIME
## WE PUT PAID TO
## SELF-RIGHTEOUS

**BUSH BIGOTRY** Some plain speaking on a touchy theme. I hope only that it will stimulate dialogue rather than diatribe.

The theme concerns the growing cultural conflict between the backward, egocentric, conservative and largely ignorant rural Australian community, and the increasingly sophisticated and enlightened values of both the urban and (pace Barry Humphries) suburban denizens of our fair land.

The sources of this impending conflict are bound up with our national social history, with The Australian Legend, as Dr Russel Ward has defined it historically. Once the Australian tradition was a bush phenomenon, defined by the liberalism and tolerant humanity of a rural proletariat, philosophically crystallised in the unique, repressed, homosexual conventions of mateship. Its literature was the balladry of itinerant workers, its homeric phase the long, drawn-out century of exploration. It was a great tradition, and Australians are rightfully proud of it. Some of us spend large amounts of our intellectual lifetime studying it.

But this tradition died, and it died suddenly and recently. Writers like George Farwell, Douglas Lockwood, Bill Beatty, traipse around the country trying to find the surviving presence of this great tradition. But they're having a hard time of it. Warm-hearted, open-minded bushies are thin on the ground. Even though the 'real' Australian tradition has disappeared, and the country now represents only specific economic, self-interested pressure groups, there is a tendency for these groups to assume the posture of superior 'Australian-ness' to declare that they symbolise the genuine decencies of the country, and to demand unreal economic privileges because they make their profit out of one kind of product as against another.

Queensland is probably the State where loud-mouthed ruralism survives strongest, and Queensland has become a notorious cultural shambles because of it. This rich and fascinating territory is becoming a stewpot of aesthetic outrage, unredeemed vulgarity, rampant philistinism, and backwoods morality, and I think it's because the rural voice is all-powerful.

'The appeal of the play "Hair", could only be to those who could be regarded as sexually depraved, or a group of homosexuals, lesbians, wife-swappers or spivs,' declared that notable authority on theatre aesthetics, Mr R. J. Hinze, a Queensland Country Party MP. With exquisite delicacy, this bucolic gentleman then proceeded to describe university radicals as 'a group of ratbags bringing a great institution of learning into disrepute by filthy expressions and a complete disregard for law and order . . . contemptible hooligans.'

The Vice-Chancellor's reply was perfect irony: 'I don't know what to say because some of these people (referring to Mr Hinze) just don't apply ideas to modern circumstances.'

There are rural vocal minorities creating dissidence and disturbance all over the country. It's only a matter of time before they are hit by an educated and majority urban backlash. We can deal with the problems of the generation gap, of student dissent, of permissive artistic events, and we use the weapons of social and intellectual sophistication. 'Hair' is a success because it has great merit. Other permissive-seeming events will fail because they are phoney. Student protesters we will evaluate on the validity of the causes they put before us.

But a genuinely adult Australia will make no progress in these matters if the voice of the self-righteous bigot is too loudly influential in the land. Strangely enough, it may well be through the pervasive social education of ordinary Australians that the voice of the Australian countryside will have to change.

Sir Henry Bolte, farmer to the end, stepped up his war against margarine, for example, but can he win out in his blind championship of one Australian industry against another when, lined up against him, is the National Heart Foundation, the medical profession, the 100,000 people who've purchased the Heart Foundation titles, *The Fats of Life* and *The Anti-Coronary Cookbook?*

It's a basic public freedom that people should not be made to smoke, should be allowed to eat non-fatty meats, and to have access to as much polyunsaturated material as they choose to consume.

The conflict of the rural politicians who lower the standard of our political and public life will be resolved by the country population itself. It's the weird contradiction that Australia's intellectualism, particularly her book-reading reputation, is a rural phenomenon. It's a rural core (and I can substantiate this statistically) that consumes a relatively high proportion of intellectual and cultural products. These people themselves will, in due course, breed out the bad old strain, the image of backwardness, the bigoted public minds that have made Australia notorious for philistinism. One only hopes they don't take too long about it.

SECTION TWO

# Gestures of National Disenchantment

# INTELLECTUAL
## SNOBBERY
I have had a comment on the pervasive and deplorable snobbery of Australian intellectuals in their collective attitude to sport.

Most generalisations are open to dispute, but not this one. Sport is one of the dirtiest words in the intellectual vocabulary. It is used to epitomise the most vacuous and most emptied-headed preoccupations in the Lucky Country way of life. Along with beer and betting, sport symbolises our cultural aimlessness.

It is an unwholesome snobbery, not shared I think by many national groups.

Whether the arties and the crafties like it or not, sport is a part of the total cultural complex. Its forms and motivations are as interesting in their own right as the forms and motivations which go to make modern Australian poetry the world's dreariest, or modern Australian painting so chaotic.

It is more to the point to consider why sport in Australia, with its peculiar drive, energies, and youthfulness, has not gracefully or intelligently been integrated into the cultural picture.

The British have no qualms about this. They have never found it difficult to lay hands on a sophisticated and self-respecting literature about sport.

It is the opposite in Australia. It is something of a confession of second-classness for an intellectual to admit to an interest in a sport, let alone write about it. And Australian sport could gain a great deal from intelligent appraisal: from cultural recognition, in fact.

The process has to start at the grass roots. The sporting journalist considers himself through some sort of inferiority process as a race apart, as the plainest and most uncerebral of tradesmen. It would be sissy, contrary to reader-interest, to write well and literately about sporting occasions.

But sports writing in Britain is a supremely developed literary skill, and those who write for the Sunday papers there are national names, in the groves of Academe as well as the pubs of Islington.

The Australian attitude of write-down-to-our-drongo readers leads on to the endless flood of bad sporting books. We produce a lot of champions and they all seem to produce those as-told-to-Joe Goat books. These Australian books are excruciatingly arch, gossipy, trivial, and conducive to the belief that sportsmen are empty-headed egotists.

I don't think this is the fault of the sportsmen. It is the fault of the writers who interest themselves in the subject. Even though the books are bad, the literary pages of the newspapers and the journals don't help to improve them. I'd estimate that some thirty sporting books on Australian themes have appeared in the last year. I can't remember one of them being considered worthy of critical scrutiny in the pages of any newspaper, journal, or quarterly.

We are all too busy impressing the public with our knowledge of the role of Tashkent in the sixteenth century or Joyce's use of the word fuff. I don't think Australian sporting books will become literate until we look to them to be so.

There is a literature ready to emerge all right. The Lansdowne Press *Six and Out* showed that there can be writing of great imaginative calibre at least on the subject of cricket in this country.

But the Donald Horne sort of denigration of this part of our life has to disappear as a sorry sort of snobbery.

I'll help the process. Did you know that Vincent Buckley, no less, and Clement Semmler are keen on the gallopers? That Geoffrey Dutton hero-worships Jack Brabham? That Patrick White is about the wisest man I know on the subject of dogs. That the poet, Flexmore Hudson, is a rowing expert.

In short, it's time the secret vices of the intellectuals came to be deemed as public virtues.

There are rewards to be won. When first I declared myself an Australian Rules devotee, albeit very nervously, I wrote that a footballer took a 'cantilevered mark'. It caused more reader excitement than any observation I've ever published.

After initial shock and hostility at this curious word appearing on the sporting page, after the furtive consulting of dictionaries, I found myself being patted on the back by unknown readers at a variety of football ovals.

Anyone would think I'd taken the mark myself. But at least it convinced me that the Australian public don't want to think of their sporting preoccupations in a wholly empty-headed way.

# THEY THINK
# WE'RE
# A WEIRD MOB,
**MATES**   It is surprising to many of us that there should be any
degree of public stir about Sidney Baker's suggestion, in
*The Australian Language*, that the Kelly gang might have
been homosexual.

It is largely surmise apart from the established fact that
the gang were rather keen on appearing in 'drag'.

On the other hand historians have come to accept fairly
calmly the notion that the Australian national philosophy
of 'mateship' emerged from what was perhaps the world's
only homosexual social ordering of things. This idea was put
forward in the Nation during its first year of publication.

It was based on a study of the social response to two
conditions of work in early Australia. Firstly, in the rural
working environment there was a population disproportion,
as large at times as eight males to one female. Secondly,
during the shepherding era of the wool industry, the isolation of the shepherd from the home station for extended
periods of time led to 'bush madness'.

The answer to this shepherding problem lay in providing
the shepherd with a 'mate', another man whose chief function was as hut-keeper, cook, and general factotum.

The same principle applied to any number of rural tasks.
The bush carpenter always went around his itinerant tasks
with his 'mate'.

This ordering of labour in terms of the worker and his
camp mate (no pun intended) became very extensive, and
led to loyalties of a fierce and irrational kind which go a long
way towards explaining some of the unique facets of the
Australian character. A man defended his 'mate' as fiercely
as he'd defend the honour of a wife—even though the mateship often had a love-hate basis to it.

There is no suggestion that this male conjugality was
accompanied by overt homosexuality. It may have been;
there's just not enough evidence to establish the fact one
way or the other.

But as working groups changed their character and size,
the mateship principle was taken over and applied to larger
and more proletarian groups. It became Henry Lawson's
'mateship', the ruling code of the bush, and the foundation
stone of the Australian philosophy.

From its origins mateship held sway into the twentieth
century, manifesting itself in the male sanctity of the bar and
the tradition of men foregathering around the keg at parties.

Michael Powell clings to this image in the 'Weird Mob' film by making the leit-motif of the whole show the theme that Australia's a 'man's country'. If we are still a weird mob, and let's hope we're not, it's because we are the only country on earth that holds to homosexual group values; even though Australian males are mostly too ingenuous to recognise the fact.

Next time you see a mob of blokes gathered round the keg at a party, with the women isolated in the parlour, I don't suggest you go up and tell them they're unconsciously adhering to a traditional Australian code of effeminacy. You'd probably get clobbered for no really good reason.

But I suggest a reading of Alexander Harris' early classic, *Settlers and Convicts* will give you a fairly clear picture of a colonial working world where the little woman was another man.

# THE
# LARRIKINS
# IN
# WEIMAR

From all directions they converged on East Berlin —300 writers, Africans in flowing regalia, impassive Mongolians, impeccable Cubans, noisome Americans, West German poets looking youthful and ill-at-ease, plus the gregarious and omnipresent band of Australians. Where the guffaws were loudest there they were.

But it wasn't basically all fun and games for the hosts from the 'unstable city-state of East Germany' who had spent an astronomical sum in organising an International Meeting of Writers as a cultural counter-measure to the royal visit to West Germany.

It was a deadly serious matter to them that the cause of East Germany should be understood aright in the light of the perpetually damaging mystique built up in the West around the Wall and Checkpoint Charlie. And, for that matter, the East Germans needed desperately to change the view in other socialist countries that East German communism is the most puritanical and formalistic of all.

The East German organisers played their cards wisely and well. They prepared only one formal meeting, no guided tours or compulsory itineraries. The writers were offered a fistful of drinking money whenever they required it and allowed to attend discussions or not, as they saw fit. Manifestations of propaganda were suppressed in favour of the subtle and disarming technique of saying: 'Here we are, take us as you find us! Most of you writers are far from being communists, and you will have your own views about our society. This doesn't matter so long as you depict our way of life as truthfully as you can. For our part we are concealing nothing.'

These methods are nothing new as a cunning way of converting the liberal mind which believes in the spirit of open and unprejudiced enquiry.

Did these ingenious non-directive methods work to brainwash the ingenuous band of literary boys from the Australian bush?

If ASIO keeps dossiers on political loners, then they'd better start one on me. I'll gladly give them a hand. It's not that I, or any of my writing colleagues from the Australian contingent to East Berlin, have been brainwashed by the Mephistophelian sophistries of East European communism, but rather in my case that a direct experience of Western Europe makes one realise with a shock of shame and dismay how much of the propaganda and manifestly untruthful guff of our own side has rubbed off on us as we luxuriate on the beaches of the Lucky Country.

West Germany for instance. Here we have a country besotted with affluence and self-assurance, the streets of Frankfurt and Wiesbaden more bepoodled than any in the world; citizens fighting to pay £5 a seat to see the Italian Opera; the shops gluttonous mountains of decorative carbohydrates.

And the West Germans themselves? Not bitter and still arrogant as they were when I last saw them a decade ago, but suave and possessed of an all-embracing self-assurance. It is the unpretty affluence of a discreetly powerful emerging middle-class, dressed, young and old alike, in the uniform of current fashion and with the omnipresent expensive leather brief-case.

They were to a man much amused by the royal tour of West Germany, much amused in a tolerant way that Britain's desperate need to secure a better economic toehold in the Common Market in the face of de Gaulle's capriciousness had led to such an elaborate act of flattery on the part of Britain. Being obedient Germans they took their little flags, lined the streets, and benignly accepted the decorations that were strewn over Germany like confetti from the royal fingers.

Nothing shameful in Britain using its royal paraphernalia to strengthen its hand in Europe: it demonstrates clearly the value of a monarchy as a device even in modern political psychology.

But this was not the story reported in Britain or Australia. Day by day, hour by hour, the BBC, the popular Press, even journals like *The Guardian*, which should know better, reported endless vistas of jubilant Germans transported at the thought of being finally forgiven their past—'their queen is now our queen too'. This nauseous guff of old Bavarian women saying to children: 'Now we really belong to the free world again' saturated the British and Commonwealth mass media so that one was aware of a compulsive 'party line' on this event—that it symbolised to the Germans British forgiveness of their nazi past.

But it was just untrue! And dangerously untrue. The West Germans know their commanding strength in the Common Market, that 1,000,000 Italians have been absorbed into their work-force like a flash, and that they can well afford the luxury of old hard-core nazis in their new army and to hell with ancient remorse.

And they can increase their pressure and intensify their manoeuvres towards a German reunification (which wise editorialists, like those of *The Sunday Times*, see as historically unrealistic and politically dangerous in a period that hopes for American-Soviet rapprochement).

One sees present history falsified and this leads one to wonder about past history and to worry how far one has brainwashed oneself in one's own environment, where free and unimpeded intellectual enquiry is the greatest merit of our social order.

For my part, out of laziness I had become attuned to a Hopalong Cassidy goodies-and-baddies image of the division of Berlin and the lethal terrors of the Wall. As I flew up the Corridor to Tempelhof I began to suspect with some shame that I had become habituated to seeing the world in terms of over-simplifications just as stark and untrue to reality as the views of the West that prevail in Iron Curtain countries.

In fact there probably only exists a world of confusing, diffuse and kaleidoscopic greys.

West Berlin, a vital, vibrant city of work and happy fleshpots set against the grey, dazed poverty of communist East Berlin, bleak and rubble-strewn over the impenetrable Wall?

Not a whit! My mind had been filled with two half-truths together constituting a dangerously viable untruth. West Berlin is as sad as East Berlin in a different way. The vestiges of war destruction are less evident; the true sadness of the town lies in the crass vulgarity of its modern architectural splendors, often donated by an over-grateful United States, and the weary effort to affect the gaiety of Americanised affluence. Your true Berliner, East or West, is invariably sardonic rather than gay about his world.

East Berlin? As quiet and repressed as Melbourne on a Sunday—in fact a bit like that noble if uninspiring city. East Berlin now proffers a variety of splendiferous restaurants that still manage to purvey amateurish and down-at-heel variants of Western culinary luxury.

But you can wander into the remotest suburb of East Berlin and the citizenry eat as well and as modestly as they do in any unpretentious London pub (German beer's better) and they are clothed as well as the suburban Britisher. If they have lived twenty years under the most puritanical communist yoke of them all, then they must have come to terms with it in some way, for they do not appear to move under any obvious shadow.

The influence of the republic's most jaundiced TV polemicist is made negligible by a universal nickname of unwritable obscenity. The police are known affectionately as White Mice, and there are no Russians to be seen by the naked eye in the way that West Berlin exudes Americans at every pore.

To sustain one's conditioned reflexes there is only the Wall. And here, shocking and perhaps controversially, one's Pavlovian images dissolve to a confusion of doubts. People have died at the Wall. There are graves on both sides. (In this world of chop-logic the East Berliners view the deaths of young guards killed in cold blood by escapees as tragic and useless sacrifices).

But the Wall, as one stood before its length, appeared deserted and meaningless. No bristling of guns and guards on either side. And Checkpoint Charlie appeared to be about as formidable as the toll-gates over the Sydney Harbor bridge. Tourists and West Germans (not West Berliners) pass through with ridiculous ease. The only, and legitimate, preoccupation, is with the smuggling of currency, a preoccupation logical enough in the light of the frail situation of the East German mark. East Berliners do not pass so easily through in the opposite direction.

But on this grim question, one has, these days, in the calmer retrospect that comes with the knowledge that German reunification is a long-range dream, to consider the views of liberal Western commentators that Adenaeur and Ulbricht, the Americans and the Russians, built the Wall between them.

It may not have been Allied policy to set out to make Berlin a Caucasian chalk circle, the scene of a trial by ideologies, but the present psychological shape of East Germany has come into being, and we have to look at its existence with wisdom as well as guile.

East Germany is a city-state of seventeen and a half million people. While its socialist organisation, its economic life-blood and its alliances are linked with East European communism, its gaze is hypnotically and perpetually fixed upon the West in a way which puzzles and frustrates the self-contained Poles and Czechs and Russians.

For twenty years seventy million Germans across the frontier have been claiming them, agitating bitterly to get them within the folds of the most luxurious way of life in Europe. What dreams the East Germans have had about the Day of the Fleshpots have long since gone, and reconciliation of a sort to the historical realities has taken place.

Those of us attuned to meetings in the style of the Congress for Cultural Freedom, sodden with motions, speeches and heavy intellectuality, were ill-prepared for the East European new style of handling such affairs.

After luncheons of some substance one proceeded at will to meetings on themes of poetry or literature or films which were held around a banqueting table.

It is a fearsome European custom to begin a meeting with cognac all round. Then, while the first and only speaker unburdens himself of his brief remarks, flunkeys circulate with fruit and light Hungarian wines.

The discussions begin to warm up—and the flunkeys are in action again with massive arrays of hors d'oeuvres and Hungarian champagne to make sure that the discussion doesn't dry up. That moods should be finally mellow, coffee and cognac circulate, and the meeting breaks up in amiable and inconclusive disorder so that visitors may prepare for the massive parties and orgies of the evening.

The scale of the hospitality ensured that political overtones would be impossible and that our impressions of a communist social order would be ones of the utmost urban normalcy broken by ancient conventions of high life.

This worked to perfection in Weimar, the town of Goethe, Schiller and Bach, a town corrupted from its ancient peace by neither tourism nor commercialism, as is a town such as Heidelberg.

The impressions that crowded in on me only firmed into a single resolute point of view about one thing: and that was that the occasions had more of the stuff of life about them than the celebrities who attended. It was an assembly of dead reputations, aged characters living off forgotten books and great moments of past triumphs.

If the East Germans had called for the literary whirlwinds, they had received only the sunset zephyrs of early autumn.

But West Germany, with American assistance, is maintaining the barrage of propaganda on the theme of the 'suffering' East Germans, and the East Germans respond bitterly to an image of themselves that is blandly untruthful.

When the West German newspapers to a man reported the vastly expensive East Berlin writers' bunfight in single paragraph stories along the lines 'a meeting of communist writers is taking place in East Berlin', the general bitterness seemed disproportionate to the realities of European propaganda cynicism. Having gone to such lengths to eliminate the usual machinery of communist manipulation and dominance of such occasions, they were surprisingly rattled by the picture of the occasion presented over the Wall.

This is the crux of the East German mood. It springs from the fantastic youthfulness of the society and its vulnerability, not towards its Soviet pastors and masters, but towards its vast and hostile mass of fellow-countrymen across the border.

Here was a national climate—in which criticism, not only of literary ideologies, but even of beer and beds, is disposed to stir up silent pain close to the heart, rather than hearty discussion.

From our antipodean burrows, Australians are disposed not to be over-sensitive to a national climate in which criticism, not only of literary ideologies, but even of beer and beds is disposed to stir up less hearty discussion than silent pain close to the heart.

How then did the Australian larrikins fare in an environment calling for a hypersensitive response to realities we have been traditionally disposed to praise or rubbish at will? Not too badly. They did appear to me to have some of the appropriate quantities of vigorous and enquiring young nationhood in their participation.

It was not inept, even if politically ludicrous, that the rumbustious Russians, the quicksilver Cubans and the ratbag Australians seemed to form one of the many enclaves of human affinities that had developed by the end of ten days.

Now, retrospectively, I wonder how many of my Wall-climbing mates feel the weight of a cloud of intellectual unknowing as the outcome of it all? Australia and Australians are so well insulated from the labyrinthine realities of Western Europe and communist Europe, that we don't see through our glass newspapers darkly. The values of the world we inhabit are clearly defined for us.

The direct experience of European communism wipes away all clarities of definition. If ASIO were to ask me point-blank if I was pro-communist I should certainly say 'No'. If I were to be asked was I anti-communist I should reply: 'No, not of communist societies that think and behave in terms of the civilised and peace-loving man' and I should then in turn have to ask Colonel Spry: 'Have I been brainwashed?'

# THE DECLINE
# AND FALL
# OF

**EXCELLENCE** A homily, but perhaps more an elegy, as precursor to another year, lamenting the decline and fall of material excellence in the present age.

This may run counter to the more high-minded of prevailing ideas, since the concern is with material quality, standards of service, attitudes towards what should constitute the superior amenities of an affluent civilisation.

Since these hedonistic indulgences are mostly to be enjoyed by the rich, there may seem something depraved in showing an analytic concern for them. They mean nothing in Bangla Desh or other areas of vast impoverishment. They may well be irrelevant to the quality of life aspired to by the ascetic intellectual.

Yet they have to do with self-respect, pride in work, calibre of commercial achievement on the one hand—and with the quite legitimate subjective pleasure one derives from the experience of excellence on the other. This latter pleasure is not to be deemed vacuous nor the hobby of those with more money than spiritual sense.

A plumber who prides himself on prompt response and good workmanship is a rare jewel of the age, pursued like some Holy Grail by just about anyone who lives in a house. A night of exquisite service and solicitous attention at a restaurant, can refresh the inner spirit of the child-plagued suburban mum as effectively as a reading from St Pancreas the Liver, a most spiritual author.

My lament is that excellence in all fields is a disappearing commodity. But it has been cunningly eroded, the excellence has invisibly disappeared by a process of gradual attrition and technological trickery.

It is one of the most hilarious myths, for example, of the advertising age, that the world is full of expensive, elegant, luxury hotels in which you raise the little finger, pay the appropriate exaction, and a bowl of peeled grapes appears instantly on a silver salver.

The image is a masterpiece of brainwashing. The fact is the more famous the pub, the more sloppy and dilatory are the services. In the massive super hotels of New York or London, it is routine room service procedure to require up to one hour to deliver a pot of coffee. Room cleaning is sloppy and perfunctory.

Desk services are adequate, but there is an unseemly passion for confusion. It would be malapropos for me to name rank and regimental numbers of those grotesquely high-priced hostelries around the world. At best I can say that what passes for service excellence in New York and London would be diagnosed as fourth rate by even the most tolerant of standards.

In a sampling over the years of over one hundred celebrated international hotels, I have found only three—the Grande Bretagne in Athens, the Crillon in Lima, and, unexpectedly, the vast, gothic Caledonian Hotel in Edinburgh —that exhibit an unequivocal pride in, and self-respect for, professional standards. None of these are in the really high-priced bracket.

Air transport, expectedly, is preparing for the Stockyard Age of travel, and those glossy advertisements depicting the sophisticated elegance of first-class flight, are increasingly becoming ironic jest. Not that cabin standards of solicitude are declining, but these days the food comes with its cafeteria origins barely disguised. The airlines are busily cutting costs at the luxury edges. The hot towels come—but no longer charmingly impregnated with cologne.

The little gifties of correspondence kits, or what have you, have gone. The thoughtful courtesy of offering to post your mail at stopovers is now no longer offered. It has to be requested by the seasoned travellers who know the ritual drill.

Along with pinch-penny cost economics, not, fortunately, yet practised by all airlines, goes a new system of clobbering the long-haul Australian colonials. Because they spend a huge sum of money on very long hauls, it has been traditional practice over a decade for airlines to turn a blind eye to overnight luggage for 11,000 mile flights as against a short European haul. This civilised bending of the rules has been abandoned by certain airlines in favour of squeezing the last ounce of revenue out of any excess of weight.

And it is proving a lucrative squeeze. On my present overseas junket, my chosen airline received $4000 in fares, plus $288 in last minute excess baggage charges by virtue of weighing everything within sight and asserting, without any adduced or visible evidence, that this was an extra amount due. Unlike at your local butcher shop, you never get to see the scales. Excellence, alas, has given way to avarice.

This attrition of excellence in international areas may be lamented only by the jet-set minority. But surely you have experienced it closer to home and in more modest ways?

In relationship, for example, between menu pretensions and the product served in your restaurant? With due respect to epicureans far more expert than I, perhaps the best eating house I have visited in recent moons is Robert Carrier's tiny establishment in Islington, London. Grimly suspicious of that celebrated name, I was startled to find the dishes served were of disarming and almost plebeian simplicity.

But each item was the freshest and best of the season's materials. There was no cutting of corners by judicious use of the deep freeze cabinet or the can. And the meal was organised in a healthy and balanced sequence of culinary relationships. I have found gastronomic zeal and enthusiasm in Australian restaurants, but not this subtle and uncompromising sense of total excellence.

The absence of excellence is very often a matter of the presence of ignorance. Australian insularity may explain the intolerable averageness of practically everything we do. To illustrate this I shall take a fairly innocuous and uncontroversial field of comparison.

Our cities are, I think, fairly complacent about what we must jokingly describe as Botanic Gardens. In fact, certain Australian cities imagine their gardens are pretty crash-hot. We have the climatic potential to offer gardens of breathtaking beauty—including the unbelievably exotic gardens at Lae in New Guinea.

But we complacent, insulated folk haven't begun to understand the first principles of gardens as integrated, educative, intellectually stimulating areas of formative experience—such as the Royal Botanic Gardens in Edinburgh!

A bitter Scottish deep-winter, a climate of unrelenting harshness, but there, in Edinburgh, the wattles all in aromatic bloom. Enough to craze any homesick bushwacker! But apart from this, the Scots have placed their Henry Moores and Epsteins in long garden perspectives. The Gardens house a gallery of modern art to diversify one's botanical musings.

There is a bird-feeding point with identification boards to set both children and elderly duffers on the path to ornithological interest. There are audio-guides you can hire to provide taped information as you work your way through the glass-houses. The culminatory experience of a walk through the gardens is a superbly mounted and intellectually inspiring exhibition of botanical principles and ecology, using living examples, colour-slide sequences; every modern inducement to stir the scientific imagination.

In Edinburgh there's been passionate devotion to the idea that a visit to the gardens should be a dynamic total experience, rather than a desultory Sunday walk with one's bored and teasy children.

But in Australia has anyone yet had the first notion of associating intellectual excellence with such a conservative amenity as the local Botanic Gardens? I think not.

It is not very original to record the decline and fall of excellence in an age of standardised sub-service. And it may be that, in the pursuit of excellence, one does not rate Australia higher or lower than most places in the advanced West. It would be parochial bias to claim improbable virtues for our rough-hewn national community.

But we do have our field of capricious and erratic excellence—it's a sort of humanistic excellence. You find it in one in six throws of the social dice amongst the Sydney proletariat; in four of six throws of the dice in beaut old Perth; and so on. It's the splendour of people responding to people as people, if you know what I mean. If you do, then you share my belief that we possess an Australian mystique. It compensates completely for our subservience to the sub-standard standards of the age.

# THINGS
# MORE URGENT
# THAN
# DETERGENT

My God, am I bored to distraction with ecology, environment, and pollution! Through the sheer insistent, relentless, pervasive sanctimoniousness of the movement I'm often tempted to establish a one-man devil's party.

A paean of praise for the cluttered unkempt squalid vitality of Carlton, Collingwood, Redfern, Port Adelaide! An aesthetic appreciation of the beautiful nocturnal linear rhythms of some of the British motor freeways! A simple-minded appreciation of the importance of the Concorde supersonic project in terms of what it will mean for tomorrow's less smugly insulated Australia.

I have this perverse desire, but I can't work up the intellectual conviction to make it credible.

It would be plain idiocy to pretend the actual issues aren't valid; don't exist as the largest single global problem of our age.

Yet the fact remains, although most of us won't admit it, that the conservationists are rapidly becoming a pious pain in the posterior.

Can't we at least say that the time for the holy preaching is past?

Our weariness with the anti-pollutional conservationist cause is simply because it is the most impeccable, the safest, most unquestionable, the cosiest of all high-minded band-waggons.

It's just about the goody-goody cause of all time.

The ecology cause stinks to high heaven with the rotting-fish odour of double standards. The fact that these double standards aren't deliberate, are the end-product of simple ignorance, doesn't reduce the level of olfactory offensiveness.

Let's do a head-count. How many of those who deplore urban smog have abandoned ownership and use of the private motor car? Hands up. After all, it's a simple and not particularly troublesome way to eliminate one of the nastiest carcinogenic problems of all. The deprivation isn't too bad. I gave up car ownership ten years ago and felt no pain at all.

The absence of any sea of upraised hands in answer to my question shows the underlying hypocritic affectation in the ecological crusade. The crusade exists for many as a holy Joe accusation directed against an anonymous 'them'. The mind goes blank when it's a matter of 'us'. Even the nicest ecological idealists can summon up a ratbag reason why the family car is essential to themselves.

One would have greater respect for the goody-goody pleasures of ecological preaching if one felt convinced that the crusaders were capable of a sophisticated understanding of complexities. Too often one suspects that there's a reflex parrot squawk motivated by the natural desire of human beings to appear in favour of the self-evidently good, the transparently virtuous value.

Except that matters aren't always comfortably simple. There's usually an either-or factor.

I've recently been deluged with ecological propaganda directed against the supersonic Concorde project. Windows may be damaged at Uggabugga Station in the North-West. The noise will send citizens scrambling up their suburban walls. The entire upper atmosphere will be poisoned or explode or something.

The anti-Concorde campaigners may be correct in their shrill protestations. But I require the anti-Concorde lobby to lay before me a calm, rational set of facts.

Intellectual, emotional and moral pollution concerns me just as much, if not more, than the obvious physical environmental problem.

What shall it profit mankind if he gains a lovely pristine world to live in, and then inhabits it with ugly fascist bigots? The Australian social psyche is well and truly polluted with arrogant insularity, complacent ignorance, and global dimwittedness. Anything that brings us closer to the common civilised conventions of the dynamic and morally evolving modern nations may well eliminate our occasional affinity with the bible belt of the American deep south.

If the Concorde brings us into an even more immediate touch with the rest of the world, then it may contribute valuably to eliminating the pollution within the Australian skull. The Concorde may be a boon to us, albeit a dubious blessing for the British or Europeans who are already in a situation of cultural cross-fertilisation. For Australians it may represent a technological development to be welcomed rather than rejected. A social kind of environmental gain may outweigh a purely physical sort of environmental damage.

I don't know. Except that I won't fall for the anti-Concorde public lobby until they offer me thinking more complex than the amoeba reflex.

There's one comforting thing about the comic hypocrisy of ecological idealism as it as present manifests itself.

There's no generation gap.

The young have made it their pietistic thing with a zeal equal to that of enlightened suburban mumhood, or of news media desperate for an innocuous popular crusading theme.

The young have revolted heroically against the technological pollution of mother earth. They buy their Whole Earth Catalogue, tens of thousands of them, ingest their macrobiotic food, gobble up organic vegetables, endorse zero population growth, then race off to their pads to worship the household god they really love best—the stereophonic headphone attached to a sophisticated technological sound producing machine which belts out sounds produced by technologically-controlled musical instruments orchestrated by technological engineers.

When they get bored with this, they go out and idealistically demonstrate against the noise pollution of modern urban living.

Suggest to the young that their cultural experiences would be freed of a measure of pollution if there were a ban on amplification and they'd wrathfully shove a hand microphone straight up your left nostril.

Grown-up critics overseas have universally found cause for compensatory hilarity at Jesus Christ Superstar because of the comic shambles of technological confusion that alone alleviates the unadulterated vulgarity, grotesqueries, and teeny-bopper stupidity of the entire conception.

Jesus Christ, Judas Iscariot, and every vocal biblical dignitary drags a microphone cord in his trail. The cast keep changing microphones in mid-action in a singing relay-race. The apostles kick away at a confusion of trailing cords.

The effect is not so much that the young have discovered Jesus but that Jesus has discovered technology.

I challenge you. See if you can convince one single ecologically minded youngster that a youth culture polluted by technology is as dangerous as a river polluted by industrial effluent. See how you go.

While on this subject of the young indulging in the spiritual pollution of Christian mythology, it is remarkable how the elders of the established religion have assumed their mantle of responsibility in helping to preserve spaceship earth from environmental destruction.

They're doing a noble, dedicated, selfless job in fighting to preserve the world as a fit place to live in.

And what an extra-beaut cause it is. You feel so good about the good you're trying to do. Above all, no nasty self-doubts or destructive confrontations. Heroism without danger.

But there's total silence on the possibility that there could exist such a terrible and debilitating phenomenon as spiritual and moral pollution as a social problem. Fight the smog-producing chimneys of the industrialists by all means, but take on the spiritual and moral degradation of religion as a pop phenomenon?

Can't be done.

It might alienate the arrogant and touchy young if they had to be tackled as themselves causing an environmental problem of the mind.

The rush by oldies to abandon the fundamental dignity and loftiness that attends all genuine religious expression, Christian or otherwise, in fact to endorse the freakification of religion, leaves the Gadarene swine looking like a tray of day-old chicks.

It is my duty, I am told, to be temperate these days. Harris in outrage is not apt to the tonalities people wish to hear. Latterday Aldous Huxleys, buzz off. So temperate shall the conclusion be.

Is there not a possibility that our religious pastors may have a small pollution problem of their own to help us with? A problem which calls for some troubledness of mind and long nights of the soul.

Smoking chimneys are easier, visible, tangible. Even so, won't one single clerical gentleman abandon the strength, and join my loneliest of ecological crusades?

The conservationists—the specialists, the do-gooders, the anti-technological youngies, worried mums, deeply concerned television reporters—bless 'em all. And may they never forget that there's a certain something that speaks a lot louder than all the words.

# DRINKING
# THE
# BALI
**BROTH** Sometimes it seems too characteristic. Comically so. Australia's most publicised business investment in the Indonesian scene is a horse-racing industry.

On the face of it, it would appear there's no enterprise less relevant to an underdeveloped economy than a fat-cat's gambling speciality.

This surely can't be all the Australian-Indonesian story in terms purely of private enterprise investment in the social growth of our nearest neighbour?

I am reporting once again from Nehru's 'morning of the world'; and a year has brought some interesting changes to Bali.

Bali is Indonesia's greatest tourist income-earner, and the miracle is that this most paradisical of all lands tended by the most ethnically beautiful race of people on the globe, can absorb an even greater tourist inflow without destroying the basic economy of the island or disturbing the conservative and unself-conscious pattern of village life.

That Bali should not be destroyed by tourism has been a matter of committed concern for tens of thousands of people who are besotted by the place. I sense this from the correspondence I received when I discussed the subject a year ago.

It is pleasurable to confirm now that one doesn't study Bali and come up with the glum warning of the ecological doomsters.

The village art forms, which are far more integral to the community group than football is to the suburbs of Melbourne, I found immensely strengthened even after one year.

If there have been touristic variations to the Ramayana and Mahabarata stories, I certainly can't spot them as distressing Westernisations. And whereas the Peliatan Legong group is priced outside the casual tourist market these days, there are other Legong performers who can produce the breathtaking beauty of a dance idiom that convinces even Blind Freddie of the effect and vacuous inferiority of the Western balletic nonsense we attempt to support in Australia.

Barong has begun to thrive all over the place. The Mask Dance is alive, and with it the demand for the mask-carver's art. The gamelan orchestras are numerous, disciplined, competitive, and ravishing. This all feeds back to the villages, which are thriving in terms of pride, tradition, and enthusiasm, in response to a growing audience situation.

This sweet excellence can only continue if a sophisticated tourist ecology is balanced, maintained and controlled.

To this end, the policies of both the central and regional Indonesian governments are remarkably praiseworthy. Tourist features, such as the Bali Beach Hotel, are usually effected in association with government, and development is being rationally controlled on sound ecological principles. For the ugly tourists the vast air-conditioned hotel ghettoes are devised so that the vulgarians can live out their tropic delights within reach of a hamburger. They can huddle happily around the swimming pools, and bars.

Even so, high-rise is banned from future projects. No luxury complex can project above the height of the coconut palms. For the rest, American and Japanese capital is flowing in to extend the hotel bungalow system traditional to the area. Within a few years Sanur Beach will be the world's most admirable resort.

The dual system successfully sorts out the ugly and the beautiful tourists. For the most part.

When tourism has threatened the animistic systems of the Balinese, the Indonesian Government has acted rapidly and wisely. Since last year tourists have been banned from all trance dance ceremonies. The official reason advanced is that the purely religious integrity of this primitive and mysterious ceremony is in danger of being corrupted into a tourist entertainment. Therefore it must become once again a private spirit manifestation for the villagers.

Knowing the casualness and tolerance of the Balinese I personally suspect that the prohibition has resulted from the intolerable behaviour of Ugly Tourists, that their Master Race camera-arrogance has put the safety of the fire-dancers at risk.

In their art activities the Balinese are masterly in dividing their unbelievable carving skill between tourist rubbish and traditional ethnographic works. The bad, as far as I have been able to determine, does not debase the good.

Except in one tragi-comic instance.

While impeccably moral in their marital patterns, and touchingly modest in their behaviour, the Balinese are unable to conceive such notions as obscenity or sexual guilt. They just can't latch on to the Christian sexual hang-ups of the West.

It so happens that the most miraculous ethnographic wood carvings of all Asia emanate from a small paddy-field village near Ubud. These small blackwood carvings display such a fertile and comic erotic imagination that they make Rabelais seem as pedestrian as the thoughts of our Chairman McMahon. These carvings are guiltless, fantastic, instinctively skilled, and little known except to local experts.

Alas, in the last short year the Rodins of the ricefields have discovered that the insane tourists have a preference for exotic copulatory themes, and erotic art has turned into a splendid pornography.

But pornography rather than ethnic sexual humour for all that.

I urge the Indonesian Government to retrieve this situation or the primitives of Ubud will cease to exist within the next year. A small but urgent matter, for it concerns one of the last great folk arts of the world.

How are these traveller's topics relevant to Australia?

I believe them to be relevant in a multitude of ways.

The islands of Indonesia in one direction, and the Pacific in another direction, are certain to be the great recreational magnets for Australia, above any other nation except the Japanese, over the next decade.

To us they are proximate, just as the south of France is accessible to the British. A vast annual tourist exodus from Australia is certain once these exotic places are geared to tourism more adequately.

The time has to come when Australia has to play an initiatory role in not so much a South-East Asian Common Market, but a Trading Community.

To the idiot traveller such as myself our trading initiatives seem sadly enfeebled. In consequence I'd like to direct a few simple-minded questions to the Australian Department of Trade and to the Indonesian Embassy.

Apart from the bloody horse-racing, how much joint development capital is Australia injecting into Indonesia, since it will be largely Australian tourist money that will be spent there a decade from now?

A hotel-casino out from Denpasar (gambling again!) is projected. But for the most part Japanese and American investors will harvest the profits from the Australian holiday-maker. The Indonesian Government can be difficult—as evidenced by the withdrawal of the Hilton Hotel organisation from its Bali plans. Australian partnership should be another kettle of fish as it would produce reciprocal benefits within the region.

Next question. Is Australia incapable of product competition within the region, despite our geographical advantages? In the good hotels one washes with soap from the People's Republic of China; the lavatory paper comes per courtesy of Chairman Mao; the gigantic bicycle industry is dominated by remote Germany, Britain, and Japan. All the textile dyes

I saw were Japanese. One munches biscuits from Singapore or Hong Kong. And so on.

If Australian products are about the place, they certainly aren't evident to the naked eye.

If in fact our trading situation isn't booming, then surely it's time some dramatic and preferential agreements were effected.

By the same token it would appear about time for the Indonesians to pull out the proverbial finger. Their cottage industries are capable of indefinite expansion, and it seems a howling disgrace that there aren't flourishing batik departments in David Jones, Myers, Farmer's and the rest. The Balinese produce the world's best and possibly the cheapest tie-and-dye handloomed textiles. But just try buying a sarong-length for Australian beach wear in our rag-trade outlets?

Have Indonesian trade missions attempted to convince Australian consumers that our dress conventions are climatically comic? (Well, the failure of the Queensland male to use the sarong in that ghastly climate is a pretty funny survival of pukkah British colonialism. It really is. Those crutchy ugly shorts or skin-tight jeans in humid atmosphere!)

We should be disposed to prefer the exquisite jewellery, the silver and gold crafts of Asia. But as rigidified mock-ups of the European nexus we prefer to remit profits back to Scandinavia or France.

It all gets me a bit whacked. The orientations of our economy destiny seem to be clearly defined. We may be cognizant of this at the level of goodwill tours come election year, but there's no sign of real action in the economic bazaars where it really counts.

The only leader who sees the situation whole in Australia is Donny the Dunstan. And he's just dreaming a dream in a hick town.

Meantime—it's Advance Australia. Downwards. Land of the economic dinosaurs.

If all this gloom-gloom is a matter of sheer lay ignorance of the facts on my part I wish to God the Indonesian and Australian trade experts would tell us the nice, surprising, dynamic truth. I'm all ears.

## ALF GARNETT
## YES;
## AFRICAN ASIANS

**NO** On reflection I tend to think that Australia is not very good at what one might define as political humanism.

It's not that we as a people are viciously egocentric and selfish, or that our politicians are deliberate opportunistic villians. It's just that we are a bit on the stupid side. In consequence our politics exhibit the dramatic qualities of gutless wonderdom; and vox populi, via the media, expresses itself in terms of a predictable mental dimness.

Think back, if you will, to the expulsion of the 35,000 Asians from Uganda with their British passports and bitter destinies. Think of the face we presented to the civilised world when the arrogant Poms, blast their eyes, had the bloody hide to ask for our assistance in providing a refuge for these hapless Asians from Uganda.

Of course the Poms didn't have a leg to stand on in asking us and the Canadians to help them cope with a problem of their own historic making. They brought the Asians to Africa in the first place to fill their own imperialist pockets. They gave them the choice of British or Uganda citizenship and passports in 1962. They then tended to renege on the rights of these British passport holders to enter Britain except under a minute quota system. Now a problem engendered by imperialist profit-making has landed fair and square back in their own lap.

Those odd bedfellows, Mr Arthur Calwell, and the Minister for Immigration, spelled it out loud and clear, each in his own firm if offensive fashion. Let Britain clean up its own nasty little mess. We have problems of our own.

Canada, a much more advanced and humane society than our nasty big Antipodean moral waste-land, said let the Asians come.

But when you think of it, the cunning Poms put us behind a celebrated eight-ball the size of Ayers Rock.

For the world deems us to be racist. They deem us to be racist in terms of hostility to racial admixing with any significant Asian component in our society. They deem us to be racist in furtively favouring South Africa's ambitions and ideals, in secretly admiring brave little Rhodesia. They deem us racist in that our policies for Aboriginal rights and development are both tardy and inadequate.

The world's opinion of us may be wrong; may be savagely and unfairly distorted.

But right or wrong, that's the regard in which we are held by governments and individuals. The customs officers at Miami gave me a right royal welcome to the good old US of A because of his unstinted admiration for the way we keep our niggers in their place.

Therefore when there is a situation of crisis, when the world looks around to see who will make the humane gesture at the immediate moment, Australia is either looking the other way, making governmental evasions, indulging in rationalisations, or watching idiot-box presentations which fail to offer the facts let alone present the public issue in the round.

You will remember that the Minister for Immigration responded to Britain's embarrassing request with a quack of platitudes about our stated migrant policy. All of which had nothing to do with proffering help in solving a vast and tragic human problem.

But this is because the Minister for Immigration believes in the game of political survival as the ultimate law of laws. If he, or his Prime Minister, or his ministerial colleagues are confronted with statesmanlike demands that call a common transcendent humanity into play, then national stature has to go by the board if it conflicts with the opportunistic exigencies of the political power game.

It's sick, but it's the system we've chosen.

And can we expect a Minister for Immigration to rise statesmanlike above or in conflict with the nasty little set of party ground-rules which have all the fundamentalist authority of religious doctrine in his limited vision? Of course not.

The only way in which the political Saul could have become the statesman Paul would have been if he could have pretended to respond to a pressure of public enlightenment.

This would be difficult since a preponderance of Australians are mute and unconsciously racist anyway.

The ultimate Four Corners filmed reports gave some of the facts—after the game was up.

I will elaborate these facts even more belatedly just to show up the ultimate exquisite irony of the politically inhumane face that Australia has presented to the world.

The Ugandan Asians are almost exclusively middle-class, an educated group, ideally equipped psychologically 'to merge themselves into the bourgeois landscape'.

They present no problem of assimilation in fact.

In migrational terms they would prove easier to assimilate than the proletarian British who come to this country for ten pounds and substantially race back to Britain again after a few disgruntled years.

It was made no easier by the instant idiocy of the mass media. To whichever television channel I turned there was the ancient Arthur Calwell sounding off with an air of doctrinaire pseudo-authority. Everyone in the media business knows that the old Arthur is a bit of a ratbag on the race theme, and has finished up in his old age with a rare old bee in the bonnet.

The responsible thing vis a vis the media would be to let predictable old odd-bods live out their sunset years mumbling into their can of Fosters.

Mike Willesee and This Day Tonight could have summoned a better flow of cool information and an educated balance of opinion.

It was at least a week after these idiot news commentaries and the devious back-turning by the Minister for Immigration that some of the facts about the Ugandan Asians filtered through—facts thoroughly known by the Minister for Immigration and facts which should have been known by the media-mongers when they called for Calwell.

Thus it has come about that despite a clear knowledge of these seemingly well-known facts our Migration Minister could not rise to a statesmanlike response comparable to that of his Canadian counterpart, even in a crisis situation which involved no assimilation, linguistic, economic, or cultural problem for Australia.

If the minister were at this retrospective stage to attempt to answer the facts of the matter (and he is not one to answer anything except by party political rote) he might well escape by saying Australia cannot cope with more migrants at the moment given our internal level of unemployment. This is what many people might reasonably say.

But here the minister cops it sweet with the ultimate irony!

On the very day our political population commissar was declaring that Australia will do no special thing for an educated and British-Europeanised group of Asian refugees, he had his chief migration officer in London advertising stridently in the London Press for ten-pound-a-passage migrants to come racing out to Australia. Page two of the Sunday prestige papers was filled with human reportage on the Uganda situation. But there was still room on the same page for the minister's advertised invitation to the Alf Garnetts to come out and substantially non-assimilate in Australia.

'Australia—a place to live,' headlined. 'Adults can go to Australia for £10 and family members under 18 travel free.

£10 assisted passages are available only to residents of the British Isles.'

The minister is probably quite right. Australia is a place to live. Just so long as you don't experience too many moral scruples about the condition of man. In which case I suggest the civilised Brit. migrate to Canada. It seems that there you can live with your global conscience. And with your Minister for Immigration.

# THEY'RE SELLING
# WHICKER WARE
# IN
**AUSTRALIA** The trouble with being one of the local prime examples of the village two-headed freak is that there's no place to hide. And where I come from, we're a very small fraternity. So we cop it.

There is a depressingly large band of itinerants from overseas who market this new product—Instant Australia. The technique for manufacturing this refined consumer item is to blow in, seek out the local freaks, do a quick brain-tapping, and bingo, you've got the outline for a telly programme for the BBC, an article for *Life*, or another chapter for the new book.

If you take evasive action, as a lot of us do these days, you still haven't opted out. You've let the country down. The distinguished itinerant becomes convinced that part of the Australian character is insular, stand-offish, churlishly uninterested in the wider world represented by them, the big noises who have blown in from wherever.

I'm only a small-timer, the best of a provincial range of minimal possibilities. But take Patrick White. I bet you've heard that he's stand-offish, patrician, a deliberate isolate. What this really means is that he's sociable, gregarious, intensely busy about his own affairs, but allocates his time to his own friends rather than to Joe McGoat who's going to do the definitive interview for the Glasgow War Cry.

The most guilt-riddled situation of recent date for me was the advent into Adelaide of that Inside specialist, Mr John Gunther. There was an old-fashioned New England courtesy about Mr Gunther, delicate but persistent in the pursuit of his informational quarry. Mr Gunther makes a lot of money, more possibly than I'll ever make, but when you come to think of it, his income and delectable wandering life are largely derived from chewing up other people's earning time free of charge.

Last year, the boys from BBC television blew in. Alan Whicker had come to Australia to direct six programmes about the Lucky Country.

This time, I instantly leapt into action in response to a stirring sense of patriotic duty.

After all, Whicker is the world's most accomplished front man in the presentation of critical penetrating BBC documentaries. Whicker's recent portrayal of Papa Doc, the sinister Haitian dictator, became an immediate classic of television reportage.

Whicker's producers, it seemed, were hedge-hopping around Australia doing their advance homework. The Yorkshire whizz-kid duly fitted me in between lunch at the Adelaide Club (paper tigers, no visual material there) and a tally-ho session with the Hunt Club.

Well, what gives? What's the score on this place? The whizz-kid bleakly waited for me to strut my paces.

God, how to avoid all the overworked cliches of these instant Australia presentations? They seem to have been going on for a thousand years!

I launched into a scintillating and brilliant analysis of Australia's cultural dynamic and how its character is formed precisely through conflict with entrenched reaction and established illiberalism. I tell you, mates, it was sizzling stuff. I didn't mention Abos or the outback once.

At the third beer, I panted to a triumphant halt.

The whizz-kid still stared at me bleakly. Whicker doesn't like the culture bit; not at home with it.

Rather desperately, I changed cerebral gears into overdrive.

'How about a change from the usual thing? These days the boot's on the other foot. Australians as an emergent confident people are prone to patronise the British, reversing the situation that has applied for a couple of centuries. The British antipathy to the work situation, their inability to get over their endless sex hang-ups, the literary and artistic incestuousness. Why not Whicker conversationally confronted?' Names flashed into vision—Donald Horne, Richard Walsh, Phillip Adams. Sounded rare old fun. Australia on the attack instead of on the defensive for once.

The whizz-kid looked at me as if I was the Monster from the Wagga Lagoon. Very bleak. Very disappointed. Local freak not delivering the goods. Proper ratbag.

'No good at all. Whicker does the interviewing.'

Of course. Of course. I realise that Whicker gets his victims to talk, and does his demolition bit, where desirable, by recording voice over film at a later date. The poor bunny who's expounded to camera doesn't have a chance to answer back. Lucky Whicker. Poor bunny.

Defeated, exhausted, dribbling beer down my tie, epic picture of the colourful personality who failed all his Instant Inspiration tests. I enquired: 'What exactly are you thinking of doing?'

'Well,' replied the whizz-kid, 'We're calling the programme Whicker's Walkabout. We've done the Abos. And there's a country race-meeting—there ought to be a programme in that. And, of course, the mining boom, that's automatic. Down your way we were thinking of the wine industry or British migrants.'

Since I'm not a migrant or a wine-maker, I gathered together my cane and my dignity and we parted company.

I suppose it has to be the old, old thing? Again and again. For ever and ever. Amen.

Life as we live it through the media has to be a set of established cliches.

So remember me a year from now when you see the Whicker ware being flogged on the square box. I did my best, such as it is, by a nation that deserves better than the inevitable celebrity doing a Trotabout over the geographical and sociological surfaces.

What's more, won't you support me in a scheme I've been championing for years? Give me a camera crew, a couple of whizz-kids, a slap-up budget and two weeks. We'll return the compliment and do an Instant England. There'd be one programme on Kings Road; a quickie on race relations; that's easy; a couple of interviews on the odd Paki and West Indian; some Enoch Powell stock shots for the archives; Liverpool and the pop scene; the pollution of rural England. No trouble at all. Maybe Yorkshire Television will buy it. Honour will be satisfied.

# IT'S ABOUT THAT FLAMIN' NEW YEAR HONOURS LIST, MA'AM

Dear Your 'Royal Highness':

One of your humblest liege subjects makes bold enough to address himself to you on behalf of the loyal but bemused citizenry of Browser's Gully, a roughneck and tiny part of your domain.

We have a problem akin to that of the late Samuel Johnson (not on the Honours' List, I believe) who could well have been a philosopher, but that cheerfulness kept breaking through.

We members of the Browser's Gully Euchre Club and Buffalo Lodge could out-Menzies Menzies if only we could understand the way you bestow your new year favours on those subjects who happen to please you! You are not the only one who moves in a mysterious way your wonders to perform, but need you be all that mysterious!

I am grateful that Sir Alex Downer's chauffeur has found favour in your eye and been honoured, presumably for his services to the transport industry. I've seen him in that Rolls Royce with the plates AUST 1 choofing around London, and right posh he looks, too.

Now, we peasants are perfectly content to pull the fetlock and acknowledge that men are not all equal. A bloke called George Orwell (not on the Honours' List, I believe) proved that to our complete satisfaction. But how less equal are we?

Like, I mean we all know that Sir Alex Downer (gosh, how I love all those English trees he planted in the Adelaide Hills after rooting out all the scrubby Australian natives) is of more import than an ordinary Aussie citizen, and that his chauffeur bears a great public responsibility chauffing him around.

But how many Aussie citizens equal Sir Alex Downer? This is the hub of the matter. The High Commissioner's chauffeur has certainly served public transport well in his Rolls Royce; yet a Sydney taxi-driver, often in a clapped-out Holden, safely transports a hundred citizens a day. I never heard of a Sydney taxi-driver being made a Member of What British Empire.

Then there's this matter of the public service lady steno-secretaries. We can't work out what makes them (and country post-mistresses) so special in your regal eye. This year, you honoured a great swatch of them for doing steno-secretarial work. Well, what else, bless me, does a steno-secretary do but steno?

As humble subjects, could we point out that it's Miss Thelma Bloggs, steno-secretary to a bloke in the Flinders Street rag trade, who works like a drain to keep the old economy buoyant, plus ten thousand like her. Go on, Your Majesty, be a devil—give 'em ALL a Damehood. Like Sir Robert Menzies told us, you believe in scrupulous fairness to all your subjects.

As it is you quite rightly honoured the lady who works the switchboard at Government House. But, your Royal Majesty-hood—have you ever copped the way those girls serve the community at the Sydney Telephone Exchange? Flat out all day long I do assure you. Next year, give 'em ALL a guernsey. They'd be that grateful.

While on the subject of making suggestions for next year, there's the matter of the big weight-for-age events. That is racing parlance, Your Majesty, and I am referring of course to the subject of Knight Hoods.

Out here at Browser's Gully, our collective eyes popped when we saw that among the few Knight Hoods bestowed in this modest realm to begin the new decade, you decided to give one to a nicotine pusher from Sydney and another to an alcohol pusher from Melbourne.

The Prime Minister is too well-bred to have said any-thing, I know, but I reckon he wasn't all that pleased with you about this. He was about to bring in new legislation to make nicotine pushers label their products as not too healthy, and you gave one of the boss-cocky pushers of the weed a Knight Hood.

I know they call them company directors, and when their operation gets pretty big then it's not the same.

Size makes the difference, let's be reasonable about that.

And there's a guy pushing pot and speed round the Cross who's getting pretty close to the tycoon class, I hear tell. Ted Noffs will give you his name. (When's the old Ted going to cop a Knight Hood, by the way?) He might be worth considering for the big money next year.

I do apologise for taking up your time with these insigni-ficant colonial puzzlements. But you'll understand. After all, I did see you passing by, and yet.

I remain,
Yours by the bootstraps,
Snowy Harris,

# A
# TIGER-SNAKE
# MESMERISED
**BY A RABBIT**   I came to the mysteries of Bellbird late in life, and consequently I can't boast a high level of comprehension. I've engaged in no consistent study of our national troglodytes during their nocturnal crawl from the television woodwork; so I beg indulgence for the following interpretation of what Bellbird means to our modern Australian nationhood.

It will seem a bit tired to discuss the indestructible facts of Bellbird life after a number of years, and long after the satirists have had their bit of fun.

For all this the itinerant critics may have failed to realise that a national mythology consists precisely of the social platitudes people have come to believe in as enduring fact. Contemporary Australia is Bellbird, just as the Australia of yesterday was that nauseous world of Dad and Dave buffoonery invented by Steele Rudd.

Bellbird provides us with the only authentic stereotypes for a modern swinging urban Australia in terms of a contemporaneous mythology, and it is in this light that I propose to examine this television mirror-image of Australianism.

From Bourke and Wills to the Kokoda Trail via the climatic preoccupations of Dorothea McKellar, the weather has been the blinding Australian fact of life. People do perish traversing waterless horizons; hairily sweat out the humidity of Brisbane; wait for the Todd to come down in flood at the Alice.

This sort of thing is just not on at Bellbird.

There is no weather at Bellbird.

Day by day the sub-normal citizenry foregather at an outdoor cardboard coffee shop, fronting a unique dress boutique in which some bird spends all day every day taking stock of the sixteen dresses on the rack.

All this coffee slurping occurs in a declimatised balminess. It's never hot, cold, wet, dry, windy or changeable. The world is as immutably weatherless as the dialogue of the citizens. Thus it's the stereotype of the new insulated air-conditioned swinging Australia. Clever ABC. Clever script-writers.

Mark you, they did have a bash at the weather, I remember. That was the time when the local lawyer went off his wick during the disastrous Bellbird floods, had the amnesias, and died in solemn state at the Bellbird Repat Hospital. It was shock that killed him.

The truth about contemporary Australian Nationhood is revealed in all its complexity in Bellbird. We have there all the modern problems—from revolting youth stealing Bex from the doc's little black bag, sexual alienation, to a refugee from Haight-Ashbury turned zombie after a nasty encounter with horse (the drug, you idiots, not the kind you ride in cigarette commercials). We all breathlessly await the fate of Pate.

But the social caste system of Australia remains unchanged.

At the top of the pyramid is Colonel Witherspoon-Witherfork, the local squatter. He has taken unto himself a Dago-Balt New Australian bride because Australia is full of 'em and they're just as stupid, thank God, as us long resident molls.

Bellbird's villian is the local stock and station agent. In classical Hopalong Cassidy western tradition, this is made clear each night because he never takes off his hat.

The good squatter spends his life taking the bad stock agent down several pegs. The bad stock agent spends his life apologising and promising to make amends in future, because the ABC don't want to have a writ slapped on them by the big rural stock companies who must be having an awful tussle recruiting clean-cut types for their country offices.

The most radical change in the Australian myth as presently enshrined in the folkways of Bellbird is the changed character of the Victoria Police Force since the goldfield days and O'Hara Bourke.

The Bellbird walloper is Des or Derek or Dolly somebody, and he's soppy as all getout. The citizens love him. If they had an apartheid demo at the Bellbird oval, Derek would be bringing the protesters tea and bikkies while sportingly barracking for the Springboks. He's that type.

When I watch Bellbird I find myself in the idiot situation of a tiger snake that's been totally mesmerised by a rabbit. I'm dumbfounded, no, paralysed, by the appalling ordinariness of the ordinary. To indulge in Wildean paradox, there's nothing quite so incredible as the relentlessly credible.

People can't be enthralled by the fifteen-minute drama of mum boiling saveloys for dad's tea. This can't be the stuff of entertainment—and yet, it is for a vast tribe of the community; people who vote, elect governments, and fight or reject wars. What's more, it's our greatest surviving point of contact with the once beloved Motherland; the battle between Bellbird and Coronation Street—for the palm of platitudiousness.

It is true that great creative insights can be derived from the response of commonplace humanity to both the comic and tragic pressures of ordinary events. It's his sensitivity to the transcendent implications of ordinary experience that makes Chekhov the Shakespeare of the novella in my judgment.

But the unrelieved ordinariness of the ordinary, the insistent crude predictability of characterisation, the lamentable abandonment of acting abilities by players content to pound out a nightly unconvincing stereotype—how can the Coronation Street and Bellbird phenomena possibly entertain or hold the interest of even the addicted denizens of Supermarketland?

I'm mesmerised by the sociological reality of these two television creations. They do appeal, hold their vast audiences—so much so that the purveyors of the product don't have to bother about professionalism of production, advanced scripting abilities, or talented acting.

The answer, irresistibly, is that ordinary folk are ferociously narcissistic. They are in love with themselves.

To be this way you have to be defective in the self-critical faculty. Otherwise, of course, the insistent dream is of ordinariness transformed into something richer, more individualistic, unique.

But the value-judgments of society usually attribute self-centredness and rank narcissism to the ambitious, the creative, the intellectually endowed, the idiosyncratics. In fact these are the people riddled with self-distrust, their surface egotism aimed only at convincing themselves of their unquestionable human worth.

The citizens of Bellbird are thus not the salt of the earth, but the petrified monsters of Don Giovanni. The thought terrifies me. In some way I must be reassured that the average citizen doesn't revere his own mediocrity of thought and aspiration.

Otherwise, if I keep watching Bellbird I could well make it in the Guinness Book of Records as the first tiger snake to finish up inside a rabbit.

# RAISING THE LOLLY WITH

**ALLIE AND OLLIE** Dear Allie and Ollie—You've got to be joking. You've just got to be joking. You two beaut blokes leading what must surely be the least worthy charitable fund-raising cause.

Before expatiating on this quarrelsome theme I must apologise for the familiar form of address. To attribute the qualities of a comedy duo to my old sparring mate Alan Marshall, and to Professor Sir Mark Oliphant, KBE, FRS, is most disrespectful and I apologise.

The fact remains, however, that I have received a circular letter from Allie and Ollie (Oh, my God, there I go again!) beseeching me to make a financial donation so that 10,000 Australian books can be presented free, gratis, and grandiloquently to the Central Lenin Library in Moscow as a goodwill gift from bonzer Australia.

This charitable appeal is apparently sponsored through the agency of the Australia-USSR Society, and the signatories of the appeal are Professor Sir Alan Marshall and Mark Oliphant (I'm really dreadfully confused at the moment).

The prime result of this 10,000-book gesture is that it 'could inform Russian scholars and others of the Australian way of life, and where Australia stands in the face of the problems of today'. (Oh boy, I bet those Russian scholars will be wild with delight when they come across their free set of the collected writings of B. A. Santamaria and 'Carpet Snakes', the most recent verse volume of John McFinley McLeay.)

Such ruminations lead me away from the essential fact of life that Allie and Ollie and the Australia-USSR Society seem never to have learned; viz—

The United States and the Soviet Union are the two global super-powers!

It's true.

Between them they can raise the astronomic billions of dollars or roubles to send men skittering out into space. They have the unbelievable wealth to create instruments of nuclear destruction capable of destroying each other completely, and the whole world as well just for afters.

And you want that I should write out a cheque to give cerebral Aussie gifties to these millionaire super-powers.

Cripes, I don't know what the world is coming to. If the Australian-American Association launches an appeal for the

Australian people to present a free Holden to the chairman of General Motors I'll put it at the bottom of my list of charitable priorities.

Likewise, without being the teensiest bit anti-communist or anti the mighty and powerful Soviet Union, I'm going to do the same thing with the invitation to fork out from Allie and Ollie.

The deprivation endured by the Russian scholars at Moscow's Central Lenin Library due to the lack of 10,000 proud Australian volumes may be heart-rendering, but I still think my charitable duty is to keep my eye on the sparrow. While there's starvation, malnutrition, persecution, injustice, and the whole blinding spectrum of human misery, there's plenty to keep my cheque book at the ready.

I know what the answer will be to this. A national giftie would be in effect a contribution to international goodwill and understanding; and even a tiny library gesture from Australia will constitute one small action to reduce international misunderstanding, etc.

I've read your romantic pamphlet carefully. Additionally, you say, it would be an action in Australia's interests. We are a very small and insignificant country in the eyes of the Russian scholars and a gesture such as you are making will help the Russians to realise that we actually exist.

But Allie and Ollie—the USSR is a global super-power.

If the accessions of Moscow's Lenin Library are so feeble as not to include our glorious country's literary output, then that's hard bloody cheese for their English-reading scholars. Let them con their government into short-changing the Syrians, let us say, by a mere quarter of an armoured tank and they could have 30,000 Australian books. A mere nothing.

Canada is not a super-power, but the University of British Columbia has a superlative collection of Australiana. And pays hard cash for every single book.

The University of Pennsylvania is not a vast State-financed institution, but have you ever seen their catalogue of Australiana? All paid for.

If you want to study Aboriginal culture you can do it in Munich as well as in Canberra.

Other countries with limited resources, and by no means in the category of the USA and USSR, find it part of their ordinary academic responsibility to provide for the study of international cultures—even one as remote and unimportant as ours.

You infer that the Russians will continue to ignore our intellectual existence if we don't all club together to offer them our literary heritage as spectacular gifties. Well, that says damn-all for the self-respect and required internationalism of Russian scholarship.

If they don't care to study us after the fifty years of library building, let them stay piss-ignorant.

Let's get together the 10,000-book library and let the Australia-USSR Society donate it to certain under-developed countries which have a passionate and important cultural interest in Australia, but which are poor as temple mice.

There's a little university in Denpasar, broke to the wide, which is begging for even a collection of secondhand cast-off Australiana. You blokes will surely have heard of the University of the South Pacific. Now they could really do with a collection of Australiana.

And if we are to consider self-interest, surely it's more important for our immediate and impoverished Asian neighbours to be given the resources to study our culture (as they passionately wish to do) rather than for the indifferent fat-cat Russians or Americans?

I feel sure you'll see things my way and change your project as an act of moral responsibility, and in terms of reconsidered priorities.

If so, then my cheque book is twitching at the ready. So is my bank manager.

# RAGING IN PARK

**AVENUE**  Long ago I swore a solemn swear that I'd never sound off on the subject of New York and the Americans. Yet here I am about to bray forth loud and clear.

My reluctance is based on the fact that blowsy old New York is everybody's literary whore.

Australia maintains Press bureaus in Washington and New York and there's an army of expatriate reporters who have to earn their hamburgers and thick-shakes with instant portraits of the strangulating agonies of New York for us denizens back in Fredland. But these fellows are strictly peasant class.

Theirs is not the New York of us jetsetters. Like the antique song says, they just go slumming up the Park Avenue that is the home from home for the colonial creme de la creme.

I have before me a sentimental relic of my Park Avenue sojourn. Rheumy eyes dim with tears as I turn the Room Service Directory of the Regency Hotel, of recent and hallowed memory.

How to eat breakfast without finishing up in the bankruptcy court— an exquisite problem that I study afresh right now. One could survive on a small bowl of cornflakes with a sliced banana. That's $1.75 plus 75c service charge, plus 50c tip. A bowl of the old breakfast horse fodder for $3, that's not bad.

I won't tantalise you with the luncheon and dinner offerings. Suffice it to say that the astute Australian culinary economist can work his way past such offerings as a crummy old sirloin steak for $9.75 to winkle out the bargain dish—a couple of English lamb chops for a mere $8.50 with spuds and peas for another $2.50, a tomato salad for $1.75, an espresso coffee for $1.25, plus service fee of 75c plus $1 tip. By sticking to one-course meals only you can lunch at the Regency for as little as $15.75.

Back in my hotel room, I contemplated a new and radical revolution on behalf of a grateful American people.

No one was the slightest bit impressed with my frenetic campaign to give back to the Americans a long lost civil right. My American acquaintance thought I was bonkers.

I had bought the latest Ross McDonald and John D. McDonald whodunits from Brentano's Bookshop for $6.95 and $5.95 respectively. As I painfully parted from all that cash the assistant bunged on another 80c or so for 'tax'.

In New York State, and many other places apparently, they slap a bloody great luxury tax on education. The technical book, the text book, the child's primer; all books, along with bourbon, petrol and mink coats, carry a tax impost.

Surely this doesn't happen in any other Western democracy (or does it?) Certainly it could never happen in the communist countries?

The hard-bitten New Yorkers were not impressed. A tax on the ticky-box? Fair enough. We've been doing it with enormous success for years, they declared. So I had to shrink off to Park Avenue and read my McDonald crime tomes—and hated every stinking word on every overpriced page.

America produces an almost uncontrollable moral anger in the Australian or European tourist—for which one has to blame oneself rather than the unaware Yanks. One feels a combination of guilt and anger at the suckerdom which has brought one to such a financially virulent environment.

There is some point in parting from one's antipodean dollar in underdeveloped countries where any tourist income helps to feed someone in real need of feeding. But in New York they extract from you in three days more than you part with in three weeks in Greece or Bolivia or Peru. And the vast sums you part with mean SFA in the scheme of things.

It's intolerable to be in New York, and yet it would be a deprivation not to have been there and learned the lessons of the mind and heart and conscience that just haven't seeped through yet to the average home-bound, stunned-mullet Australian consciousness.

In America one discovers exactly how implanted is the Great Australian Stupefaction. Our awareness of social issues is defective and distorted. Our response as a public to social issues is selective and dishonest. The Australian spends half his life determinedly not wanting to know.

The Americans are different—to the point of national masochism.

For this reason the age of America is likely to be short-lived, and communist dictatorship the dominant world system by the end of the century. Power breeds and thrives on tougher, less humane material than the tortured omni-present tender conscience of the Americans. Even at the height of their technological brilliance there's a feeling of dinosaurian survival about the lumbering yet democratically admirable American presence.

The most significant element not present in our dim social schemata is a restless, probing, accusatory mass media. The media could and should prevent any passive acquiescence in the machinations of government, institutions, or corporations.

In Australia the ABC is a sociological eunuch, dead scared to confront facts, let alone thump home conclusions. The commercial media tend to bypass public affairs completely on the grounds of economic survival, ratings, the alienation of advertisers.

CBS in America are not at all averse to taking on the President himself, Spiro Agnew, the FBI, and most riskily of all, the political meddlings of the Pentagon. The public affairs men, like Walter Cronkite, are seasoned, expertly informed, and totally respected. The television channels actually produce nightly editorial pieces which are frankly opinion material. Yet the media convey a reasonably just balance of views.

The Australian imperative is that the public conscience should not be agitated on controversial issues, and our way of doing this is to sidestep hard-core controversial issues in favour of bland and unequivocal non-issues.

We'll devote endless hours to deploring the crown of thorns starfish menace; but how many sustained television confrontations on a Vietnam policy have you viewed in the past twelve months?

There the American distress is not a public pose. It is deeply implanted in the individual mind, whether he is educated or not, a liberal do-gooder or a savage cab-driver, a Harlem hothead or a solid Yonkers citizen clinging to the uncertain values of garden suburbia.

You are not restricted to sport and beer conversations in America. The central themes of our particular national idiocies have little dominance in the cerebral scheme of ordinary Americans. The Brooklyn taxi-driver is fully aware that his proud city is dying on its feet; New York is invariably nick-named 'the zoo' or 'the jungle'. Living in a strangulating megalopolis produces an almost Dostoievskian troubledness of spirit which, believe me, came as something of a shock to my inane she'll-be-right brand of consciousness.

I even looked a proper yahoo out in the Sunday tranquillity of Yonkers and Westchester County. Here in the Andy Hardy or Dick Van Dyke country of the American suburban dream, the subject of burglary protection systems came up over the brunch table.

'Do the New York druggies manage to find their way out to these tranquil havens to carry out burglaries and muggings?' I enquired.

The whole table boggled in my direction.

Burglary systems are a necessary protection against our own kids, they patiently explained. Did I really believe that the drug problem or compulsive violence was a Thirty-fourth Street exclusive?

Supersonic aircraft pollution, Pentagon malfeasance, Vietnam, Vietnam and Vietnam again—they are all real to the individual, and not the casual newspaper abstractions they are to us here. Sometimes the thinking is straight, quite often it is crooked, in this land of endless agonising appraisals. But is episodic wrong-headness more desirable than blank-headedness.

This is the gigantic cultural energy that we must eventually accept without tariff barriers as an American export. Or must we continue vigorously to invoke the Slight Australia Policy of small-town sociological isolationism?

# THIS IS YOUR CAPTAIN, BLIGH, SPEAKING

It's the new colour thrill of the season—tulla-marine!

This ravishing new tint has set fashion-conscious Melbourne by the ears, and it's certain to be well in evidence up the Istanbul end of Collins Street during the spring season.

A daring combination of midnight puce, apoplectic red, and shrivelled orange, tullamarine is the dominant colour chosen for the interior decor of the club bars, restaurants, diddies, and for the murals of Melbourne's great new international airport building. The colour motif has been subtly borrowed from a combination of Edwardian bordellos and the dimmer strip-joints of Soho. It suits the Melbourne mood.

Somehow, both architectural and art critics, a notoriously chicken breed, have managed to avoid an intellectual confrontation with the Tullamarine erection. The task devolves on your fearless Saturday commentator to brave the wrath of a Melbourne besottedly proud of this immense new airport pile.

The building style can be described as Stalinist Ceremonial at its most relaxed. That is, the external visual impression is as if some comedian had memorialised the moral fixities of Sir Henry Bolte and decorated the result with the late lamented Joe Stalin's ziff.

However, I believe the rumour to be untrue that Bruce Petty was aesthetic adviser to the project.

The airport car park contributes nobly to the national level of petrol consumption as desperate drivers cruise round and round the packed alleys seeking non-existent spots to deposit the vehicle.

If he ever manages to find a spot for the vehicle, the driver's simple mind is going to be thrown into turmoil by the inspired split-level logic of the creators of this cathedral of architectural confusion. An endless multiplicity of signs will head him every which-way, up and down escalators, through Alice-in-Wonderland doors going through murals, and it will be no surprise if he finishes up in Sir Reggie's personal office asking for his Four-and-Twenty pie with dead-horse.

There's an evening's fun to be had for mum and the kiddies once you find your way to the boutiques, to the bonzer news stands and the beaut cafeteria. There is still room for improvement in modest ways. A Colonel Sanders Kentucky Chicken edifice would be a most useful and graceful addition to the main international departure area, and wouldn't conflict with the general stylistic feel of Tullamarine.

All this jollity and messing about comes to an end once you cease being a visitor and set about the business of actual air travel from Tullamarine. All airport systems transform human beings into self-actuated components being processed through an endless pipeline, until they are eventually funnelled into their Ansett Tiger Moth or TAA Wirraway.

But very few culminate in the stark humour or what is described with undisguised risibility at Tullamarine as the 'departure lounge'. This is a sort of open cattle pen carefully devised to boast fewer seats than there are departing passengers. Here the bovine traveller is herded in panicky confusion to trample around, wild-eyed, bloodshot, until he is goaded up the ramp into the slaughterhouse—sorry, pressurised luxury aircraft.

I am a little sad to have been so cynical about Tulla—if only for the fact that Melburnians have treated its advent as disproportionately eventful in the life of their fair city. I will gain no additional friends there by conceding that Sydney Airport is in the first rank of the hierarchy of world airport terminals.

Its perspectives are dramatic; the lines are clean, functional, unpretentious. Above all, Sydney terminal has been conceived in terms of the comprehensible processing logic of the giant air terminal.

It is less of a snarling muddle than Frankfurt. It lacks the vertical marble simplicity of Athens. It doesn't have to indulge in the improvised vitality of Heathrow, where drinks circulate among the waiting passengers on trolleys, instead of the nervous citizenry having to stampede around a bar.

Sydney lacks the distinctive characters and unmistakably Gallic atmosphere of Orly. It doesn't engage in the supermarket conmanship of Shannon, where every single product of the wily Irish is paraded as supposedly 'duty free'.

For all the procedural logic and dispassionate architectural frankness, Sydney does offer adequate personal services in terms of comfort and refreshment. Indulgence in Sydney's very own brand of fish-shop vulgarity is only an episodic decorative abberration. Hands together for the Sydney lads.

Given the presence in Australia now of two major international terminals (and surprisingly, but relevantly, the fact of the economic unification of Europe), the time has come to bring Customs entry formalities to par for the international course.

Despite a token gesture of adopting the straight through, nothing to declare baggage clearance system, the whole Customs bit is still too much like induction into the ruddy army. What with little booths, checking passports against a big black book of international villains, yellow, pink, red, brown, grey and green exit cards to take to umpteen different channels for search or non-search. What with those speeches the poor officials keep reciting all day long about have you got any metwurst, fruit cake, saveloys or fur coats up your bloomers, there is still a modicum of outdated red-tapery to be disposed of.

The spot check system is a good one, but it doesn't require all of the present lumbering machinery. Australian procedures should be at least as simple as Checkpoint Charlie, which, at the moment, they are not. We may never achieve the limp yet deadly efficient rapidity of Heathrow, but we should aim at the expeditiousness of Lima instead of rating the same procedural status as neighbouring Bolivia with its passion for xenophobic bureaucracy.

Having disposed of these little matters, at last preparing to relax and recover from the writer's palsy, along comes a deadly and devastating Press document from beaut old Qantas.

Having evangelised furiously for an airline that, wisely or not, gave instant precedence to human safety against the monetary demands of a psychotic creep who would psychologically torture a lot of innocent air travellers for a blackmailing rakeoff, what do they then turn round and do? I'll tell you what.

Qantas introduces a 747 jumbo jet service and they report that 'the lounge decor is a radical departure from anything seen on commercial aircraft for many years. It has a distinctive nautical atmosphere—timbered and trimmed in the style of a captain's cabin as it would have been in an eighteenth century sailing ship . . . belaying pins, running lights, a small captain's wheel and a sextant are used to decorate the lounge walls.'

Now I ask you, for sweet Jesu sake, what a piece of work is Qantas man that he should disguise a thundering great jumbo jet as a wormy wooden sailing ship! Bloody nice for those of us who travel by air in order to escape the combined boredom and cruel unpredictability of the sea! The imaginative implications for the Qantas jumbo traveller are nothing short of horrific.

'This is your Captain, Bligh, speaking . . . any passenger who undoes his safety belt will be flogged.' Crew mutinies . . . blindfolded stewards being forced to walk the wings . . . weevilled biscuit and salt beef the speciality of the galley.

Marty Feldman-type flight games, with the aircraft flying in nautical undulations to ensure authentic seasickness among the guests in Captain Cook's cabin.

As a fierce hater of the sea and all its watery doings, I have even begun to consider loss of face by travelling among the economy-class peasantry.

'Furnishings in the first-class seating areas and the Captain Cook lounge are royal purple and blue, while the three economy class cabins have colours drawn from Australia's varying climatic regions. There are burnt reds from the inland . . .'

Cripes. What a shocking thought! Economy clients staggering up and down the aisles, doing a perish like Leichhardt, croaking for water. Goannas haring up the imitation saltbush walls. Jerked Camel strips for lunch (vide Egerton Warburton Journals for recipe for this celebrated dish of the burnt red inland). I wouldn't put it past Qantas, while it's so frenzied with the national fantasies, to feature bootblacked naked stewards disguised as Pitjantjatjara Aborigines with rows of desert lizards hanging from their pubic strings.

There's only one thing for it. The wise traveller will spend his holidays at Moonee Ponds. It's only a stone's throw from Tullamarine. Ideal for day trips. And there's a superb boarding house there run by a mate of mine, one Bazza Humphries. Mind you, as a true Aussie patriot of the jet-set era, the owner of said establishment has decorated it as a mockup of the original Port Arthur . . .

J

# ON THE LAWS OF POETRY

In these days of the seedier media, it's nothing, nothing at all, for 'personalities', as they are laughingly called, to perform improbable switcheroos. If you think you can do something, then you do it in public, irrespective of how appallingly or beautifully you do it.

Thus we have Dame Zara Bate, a splendid wife and mum, in the role of the Bertrand Russell of the tabloids, imparting the Wisdom of the Breast. Sir Bobby Helpmann totters off tipsy-toes to sing surfy songs on the teenybopper programmes of the square box. Models perform the function of professional intellectuals without batting their three-inch eyelids. Clerical gentlemen experimentally mainline Bex at the behest of a deity that wants them to become instant social scientists of the mysterious sub-culture of the young.

Poetry is the most obvious switcheroo of them all.

Everyone is a poet from the age of thirteen to eighteen. It's a universal pubescent and post-pubescent emotional compulsion. This innocuous, indeed desirable, activity ceases usually at twenty, the affliction cured by a prolonged antibiotic course of rejection slips.

However, some people carry on with this form of self-expression much longer than others.

A disc jockey named John Laws is one such example.

I know little about this platter-spinner or radio Dorothy Dix, as his publishers describe him, but I imagine he's out of his teens. Clearly he has not undergone the cold-turkey cure of the rejection slip therapy.

Disc jockeys don't have to. They have publishers panting up to them saying, 'Great, Rod baby. Sorry, John baby. What's McKuen or Leonard Cohen got that you don't possess? Apart from the market? The which let us grab altogether, you and us, one, two, three action.'

Thus, while two million pubescents scribble their lost and secret words, John Laws is the lucky guy who has a lovely volume published: Poems by John Laws, with posters, promotions, photographs and what-all.

Indeed, in the event we are all glad that this concatenation of circumstances has occurred, because the author has added a fresh distinction to his varied career (singer, songwriter, cynic, newspaper columnist, racing car driver, lover of women, children and dogs).

Meantime, what are we told about this poet, John Laws?

Blurb department: 'John Laws is one of the first poets out of New Guinea'. A proud but very puzzling claim. Does this mean that he's top-dog versifier of those not resident in the TPNG? Or the first poet to shoot through from that fascinating land? One has images of Mr Laws fronting up with a set of recitations at the Mount Hagen or Lae sing-sings. One can imagine the indigenes, with their impeccable sense of verbal rhythms and pragmatic clarity of sentiment, having a patient listen and then chasing our budding Rod McKuen across Torres Strait to the zing of tribal arrows.

So much for the biography. What does the blurb-writer tell us of the poetry, the real deal as it were?

Quote: 'What makes a man's man bare his soul to the world so easily? It's not easy—no fairy poet this one.'

I take stern objection to this. As a member of the Fairy Poets Guild of Australia, I believe there is possible cause of legal action in such a statement. It's bloody derogatory. I'm going to talk it over with our president, white blackfellow and golf-course grass-cutter by occupation, and our secretary, sheep-cocky and bushman.

Besides being derogatory of us fairy poets, it's a load of old cobblers. Take a listen to this excerpt from the lachrymose muse of John Laws.

> 'Does anybody have a tissue
> I think my heart's caught a chill.
> I fell asleep in the draft of love
> And a frozen heart could kill.'

What's so tough about that? Man's man, eh? You wouldn't catch Roland Robinson calling for the mortician at the first onset of the amatory sniffles.

Fairy poets, eh? How does the following grab you:

> 'Why the hell should I write poetry.
> Probably because I'm trying to find
> Another way to say I've loved.
> God, how I've loved.
> What a lousy feeling to love that much
> And not have the guts to say so.'

If you'll all stop sobbing into the sink for a minute, I'll point out something to you. We poets of the Fairy Poets Guild hold to the view that if you haven't got the guts to write about love you shouldn't be in the poetry biz. If you're that choked up you can't express yourself, you shouldn't express yourself, but rather go off and have a yarn with a shrink. That's what we tell blackballed applicants to our guild to do.

In fact, I'm certain John Laws has had too anguished a life for verbal communication, and for that reason above all he ought to take his man's manhood out of our stamping ground. That's the poetic territorial imperative. John Laws:

> 'heart
> can't start
> to replace a love gone down the drain,
> that's one love that ended up in the
>     sewer of life
> I guess.'

He's worried also by:
> 'the thought of your small body
>     thudding heavily
> on to the sand under the weight of mine.'

Such thoap thuds only have a detergent effect on the queasy reader, John baby.

At this point in this charitable exercise in professional literary criticism, it may be angrily asserted that I've played unfair by quoting excerpts. Therefore we now proudly present poem number twenty-one complete and unexpurgated. (Except for the dinky little floral borders around the poems that the publisher has revived from the days of Ella Wheeler Willcox and Patience Strong.)

Poem twenty-one, called Somewhere Else:

> 'Let's go somewhere else—
>     here is too near.
> Somewhere else is far away.'

Do tell? How inscrutable can you get!

Scanning it all through, there's only one line I can approbate in this great slop of entrancing verbal sludge. How lovely is the line, with that shudderingly execrable internal rhyme:

> 'If I could give you the ability to feel
>     humility.'

But if I could, then we would have an efficient disc jockey and singer and be deprived of a new champion in the tough racket of printing bad poetry. Long live John Laws! Long live the champ!

Any challengers?

# ANTI-SEMITES
# ON
# THE
# CAMPUS

John Keats declared it was but three steps from feathers to iron. It is an even shorter passage from student radicalism to student fascism.

It is not uncommon in the United States when the participants are emotionally overcharged and intellectually immature for what starts off to be student radicalism to take on the ugly colourations of fascist hatred.

This happened for the first time to my knowledge in Australia with the Queensland student newspaper *Semper Floreat*.

I've done a bit of championing of the student Press on previous occasions. Its sociological role is potentially important, not merely as a sounding board for underground opinion, but as the basic line of communication between the student view of contemporary society, and an outside world which tends to view youth through a distorting mirror.

Journals like *Lot's Wife* had their editorial seasons of great social value.

My chief piece of paternalistic advice to the radical student Press was to go through their sexual hang-ups and noisome preoccupations with liberation expression as quickly as possible. Too much frustrated editorial virginity was spoiling the editorial flavour.

The outburst of anti-semitic attacks on Zelman Cowen, the Vice-Chancellor at St Lucia, was the ugliest thing to have erupted in the recent history of student activism.

It is not altogether surprising that the violent sickness so obvious in some issues of *Semper Floreat* should have occurred in Queensland.

The civilised and liberal component of Queensland society has a hard time of it trying to impose contemporary patterns of humane behaviour on power structures tainted with raw and violent prejudice. Perhaps the kids aren't altogether to blame.

But blamed they must be if they are to be taken as adults and hammered as adults for displays of incipient, albeit unconscious, fascist behaviour.

*Semper Floreat* is obsessed with Professor Zelman Cowen, obsessed beyond normal reason and debate. It is not my intention to analyse the issues which made this liberal academic the subject of such raw passion—except that they seem to have dealt more with the resolvable issues of university finance than with demonstrable repressive acts of establishment authority. I am not concerned with whether the students or Professor Cowen were right or wrong. That is not my present brief.

I am concerned with the remarks of one Ruth Capillano in a sickeningly wild attack on Professor Cowen which culminates with the words: 'Cowen knows how to blend schmaltz with his chutzpah. "If you prick me do I not bleed?" he asks, as he tells us how sad/tired/unhappy/hard working he is.'

A reference like this, combined with the unsavoury talents emphasising Professor Cowen's Jewishness in the cartooning, led one to the conclusion that a direct exploitation of latent anti-semitism on the campus was taking place.

As the president of the University Staff Association remarked in a reply to the article: 'One wonders at the purpose of the use of Yiddish words and a well-known quotation from *The Merchant of Venice* in an article attacking the Vice-Chancellor. It will be an odd sort of university which is created by people who need to stir the embers of latent anti-semitism to support their claims.'

Fair enough.

What is most interesting is Miss Capillano's exquisite rationalisation to deal with this suggestion in her garrulous comeback.

'As for the Yiddish words, certainly this is a reference to the fact that Cowen is semitic. Why does Fielding find it necessary to call this simple stylistic device anti-semitism? If Cowen were French and I had concluded with some French words and sentences would he seriously have accused me of anti-Gallicism?'

Contemplate for one terrible second this mode of thinking. Forget for a while the desperate escapism of the false analogy, and that Frenchness does not involve race, colour or creed in the accepted sense.

Isn't it a slimy and evasive get-out-from-under quite uncharacteristic of the normal aggressive honesty of educated undergraduates. The 'simply stylistic device' line really is the nastiest and most devious piece of slithering.

Professor Cowen is an Australian scholar, liberal, and educationist. His race and creed are absolute and total irrelevancies to any debate or disputation. Why were the snide Yiddish references pertinent to the writer's case at all— except to play on latent anti-semitic tendencies within the Queensland student mind?

I would be making more of this one *Semper Floreat* episode than is necessary if the scurrility of Miss Capillano's language were the only isolated factor in the newspaper.

No Australian student newspaper was ever as thuggish as this in using bad manners, vindictiveness, and emotional irrationality in endlessly pursuing its victim. Most student newspapers would choose to reason their opponent out of office, not hound him. No matter how revolutionary they are, most young articulate dissenters uphold the priority of sound reason and the dignity of all men.

In *Semper Floreat*, Professor Cowen is always contemptuously referred to as 'Cowen'. If he is referred to with normal courtesy it is either accidental or a misprint.

The cartooning substitutes plain offensiveness or antisemitism for the usual satirical wit of the student. So much so that the author of one article, Paul Mariott, issued a disclaimer dissociating himself from one nauseating cartoon. This disclaimer letter is the most encouraging sign that there are people at St Lucia who can recognise when student dissent is turning into student fascism.

The evidence of *Semper Floreat* alone is quite enough for me. The smell of thuggery is unmistakeable. But Geoffrey Dutton has been up at St Lucia sniffing the atmosphere at close quarters. This hard-boiled character found the environment too much for his stomach, and he left behind a letter to *Semper Floreat* which I quote herewith in extenso:

'Dear Sir.—May a visitor who has been doing a few days' work in your library make a comment?

'Who is this Jewish rat Cowen who is being hounded through the snarling pages of *Semper Floreat?* Well, it turns out to be Professor Zelman Cowen, who in the far-away south is known as an intelligent, liberal and hard-working man, one of the most worthwhile Australians of today. But in *Semper* he is the victim of that fine old sport of the mob rushing a man and kicking him when he is down. The cartoons have a finesse that would do credit to a Goebbels or a Streicher.

'One of the genuine advantages of Women's Lib would be that Professor Cowen would be entitled to give Ruth Capillano a kick in the arse without feeling he had been rude to a lady, but, alas, I suppose he won't.

'A visitor has no right to comment on the internal affairs of the University of Queensland. This is just a plea for that basic demand of all revolutions, the dignity of man.'

*Geoffrey Dutton.*

Dutton is concerned with the dignity of man. I am more concerned with the dignity and integrity of the Australian student. We've had many an honest confrontation and I think they've been fruitful. The students straightened me out as often as I've attempted to straighten them out.

But believe me, I don't fancy, and I won't indulge in, any dialogue with the current editorial talent of *Semper Floreat*. I'd rather be asked to give Enoch Powell a great big kiss.

# PULL UP
# YOUR SOCKS,

**BRITAIN** The notorious supercilious complacency of the British is more endemic and more exasperating now than it has ever been.

Ask S. J. Perelman, the American humourist who has settled in London. Ask Henry Ford. Ask Mr Rupert Murdoch. Ask me.

The society that presents itself in London to the itinerant visitor is a shock and a sloppy shambles.

The current British state of affairs would, if it existed in America or Australia, call for orgiastic self-examination, doubt, questioning, and cultural guilt in the community. No such self-questioning psychology affects the ineffable British. Our ancestral Neros piddle while London churns. Any external criticisms of their industrial sloth, cultural shallowness, or business incompetence are greeted with the traditional reflex of lofty xenophobic superiority. My God it's exasperating!

It is commonly suggested that we Australians are ingenuously eager in our pursuit of overseas praise, and are neurotically thin-skinned when in the event we are called on to accept outside criticism.

This is something of an overblown myth, a repetitive canard we are too humble to dispute.

The truth is that we are babes in the woods compared with the British in their capacity to find the most decadent and hopeless social situations both normal and admirable. They remain completely adept, as S. J. Perelman put it, at 'putting down the colonials' in order to sustain a miasma of complete and complacent self-esteem. The only way the visitant will get on in Britain, says Perelman, is through taking a course in humblification.

Few Britishers, even the more internationalised of them, can bear to believe that the spectator gets as good a view of the game as the players. And possibly it is this phenomenon of the closed mind which has impelled certain worthy kinds of migrant to this less self-assured and more self-corrective country of ours.

While I was in Britain recently this lofty xenophobia was in full flood. Fleet Street and the media were having yet another spasm of animus towards that annoyingly energetic colonial, Mr Rupert Murdoch. The local lad had acquired a dynamic interest in London Week-end Television and, by unanimous reflex, the troglodytes of the media subsumed this would involve a vulgar downgrading of their not-so-impressive television standards.

The squawks of outrage were both bitter and insistent; the snide published asides, repulsively low-brow in style. Not a scrap of evidence was adduced or analytical material derived from the Australian situation to show that excessive vulgarisation has been at the heart of the Australian pattern of development in the news and television media. It was enough that a parvenu appeared to be taking over their sinking television enterprise.

As it happened, Mr Murdoch moved aside, bringing in the talents of Mr John Freeman, the writer and diplomat, to administer the programming of London Week-end Television. This culturally inspired appointment brought nothing more than the odd churlish grunt of satisfaction in the paranoid landscape of the London media.

Lest it be thought that I am biased, consider in more detail the harrowing experiences of that passionate Anglophile, Mr Henry Ford.

His business interests crippled by a wildcat strike, amazingly legalised by the unions post hoc facto, he gently pointed out to the British that future Ford developmental investment would almost certainly have to be diverted to Australia or Japan rather than to Britain, because industrial reason and discipline make those countries a better bet in terms of sustained productivity.

Poor old Henry! Did he cop it!

He was accused of threatening the wonderful Brits when in fact he was only mildly indicating a reasonable business possibility. The most lofty of the Sunday papers declared on its back page that 'Henry Ford does not really intend to push the British around like a mob of zombies'.

The wildcat trade unionist forces shrieked out to nationalise Ford.

Nowhere did one sense the presence of a considered reaction that the anarchic pattern of British proletarian behaviour is leading to a wholesale flight of investment out of the country. British workers are destroying the national pattern of their organised trade unionism with a perverse unreasoning bigotry; with a combination of bigotry and economic short-sightedness turning Britain into a matted industrial Sargasso.

Neither Harold Wilson, Edward Heath, nor the trade union leadership have been able to control this Gadarene process. And the chosen public attitude is one of blissful indifference.

Two years ago a postal strike destroyed international communications for six weeks. This was no matter of national urgency, an event, destructive of business confidence in the outside world, but a sort of comic inconvenience to be muddled through. Rolls Royce went through the hoop. Too bad. Very sad. Motor and General Insurance folded up, leaving motorists in a wholesale mess. Very droll. The Concorde aircraft was developed without planned consideration of the environmental factors. Curse the wicked, wicked Americans for developing hypersensitivity in the rotten environmental area just to spite us!

On and on it goes.

It's the land of eternal cock-ups. The Europeans call it 'the English sickness'.

Our problems in Australia are like those of France, of America or West Germany—they are developmental problems, the troublesome by-products of the social dynamic.

We have our strikes and inflationary crises, but these emerge from entirely different sorts of motivation. Australian workers battle to adjust to the processes of change; but they are certainly not engaged in anarchic hostility to industrial change itself. Our trade union structure is the most orderly of disorderly houses. The British chaos is the product of primitive and undisciplined working-class conservatism.

As Britain drops out of the industrial rat race, it is loudly making a virtue of its increasingly lowly position on the materialist totem pole.

The business section, would you believe, of a great London newspaper, featured a statistical table of material living standards in the Western world. An editorial rider was gratuitously added to these tables to the effect that Britain's material situation might be slipping, but what the hell, the rest of the world was desperately envious of the civilised and humane and superior British life-style. To hell with two car culture, in effect!

Indeed, it may be more civilised in the seventies for a country to opt out of the materialist race, to contemplate West Germany or Japan and to say, let us be a second rate country with a first-class national soul.

But with a little bit of thought this new British philosophy may be revealed as no more than a giddy rationalisation conjured up to make sloppiness, bad service, and social disorder more tolerable day by day.

A society may just as easily develop a sterile set of values by inertly dropping out of the technological process as by blindly responding to it.

This, I fear, is exactly what is happening in Britain.

I suppose when you get to the nub of it, a civilisation can be defined as the way you think about yourself and about others. Civilisation is the climate of the mind, and the mores of the society.

Britain's cultural self-esteem as the civilised drop-out nation of the Western world is capable of being viewed with a high degree of suspicion.

The British base their lofty view of themselves on the notion of their tolerance; but they do not care to define that tolerance as largely the oblivion of the intellectually incestuous.

The freakish thing is not the youthful permissiveness of contemporary Britain but the way mental procedures just haven't changed since the nineteenth century. The English work to a closed intellectual system—a system as rigidly doctrinaire and exclusivist as it was the ineffable days of the Raj.

This is evidenced in the hub-of-the-universe editorial tone of their newspapers, the uncritical indulgence of their creative assessments of such things as West End theatre, the idiot self-enchantment expressed over the Kings Road trendiness, the pseudo-cosmopolitanism which dares to assert their sub-average gastronomy can even be mentioned in the same breath as the French. Their utter and total provincial certitudes in short.

Take, for instance, the concept of 'fair play', which is at the core of the British pseudo-ethic, just as 'mateship' is Australia's big white lie.

'Fair play' is in working fact a set of changeable rules which are adjusted to suit any British convenience at any given moment. It is the epic national rationalisation which endows any action with personalised justification for the old British mental sanitary convenience, as it were.

As an intellectually under-developed nation, in which direction should we Australians turn in the cultural learning process? To the bland self-certitudes of the British as they petrify in postures of sublime historic dignity? Or to the blundering agonies of the heart and mind expressed in the climatic despair of the Americans?

Anti-Americanism has become the traditional reflex of the Australian. These days I'm not at all sure that that reflex hasn't been conjured up from over-simplified judgments. There's something rotten in all our Denmarks.

At least the Americans seem to know this. But the British haven't a clue. I don't think they ever will have.

# IN THE RED CORNER, MAULER MAX; IN THE BLUE CORNER, CASSIUS HAWKE

Bob Hawke, boss cocky of the ACTU, is a colourful force in the Australian social scene, although the colouration is not nearly so purple as the mass media have painted him.

The only really new thing he has done, apart from being professionally devoted to his job, is to go into discount retailing in Melbourne. Big deal.

What has caused the flurry of myth-making is his personality—a developed talent in the rough-house school of university debate, manifest in his refusal to be bluffed, bullied, side-tracked or trapped by interviewers.

Bob Hawke is first and foremost a pragmatist. What else! He could scarcely be in sympathy with the philosophical forebodings of a waffler such as myself. I view with desperate pessimism the future prospect of a social structure dominated by trade union notions of the optimum good; of Australia as one great unified continental Broken Hill.

How could the noble ideas of economic justice within a capitalist society possibly lead to a barren and sterile lifestyle, not merely for the privileged likes of me, but also for the quietly decaying masses of our endless future suburbia? For a trade union functionary worries about economic justice first and the philosophy later—if ever.

The idea that what is good for the trade unionists is good for the nation is as deeply embedded in the thinking of the ACTU commissars as the like idea is in the unconscious of General Motors executives. One would not expect it to be otherwise.

For as long as all citizens of our fair nation are not yet rewarded with plentiful wherewithal to enjoy horse-racing, poker-machines and Saturday night beer-swills, there's enough idealistic motivation for Bob Hawke. I don't think he's a great reader of Mumford. I don't think he dreams the Dunstan dream.

So we come to our little personal confrontation.

It appears that the ACTU is going into the matter of chemist shop mark-ups. Some of these Mr Hawke deems to be excessively high.

But chemist shop gross retail profits are receiving the attention of Mr Hawke and his organisation.

He hoped to be able to bring down these profit margins by the application of certain pressures.

I hope that summates the discussion scrupulously, and exactly as Mr Hawke would wish it to be summarised.

It was Saturday morning when Bob Hawke rolled into the Sturt Arcade Hotel. The course, as they say, was in perfect condition. Peter Whallin was pulling some of his best West End draught. I was on my third schooner. Hawke had the flu. The ALP conference, talking, entertainment, had all taken their toll. What provocateur could resist going in for the kill.

Harris: You've gone into a flat-out attack on chemist shop margins. The ACTU is in effect telling a lot of small retailers that it's going to make them lower their annual income and reduce their standard of living. Taking chemists' earnings over an average; I'm informed the poor sods are making a lot less than you are, while providing an essential community service. If it's the ACTU's business to haul down further the humble living standard of the chemist, by the same token wouldn't it be legitimate for the community to peg down the earnings of trade union commissars?

Hawke: Your comparison is not strictly relevant. It happens that I'm in a rather highly paid position. I question your facts. Who says that chemists are battling for a quid. Produce your evidence. Quote your sources.

Harris: You've got me there. I've spoken to a few pharmacists and all they could tell me is that for every affluent chemist in a specially favourable urban situation, there are about fifty little suburban and country blokes who are struggling for a crust. After all, the supermarts have been carving up the chemists' traditional market for a decade. Who buys toothpaste from a chemist these days? What economic motivation there could be these days for a young fellow to take up a pharmacy course I can't imagine.

Even so (Harris continuing garrulously against his seriously weakened opponent) don't you think you sounded a bit of a gutless wonder on telly? You want to mutilate the modest living standards of the retail chemist, but you didn't have a go at the big pharmaceutical companies and combines, the hiking of drug prices by the international cartels on the dubious grounds of financing research, etc.

Hawke: I couldn't agree more. The pharmaceutical companies will have to be taken on in due course. It's a big job but we're not unaware of the problem. (Momentary bonhomie and agreement.) But look here, Harris, even if marginal chemists go out of business, there's no case, repeat no case for the artificial retention of resale price maintenance, and especially on such essential things as chemist's lines.

Harris: So the marginal chemist shop goes by the board.

They close up shop in the working-class suburb. They disappear from the medium and small country towns. So the unionist is deprived of a community service. He has to drive or take a taxi three suburbs distant to get his antibiotics. You haven't saved him any money.

The country town bushie has to race fifty miles to the next town to get a prescription for a sick child. You slash incomes in an occupation which no-one seriously considers to be any more economically predatory than the butcher or the greengrocer, and the ACTU creates a real and serious community social problem.

I don't know about the rest of Australia, but in our territory there's already an unfunny health problem because of doctors moving out of marginal areas. Our big social problem here in South Australia is how to raise not lower, marginal medical incomes. The same is about to be true of pharmaceutical incomes.

Hawke: (Rising wearily to the count of seven, breathing flu germs heavily in all directions.) There's clearly a case that some subsidy scheme would have to be evolved to ensure that both rural and urban workers would have access to an essential service.

Harris: But you didn't say that on the telly!

Perhaps I have been unbecomingly jocular as a conversational reporter. But I will insist that there's no misquotation, distortion or misrepresentation.

It might also be inferred that I am a supporter of resale price maintenance, a ridiculous position to be in, considering my own business crusade has been one of stimulating interest in both books and authors as a ruthless discounter during a period of prohibitive book price inflation.

Yet surely the whole point of the debate is not one of moral causes, but of complex insights. Resale price maintenance is not just a matter of collusive profiteering villainies on the part of the capitalist system. It is a mixed affair.

Often is creates unjustifiable price levels in one area of activity and solves a social problem in another. You can't respond to the problem with one simple bovine reflex—as the British have decided in relation to medicine, and, I must shamefacedly confess, certain types of books.

Apart from the fact that it is a complex issue, there is the long-range philosophical choice that must be carefully made, between a diversified and colourful consumer culture, with its excesses and wastefulness, and a commissariat culture which is economic yet conformist.

Bob Hawke can't see this complexity. Or, if he can, he didn't care to reveal it to me.

This is how it was.

Even so, the time has come for the new-look power machinery of the ACTU to be put to question.

It by no means follows that a worthy section of the populace, motivated by its own special interests, will serve the whole community, the national identity, when it acts as a pressure group using its numerical power in general social issues.

Without examining his philosophy, his thinking, his larger social values, there's no reason to accept a Sir Galahad image of Bob Hawke as he leads the trade unions from their fundamental causes into an agency pressurising the economy and the social framework.

The trade unions already exercise social pressure anyway from within the Australian Labor Party.

There are those who would wish that the character if not the strength of that presence improved in quality. There's a closed-ranks, closed-mind quality about the Australian Labor Party, which makes outside criticism an affront to a flawless organisation. This goes hand in glove with the defensive union credo that what's good for the unions is good for the nation.

Nothing, not even film clips of the good old British wharfies chanting pro-Enoch Powell slogans, will convince a dedicated union leadership that the drear conformism of Australian life, as viewed by social idealists, is a product of proletarian philistinism as much as of implacable capitalist opportunism.

Bob Hawke starts off with these two traditional and ingrained strikes against him. He will only break new ground, contribute to a more gracefully civilised pattern to the extent that he can revolutionise the grass-root thinking processes of unionists. Can he alter the salt-of-the-earth view of themselves? Can he impose social vision on a structure wholly and properly preoccupied with battling for slices of the economic cake?

For my money, Gough Whitlam and Dunstan are your men on the Labor side of the fence. Both are capable of being motivated by a social vision of Australia, of forging a party which expresses more of a national identity than of routine sectional interests.

Bob Hawke strikes me as being more the sum total of what his job has made him.

He belongs to Australia's most classic and beloved species —the pragmatist, the practical man. His intellectuality is essentially that of the abrasive debater. It is far better to hold your ground than be clobbered by new ideas. Because his aims, his party political convictions are liberal and progressive, he will feel defamed because his personality impressed me as uninspiring in its pragmatic certitudes.

It would be surely a waste of time to talk to Bob Hawke of Australia's need for increased cultural diversity—for more boutiques, ratbag enterprises, poodle parlours, bookmakers, drag cabarets, wild little theatres, struggling experimental galleries, anything that lifts us from the lawn-mower culture of predictable suburbanism.

By contrast, I have the feeling from talking to him that Hawke still dreams of that long-since realised Australian dream of the workers' paradise—a blissful community of endless replicas where even the Sarsparilla supermart has given way to Hawke's universal commissariat. And Patrick White's beautiful eccentric ghosts have long since gone to their rest.

Hawke senses an impending period of growing power to realise this dream, if this be his dream.

And of Hawke as a man of power, I'd never quote Lord Acton's weatherbeaten dictum. He wears his power with a tight and rigid integrity. But power is a mediocre mode of travelling. It doesn't broaden the horizons. You've got to do that before you pack your bags.

K

# HELPING ANNA
# WITH
# THE LIB BANNER
I've been helping Anna hold the banner for Women's Lib since pussy, if you'll forgive the improper image, was the proverbial kitten.

The trouble with the great sociological issue of restructuring the whole state of women in human affairs is that so much territory has to be covered, and that such indefinables as 'attitude' are perhaps even more important than straightforward facts such as inequality or job opportunity.

Work inequality for women is a nauseating and common reality in this country, where I suspect idiot male backwardness is more commandingly present than in a more intellectually adult country like Britain.

My knowledge of work institutions is limited to the ABC and newspapers. I'd hate to acknowledge how many examples I've seen in the ABC of enfeebled male executive abilities bolstered by the creative and organisational capacities of female research assistants, secretaries or whatever euphemistic terms are used in that estimable institution.

The trouble is you can't pin down the anti-feminism as gross anti-feminism. It's all too subtle, ingrained, unconscious and natural to the tribal pattern of the ABC. Third-rate blokes whose talents might suit them for selling pencils sit at executive desks imagining that they're thinking and doing. First-class female talents race around in outer offices really making things work, and at the same time kidding the nongs at the big desks that they've directed the action.

It's not a deliberate policy from the administrators. I doubt if they've even thought about the organisation being structured on the basis of unconscious sexual prejudice. The work has always naturally evolved on the kind of pattern that exists. And besides, this is the humble way in which women want to fit into the work situation.

But is it?

I imagine the ABC has evolved since my dim heyday and things aren't quite as bad now. But since the ABC is comparatively enlightened in such matters, how dismally frustrating it must be for intelligent women in other working environments dominated by the boofhead variety of the executive Australian male!

Unconscious attitude is more relevant than conscious policy. Let us heroes of Women's Lib never forget this difficult first principle. It's a psychological not a sociological revolution we're after. The one will follow the other. But we must always realise the ovum precedes the foetus as it were.

Australia has some sort of chance. The temper of the place favours an easy-going balance of human dignities in the future relationship of the sexes.

Our major problem is the slobby passivity of the Australian female. She is not the prime chattel of the male. The Holden Monaro occupies that august position. On the other hand, she has no great desire to play a more vital part in the human scheme. She doesn't know she hasn't any dignity, therefore she's not in pursuit of this most important attribute. If you have any doubts about this, just listen to a few of those street interviews on the telly current affairs programmes.

Women's Lib has the first and prime task in Australia of getting through to women. Since the root cause of it all lies in attitudes, not easily definable at that, the militants must pinpoint clear isolated issues and hammer away at them until the general issue sinks in and registers among the supine examples of not-so-radiant Australian womanhood.

Avoid all profound disputation on the biological differences of men and women, the child-bearing function, the choice of home versus work. Things get bogged down in words very rapidly.

Pick on some such issue as the Dean Martin show and attack the Broadcast Control Board for permitting this vile programme to be shown.

It's a classic programme to cite.

Whereas one thousand Australian mums will rise in high moral dudgeon to protest to the authorities if someone says 'bum' on the mass media, they'll sit content through Dean Martin, too stupid to realise they're being sold the squalid ethic of sexual promiscuity each week. In the Dean Martin show women are less than chattels, they are Playboy sex toys, poor gibbering excited creatures which exist for the episodic recreation of the egocentric male.

The Playboy philosophy, this less-than-medieval view of the female, is the hardest sell that's being tried on in the late twentieth century. It's slowly taking this view that the female is a sexual fun object for the male. In the permissive era the liberated young female tries to return the compliment, to regard sex as a passing gratification and the male as her sexual fun object.

But the promiscuity philosophy doesn't work for females. They're too intelligent and too basically involved with values.

One of the cultural differences between men and women is that the sexual act is generally more deeply related to human values, to love if you like, in the female than it is in the male, for whom episodic sex experience provides ego gratification as well as appetitic satisfaction. It is precisely in their more substantial concern with the 'thou' as against the self-obsessed 'I' that women are more interesting, complex, and nicer people than men.

This advantage women possess as people comes under obscene threat if the Dean Martin fantasy world is freely projected until it becomes a grotesque social actuality.

Consequently I object to chimpanzees and dogs dressed up in hats, ten-year-old children dressed up in dinner suits mimicking Elvis Presley for the telly, women degraded in their humanity pretending to dribble with anticipatory excitement over poor weary Dino, the beauty contests in the name of charity (as if it's not possible to help some human beings without degrading others), to clowns, commentators, mass media link-men who snigger, giggle and affect the playboy manner.

These I render up to the censor as the things which are ripe for his Caesarian operations. These are the obscenities that matter. Let him have a whack at these things.

No doubt I shall be denigrated as the last of the puritans, or the first amongst the frustrates—that's hard cheddar. I'll just have to put up with it. Now sufficiently primed, give us a grip of the banner, Anna, and let's foray out into Martin Place.

And wear your Yves St Laurent midi, Anna. The most liberated and cultivated women are invariably the most subtly dressed as well. An odd addendum to these reflections, and I think partly true.

# GLORIOUS MOMENTS ON THE CHARITY CATWALK

*A pretty girl is like a melody . . . Girls were made to love and kiss, and who am I to interfere with this.*

Who indeed: The same off-key orchestras squawk out the same tunes every year. And seemingly the same set of young chooks totter down the catwalks, appearing to be in a state of hysterical semi-consciousness that no pot-smoker could ever hope to attain.

The season for Miss Australia, Miss Telethon, Miss Advertising, Miss International Model, Miss Anthropy is on.

Television stations, wide-eyed innocents that they are, rush to the occasions with their video cameras embarrassingly agape. The bloomers and bosom section of the rag trade flex their advertising muscles and cut the very heart out of their promotional allocations. And all over the country those Noble Characters summoned by God to declare the blessings of Charity rehearse the unspeakable cliches which will prepare them for the glorious moments that lie ahead as spokesmen for the recipient charities.

A mysterious and unexpected audience, the hairy unknowns of the occasion, the outsiders, yea verily the eggheads of this nation, also switch off from their normal pursuits to boggle at the glittering spectacle presented on the box from Wonderland Ballroom, the Southern Cross Hotel or the Hobart City Hall.

It's all a relatively new part of the grass-roots culture of McLuhan's Australia, and in its uniquely predictable awfulness it has a compulsive fascination for people of intelligence and sensibility.

I'm not sure whether they switch over from Homicide out in Fredland or not. I rather doubt if they do. It's Donald Horne and the rest of us much-maligned cerebrators who build up the ratings for these orgies of Australian gaucherie.

There are two sociological interests involved in this relatively new but permanent component in our cultural life, these Melbourne Cups of pubescent nubility.

The one is the sheer revelatory hideousness of the occasions themselves.

The other is the corruptions of the essential notions of charity as expressed in Christian, Islamic and Buddhist doctrines.

Beauty competitions, art prizes, literary awards, musical

eisteddfods, all reflect a corrupt streak in rational psychology. People are never content with the thing in itself, the intrinsics. There must be a compulsive human need to compare apples with bananas, to place a superior or inferior evaluation on Patrick White as against Alec Hope; on Dobell as against Mike Kitchin. Or on Myrtle O'Toole the telephonist from Cairns, as against Millie McSquirt, darling of the Werribee Greyhound Trainers' Association.

We degrade paintings and concertos in this competive way. One can't object to the same thing happening to clean wholesome Aussie sheilahs, so passionately devoted to water-skiing, sewing, reading, and just lounging around on the beach in a state of primal protoplasmic idiocy.

The girls are merely drilled to a state of zombification for the one big telly night, and one's interest in this drab aspect of the glittering occasion is severely limited to a vain hope that one of them will trip head-a-tit over their ballgown. The girls only provide a dim blood-lust voyeurism usually directed to boxing matches, trapeze acts, steeplechases, or dangerous road intersections. The last-named provides the shortest odds for the sensational situation.

But we still watch and hope. Wouldn't it be heaven if Miss Queensland's panty-elastic snapped as she curtsied to the Lord Mayor of Hobart and her drawers fell down? Such squalid non-erotic fantasies are perhaps not fit for reflection in a family newspaper—but ask yourself if you know anyone who does not have them?

In point of fact the real sociological interest lies in the gobbledegook of the official speechifiers. This is when the Freds of telly-land doze off and the eggheads come awake.

'Tonight it is my pleasant duty . . . all I can say with the deepest sincerity is thank you Australia' (thunderous applause). It is peculiarly horrible. Here is the modern Australian dressed up for public presentation, wearing all his campaign medals of community goodness, oozing egotistical humility, and insulated by an unalterable pattern of predictable cliches.

The tribal rainmaker—it invariably seems to be some laboriously jolly character when I'm in front of the box—admixes regional fatuousness with dismal reverence for the giant intellectual capacities of the contestants. It all adds up to an exemplification of the Australian way of think and talk at its unbelievably bathetic worst.

In consequence, I would vote these quests as the most educational programmes on television. They indicate clearly the task that lies before this great nation in the field of adult education.

So I'm being sardonic at the expense of worthy charities

and the worthy people who work their guts out for them?

But am I? I question the charitable effectiveness of the urban corroboree, and so do a lot of other people. There's some convincing to do on the economic side of it.

It probably costs the bloomers manufacturers and the prize donors a million dollars in promotional outlay to mount the national Quest spectaculars.

What if the cost of the carry-on exceeds the amount the sweating girlies raise for charity? Wouldn't it be more rational for the bloomers tycoon to write out a cheque for a million and satisfy his charitable instincts in this fashion?

Even if the elementary financial figures don't sustain this argument, then take into account the productivity man-hours lost in terms of people's time. This must be quite considerable.

Perhaps the most pernicious thing about the telly quest for charity is its contribution to the class structure of charity. We all know that there are rich charities and poor charities, the fashionable, the chic, the middle-class and the indigent struggling charities.

Charities for children win all the way, so long as they invoke the image of the appealing and the pathetic. (A charitable drive to combat child-bashing and child-cruelty wouldn't go all that well with a parade of affluent Australian femininity.)

Can you imagine a Miss Australia Quest, for example, devoted to the shit-work carried out by the Salvation Army among derelicts, misfits, dipsomaniacs, the indigent and the unloved. The thought is ridiculous. You don't associate a boiled shirt and champagne television climactic with stinking homeless alcoholics.

Insofar as the modern tendency is for charitable collection to be associated with promotional campaigns, advertising drives, and the sporadic attacks on public humanity to which our television pastors and masters are prone, rational people are coming to feel that the whole charity business is becoming inequitable. Rational people may even resent every dollar collected by those good Miss Australia contestants, dollars contributed not out of love of man for man, but by appeals to regional egotism through sexual blandishment.

In a rational society there would be few charities at all. Sick or disabled children, mental health, the care of the aged, would be properly cared for out of the taxes we pay. The F-111s would finance a fair swatch of these needs alone!

The present half-and-half system permits the mean to grow rich and powerful, and the generous to remain static and pious. It doesn't do either kind of human being much real good.

But we are not in a rational society. So things will go on the way they are going.

# ONE
# FOR THE
# CODEINE-CHOMPER

Next time you go to your local quack with a touch of tapioca or whatever, have a look on his desk for a fattish black book, The Australian Drug Compendium —Desk Reference, 1969-70.

If you can add the compulsive kleptoes to your immediate symptomatology, race off with the book concealed in your panty-hose and study it carefully before handing yourself over to the gendarmes.

It may be a publication you can easily buy, but I've never seen it in any bookshop.

It ought to be readily and reasonably procurable, because it provides the full range of drug information which should be presented to educated people in a sophisticated society.

It is a matter of vested interest, phoney mystique, and clinical desperation that medicos still insist on patients responding to their treatments with blind faith and contented ignorance. This dismal philosophy should only be reverted to by medicos when they are providing placebos for idiot psychosomatic cases, or for terminal situations (as it is so gracefully expressed).

I should imagine that it would be in the interests of the medical profession to have patients thoroughly familiar with the nature, function, and potential side-effects of any given drug. Many drugs in the compendium are contra-indicated if other symptoms are present.

It is notorious that people are bad at communicating their general physical symptoms. They omit, often through the sheer nervousness of the medical interview itself, to mention those facts which may well prove most relevant and significant.

There must be tens of thousands of cases day by day where doctors prescribe a particular drug without really knowing if it is contra-indicated or not. Drug procedures in a general practice must be a fairly hit-or-miss business.

This grisly aspect relates to medical efficiency. Perhaps the greatest value of the public laying their hands on the doctor's desk compendium is to counteract the current vast wave of anti-drug hysteria.

Pharmacology is going forward in dramatic leaps and bounds. Public attitudes are going backwards to medievalism, states of fear, crankiness and irrational antipathy. There is a growing attitude that drugs are unnatural, nasty things and that the citizen should take evasive action to sidestep this particular aspect of modern medical technology.

Hence the raving success of such books as Dr Ainslie Meares' *Relief Without Drugs* and the popularity among the young of mystical and cultish nutritional rites. This blanket animus towards pharmacology as one facet of medical regression is induced by mass media ignorance — plus the idiocy of doctors who still practise hocus-pocus psychology.

The information in the Australian Drug Compendium is provided by the manufacturers themselves, and there are quite a few revelations for the untutored. For example, one wonders how many consumers of codeine tablets realise how quaint it is for them to take a moral line on the kids who take soft drugs — since codeine 'is methyl-morphine and may be regarded as a weakened form of morphine'.

It would appear that mum is gorging the hardest drug of all to tackle those inevitable headaches of hers! The Drug Compendium states quite baldly (see page 431, column 1) in fact that 'codeine must be classified as a drug of addiction'.

If this information is correct, as it must be, one wonders why yet one more addictive drug, in addition to alcohol and nicotine, is freely available to oldies. More importantly, since addiction is rare because of the low level of euphoria induced, one wonders once again why certain basic facts are not publicised on the bottle or in other ways.

It appears that codeine possesses no additional analgesic potency over a certain dose. It is not dangerous to exceed the stated dose: it is plain useless. I wonder how many codeine-chomping mamas are aware of this fact? If not, why not?

One particular invaluable treatment for infective diarrhoea may result in the overgrowth of non-susceptible organisms if used for more than three days. One wonders how many devoted and gratefully cured souls continue to use the preparation with dangerous prodigality, unaware of this limiting factor.

And so on.

The chemical facts indicate that the public should have a much clearer idea about the drugs they can just walk into the chemist's shop and buy.

By the same token, if we are to grow out of our present state of social ignorance, we should have a vastly greater measure of public education about the different character, function and side-effects of tranquillisers, hypnotics, depressants and barbiturates. The more information people get the more rational their behaviour.

Befuddled by mass media sensationalism, we as an educated community have made no rational assessment of their contribution to health, well-being and longevity. We just hear the word barbiturate, for example, and shudder in horror.

I guess the medicos can erect a case of some sort for public ignorance. Since side-effects of some sort or other are relatively common with many drugs, and the idiot public is infinitely suggestible, it is possible that the more suggestible patient is capable of inventing or imagining side effects. Ignorance is an effective antidote to the lively imagination.

Many drugs are of limited efficacy. It may not help the psychotherapeutic side of the general practitioner's business to have an educated public.

Against this must be set the large sociological issue of our time. There is a crisis in drug attitudes. The subject is a loud and living and confused theme of general concern. The balance of attitude is swinging, I feel, to an irrational and neurotic anti-drug medievalism.

A new era of natural cure quackery is already upon us and gathering formidable strength. It must surely be in the interests of the medical profession to promote wider drug education, an appreciation of the values and advances of the therapy, to counteract the growing suspicion and ignorance of patients.

Medicos are an overworked lot. Conservative, too. It may take years before they realise that a new relationship between pharmacology and patients is an urgent necessity.

In the meantime, your best chance of surveying the scene in a rational and comprehensive way is to sneak off with that fat black book.

# THE SAD DECLINE
# OF VARSITY SATIRE
# INTO
# UNFUNNY PORNOGRAPHY    Is it true that young people
are developing later these days?

Here's a noble theme for a pop psychiatrist eager to make
the feature pages of the Sunday Press.

If pre-pubescence is not extending into the late university
years, then the only other conclusion is that the campus
group situation is producing a collective sexual hang-up
which is saddening, pimply, and destructive.

I have before me a sorry publication, *The Australian
Women's Monthly*, issued for the annual Prosh at one of our
universities, lavishly printed and selling in the sacred name
of charity.

One has been purchasing these Prosh rags for a couple
of decades and the traumatic change that has been taking
place in their content in recent years provides revealing
diagnostic material for any head-shrinker worth an ounce
of analytical civet.

Once, the Prosh newspapers used to be filled with irre-
verent and even defamatory satirical material, leavened by
a modicum of shy pornography so that students could re-
assure themselves of their condition of sexual liberation.

But the true business, the true impulse, the true interest
of the student community, was reckless satire directed at all
the villains, the sacred cows, the rednecks, the Establish-
ments, the religious and political bigots.

Satire is as relevant to the social scene today as it ever
was. Perhaps more needful. Yet I have combed through the
endless sixteen pages of this publication and not one line
of considered satire interrupts the steady flow of desperately
unfunny pornography.

Why has pornography—and I am using this word in its
strictly technical rather than pejorative sense—completely
ousted satire from the literary preoccupations of the Australian student?

The answer, I think, must emerge from a new era of
psychological conflict which afflicts the contemporary student, the male particularly.

He emerges from secondary school excitated by the
thought that he has joined the permissive society. He has
fantasies of sexual liberation, and Third World psychic
values.

In the event, he discovers that his Kinsey average is sub-
normal, sexual libertarianism exceptional rather than the

prevailing state of affairs, and that pot-smoking is a pretty tame kick unless you're capable of endless imaginative self-delusion.

In this disappointing context, it is only logical that the dormitory snigger of the prep school should be perpetuated into full manhood, and this is one unmistakable dimension in the pages of *The Australian Women's Monthly*. There is a sad and twittering preoccupation with women's periods, masturbation, boastful references to the size of the student genitalia, obsession with the female mons veneris, and even, God help us, a photograph of a lavatory seat with a bare behind showing through it.

It is not all sub-adolescent. Quite a section of the publication is devoted to tasteless, simple-minded fantasies of endlessly virile men and ubiquitously nymphomaniac females endlessly doing their fornicatory thing.

I understand that this movement from the intellectualism of satire to the subjectivity of amateur pornography is common to the student fraternity throughout Australia.

I believe it poses a real human problem that calls for help and sympathy, and that it will prove much more significant than the excesses of student radicalism or the drop-out tendency.

The first evident thing is that the legalisation of pornography would be a considerable help.

The whole purpose of the gross pornography that I've been shown by the Collector of Customs is to produce a vicarious and harmless outlet for two ages of identical psychological traumas. Some men in late middle age, while undergoing sexual decline, need vicarious excitements, either in written form or photographic, to compensate the sense of sexual deprivation and incapacity that comes with the later years of life. For these blokes, access to pornography is a most useful psychological prophylaxis.

Likewise, it might well prove useful to students such as these who produced *The Australian Women's Monthly* for Prosh day in my village. Their publication is a classic document of sexual retardation and psychological troubledness.

It is not their fault they have been launched into a supposedly liberated university society where, in fact, the non-masturbatory outlets for sexual experience do not match up either to the promise of a permissive life or to the needs of their youthful virility. Access to legalised pornography may help them feel knowing, experienced, and sophisticated in all kinds of heroic sexual situations they've never experienced.

There may be larger social arguments against legalised pornography. I'm not, repeat not, crusading the cause.

But what stinks in this country is that reasoned discussion of the Scandinavian-American-British fait accompli of legal pornography has begun here so many years after it became open to debate overseas.

Possibly discussion is useless while certain atavistic forces remain dominant in our society. We first need a more highly educated and more youthful magistracy, so that old legal barbarisms can be eliminated through new definitions of public consensus. We can't get very far when police and magistrates still perpetuate a primitive tribal terror of four-letter words which are, after all, simply words!

In the meantime, I'm convinced we should recognise that there is a student problem which is not the problem purveyed by the law-and-order enthusiasts.

It is clear that students outgrow their adolescent sexual problems more slowly than the rest of the community. The situation won't be helped by prosecuting their published efforts at amateur self-help pornography.

The first task, surely, is to understand the weirdness of the problem. It is a common fallacy to assume that blue jokes, hired strippers, porno-movies, and front-bar dirty jokes, are the special need of the uneducated, working-class man. In another society a decade ago, this was possibly so. But through conventional training and modest pre-marital sexual anticipations which are exceeded by the event, the image of the Leagues Club furtive pornographer is a discredited one. The proletarian voyeurist industry is about as active as the market for antimacassars.

The troubled spirits, in fact, walk the campuses. Their desperate efforts to shock an uninterested world with Prosh rags and the like is to be interpreted only as their way of letting us know that there is a trouble spot, and that they need help rather than the ignorant homilies of backward magistrates.

# TIME TO
# JUDGE
# THE
# JUDGES

I have a constant bee in the bonnet on the subject of the judicial apparatus, its modus operandi, and the intellectual calibre of those functionaries who have power over the liberty of the individual.

I suppose it's a reformist passion that goes back to those startling days in 1944 when a seemingly elderly magistrate determined that the poetry of myself and the late lamented Ern Malley was indecent, immoral, and obscene. Up to a short time ago the same magistrate was still in business, determining who should go to gaol and who shouldn't, what standards are currently acceptable and what aren't.

Of all the social institutions that fuss or fascinate those of us who explore and expose society through the media, the wit, wisdom, enfeebledness, dangerousness, tolerance, humanity or inhumanity of judicial administration is perhaps the greatest theme that should concern us.

We subject politicians to the merciless spotlight of public criticism. We expose administrations and officialdom with unflagging zealousness.

But the law, the courts, the judicial system seem to have inbuilt defensive properties which inhibit or restrict public investigation and evaluation. It is a closed system and it has an effective rule of total silence which has been abandoned in other fields long ago.

The public can now appraise the standards of medical practice with the assistance of the medical profession. The policies of a church can be subject to scrutiny, and unequivocal dogmas are now the themes of open dialogue. But no member of the judiciary will enter open public debate with any critic.

The legal profession is notably remiss in not providing the public with critical and controversial data about the standards of justice and the intellectual capabilities of judges and magistrates. One feels that there should be a constant critical scrutiny, led by the legal profession and placed before the public. After all, it's the public which is on the receiving end of the system. It's you or I who may be incarcerated or not, depending possibly as much on the mental health of an arteriosclerotic judge as on the argued facts.

So be it. Press and television lay off the standards of justice in Australia as a dangerous if not inviolate area of fundamental public interest. However the era of timorous public passivity may soon be over. The subject is breaking wide open in Britain at least. Nearly two years ago, on October 24, *The Sunday Times*, in London, got hold of and reported on an unpublished report prepared by a British committee of the International Commission of Jurists. This report was confidential and Lord Shawcross, one-time UK Attorney-General, was insistent it should not be made public. He stated in *The Times* that 'he did not consider publication justified, and regretted that anyone should think it useful at the present time to shake public confidence in the judiciary'.

What had happened was that a group of moderate, senior, and responsible British legal experts had blown the whistle on a decrepit and dangerously class-biased judicial machine.

The report proposed that the appointment of judges should be taken out of the sole hands of the Lord Chancellor and that prospective judges should be assessed and appointed by a diverse committee which would examine the abilities and attitudes of the nominated judge in the light of accepted modern social values as well as on his legal qualifications.

At about the same date and for the first time in Australia this insulation of judges from community standards was not only considered, but made explicit by a brilliant judicial mind. I refer to the radical and remarkable appeals judgment of the constitutionalist, Mr Justice Howard Zelling, in Romeyko v. Samuels.

I quote:

'In addition there is the difficulty which always confronts one in these cases, namely the ascertainment of the current standards of the community. It is often blandly asserted that judges are easily able to decide for themselves without hearing evidence what those current standards are.

'With the utmost respect that is an absurdity. According to the South Australian Year Book 1971, page 140, the mean or average of the population of South Australia at the census of 1954 was 32.8 years. The age distribution of population for South Australia is given at the same page. Some fifteen to seventeen per cent of the population of South Australia would be in the age group of the judges of this court, and if it be of any importance in this matter a less percentage still in the case of the learned special magistrate from whom the appeal is brought.

'The judiciary is of necessity cut off to a certain extent from unrestricted intercourse with other members of the community, little as they may desire this to happen, and in any case their standards do not take in the standards of the young who comprise over fifty per cent of the community. I do not find the proposition anywhere in the law books that community standards are those commonly held by persons over the age of fifty years.

'As far as the young are concerned the obscenities of this life are not four-letter words. They are such things as war, racial discrimination, the imbalance of wealth and poverty and the destruction of the ecological system.'

Reverting to the British expose in *The Sunday Times*, the skilled committee there also acknowledged a seemingly insuperable class factor that operates against authentic justice. Through class background and excessively narrow experience the British judiciary at large is unable to communicate with or understand working-class mores, and that they demand 'unrealistic' standards of behaviour from people whose social background differs from their own.

Simplified, this means the ordinary British peasant gets a pretty raw deal on the whole.

The committee recommended that judges and magistrates should be given time off to maintain intellectual contact with contemporary life, 'particularly in actuarial, sociological and psychological fields'. Bloody good idea.

In addition, a judge or a magistrate should not go into action without at least six months field training in welfare work, court study, and prison visiting. Another sensible idea.

The committee brought forward the novel idea that there should be a simple apparatus for public complaint against the behaviour of magistrates or judges in particular circumstances. This would increase confidence in the system, and improve court standards. The present appeals system, or complaint via the Law Society or Bar Council, isn't worth an ounce of civet, good apothecary! And it seems British lawyers are now admitting it.

The report asserts quite unequivocally that there exists a substantial number of 'behavioural defects, mainly occurring among the lower judiciary'. These defects range from mental attitudes such as egocentricity or capriciousness to premature senility.

When you board an aircraft you are pretty certain that the pilot has been screened for impeccable medical or mental health. This is the responsible way to conduct such things.

But suppose you are up in front of a judge, and he is an arteriosclerotic (not all that unlikely). A common by-product of the complaint is intermittent loss of memory. How would you rate your chances of receiving impeccable intellectual judgment and competent assessment of the facts in this circumstance?

Judges and magistrates are not required to possess the total health faculties we demand of airline pilots. They are not subject to regular medical examination. They cannot be removed from office 'for proved incapacity, mental or physical'.

As the evidence adds up, the judicial situation is socially irresponsible. It requires implacable, immediate, and urgent reform along the rational lines that are standard in other important fields of human endeavour. A senile priest can be retired. A senile judge can't. It's all idiotic.

Little wonder that Lord Shawcross sniffed danger in the air, and invoked copyright to keep the report out of circulation. Even his own mode of reasoning was logically shaky. To regret that anyone should wish to 'shake public confidence in the judiciary at the present time' was wild chop-logic, in all faith. If an institution doesn't merit public confidence then it shouldn't have it, at this or any other time.

But Lord Shawcross was a bit late. The media cat was among the judicial pigeons. And apparently not before time.

There is no reason to assume that the Australian situation differs one iota from the English model.

However there is one easily remedied aspect peculiar to our indigenous set-up.

The first step towards reforming the dismal standards in the Australian magistracy is financial. The second is one of status.

Any lawyer, bush or otherwise, will tell you that first-class minds won't move out of the legal profession and on to the bench unless they can earn at least as much as a sub-average lawyer. The work of a magistrate is pretty drab and indubitably tedious. Even so, it involves the liberty, the rights, the pride, the self-respect of human beings. Because of the vast human import of the work it should be made irresistibly attractive in the financial sense. To recruit the least-gifted lawyers with a Public Service orientation is a disastrous procedure in the first instance. Yet this is the traditional Australian pinchpenny system.

It's just not good enough.

For starters, surely it is time we began judging the judges mercilessly and publicly; until legislatures realise that a sane society will not put up with decrepit judicial institutions.

## PIG-BREEDING FOR BOILER-MAKERS: THE TALE OF A RETARDED BOOKSELLER

Here begins the serialising of the *Memoirs of a Retarded Bookseller*, the most searing, incredible, intolerable, and pathetic set of memoirs you're ever likely to read.

There are those in the community who become fixated at a certain point in life.

In fact I suspect that the Almighty applies his own particular form of psychological Tarzan's Grip to each and every one of us at some moment of development in our individual value systems, try as we may to retain open and shifting standards of response to an ever-changing world around us.

There are those whose minds are dominated by their school years. You've probably come across them.

Well, I got through most of my early years without feeling the hardening cement of fixative, except for one appalling patch.

I got stuck with what is euphemistically known as an Undergraduate Sense of Humour.

I acquired a sort of university degree which might best be described as Hons BA Economics (failed).

But when I left the pallor of the campus to join the purple of commerce I took with me an incurably undergraduate sense of humour.

This, then, is where the story begins.

It is no deep secret that I am a South Australian bookselling institution known as the Mary Martin Bookshop.

Its book-lists go out monthly to some 8000 people, as far distant as the Yukon and Ocean Island, up the steaming rivers of New Guinea, and into the sex-crazed executive suites of Martin Place.

At this point the more cynical of my readers will be absolutely convinced that these columns are being used for a commercial plug rather than for relating the tragic experiences of one who is afflicted with an incurable undergraduate sense of humour.

Even the most vigorous of my commercial rivals would exculpate me on this score.

After all, is it common for a commercial list of current books to be the cause of a threatened writ for libel from the Prime Minister of a young and lucky country?

How many bookshops have actually sold a copy of a quarterly magazine called *The Sex-Fiends' Lunar Monthly* for $76 for the single (non-existent) copy?

It all began, I think, when I was preparing the current list of new books years ago. The giant mimeograph press of the Mary Martin Bookshop was ready to roll.

In a weary moment I filled the last inch of the page with a title that kept popping into my mind: *Pig-Breeding for Boiler-Makers*, by L. Short. Price $16. I bunged the title in.

Now somehow, somewhere, amongst the intellectual elite perusing their book-list information about the latest Camus essays and Wittgenstein translations, there must have been a deeply dissatisfied boiler-maker with a secret and irresistible desire to breed pigs.

For in came a cheque for $16 and a request that a copy of Mr Short's tome be despatched forthwith. It was a moment of some discomfiture.

It is difficult to explain to a boiler-maker that he's ordered a non-existent book. It's even more difficult to return perfectly good money.

Ever since then I became increasingly subject to these terrible undergraduate urges. I tried aspirin, healthy outdoor exercise, cold showers, consulted my local minister, joined a church choir, but nothing did any good.

Like any alcoholic, or a mainliner drug addict, spoof titles became an incurable addiction.

At the top of each book-list one indicates the telephone numbers of one's business.

It's always been my principle to personalise this information and it can be a lot of fun.

If one indicates phone number 236274 (Ask for Mr Miller), phone number 236368 (Ask for Miss Monroe) it is rather entertaining to see how many people will actually request to speak to Miss Monroe in good faith.

Anyway, on one occasion I was particularly impressed how every decent retail business of any magnitude managed to offer after hours sales and service. Why not pioneer this modern amenity in the bookselling business?

We added to the telephone data the further information, 'for after hours service of Mary Martin books, phone Government House'.

All right, it's a feeble sort of joke, pointless and schoolboyish at best. Yet it produced extraordinary consequences.

To this day I don't know if a client came across a misbound or wrongly paginated Penguin book and phoned His Excellency, the Governor of South Australia and told him to get over smartly with a replacement.

Alternatively we could have had at that time in South Australia an imperial proconsul with an excessively sensitive gubernatorial dignity.

The fact remains that I found myself confronted by two massive detectives from the local constabulary.

'We are investigating a complaint from His Excellency the Governor that you have falsely represented that His Excellency is engaging in commerce and that in contravention of the Early Closing Act.'

You can imagine how my sallow countenance bleached like an Omo wash. This time I'd cop it good.

What is the sentence for wrongfully asserting that Her Majesty's very own representative is flogging Mary Martin books after hours?

Ten years in the stockade? Transportation overseas to some British hell-hole like Taunton or Salisbury?

I can tell you I was a worried man. Then the real Mary Martin came to the rescue and produced the book-list saying to the wallopers, 'I think you'd better see the offending words.'

Without a word, the cops moved off to a corner to study the criminal document. Minutes of agonising silence ensued.

Then I saw the massive pairs of shoulders start to heave, and then the cops adjusted their dress and their faces and returned to the desk.

'On this occasion we propose to let you off with a warning, Mr Harris.

'And our warning is this: In this world some bastards got a sense of humour, some haven't.' Then off they went.

But wasn't I lucky? To think that if I hadn't happened to get a couple of friendly cops, at this very moment I might be stitching mail bags out at Yatala Gaol instead of writing you my inspiring reflections.

# WHEN
## THE
## BITTEN BLOKE
**BITES BACK** It is only fair that the biter should be bitten. In bookselling in the Mary Martin style and fashion we, the spoofers, have in our time been well and truly spoofed by a cunning and endlessly ingenious mail-order clientele.

For one thing, there's the grisly problem of the spoof title, which apparently is taken literally. It is often hard to tell whether the enquiry is a deadpan return spoof or a genuine order.

You will remember that listed between *Meanjin* and *Overland* we once advertised the availability of another journal, *The Sex Fiends' Lunar Monthly*.

To be sure that no one would take this to be a genuine publication we priced the item at $200 a year.

It still didn't prevent some moon-obsessed character in the mysterious hinterland of New South Wales from sending a cheque for $50, requesting a single copy as the subscription rate seemed rather high.

In returning the cheque we did, I'm ashamed to admit, resort to telling a white lie about our much-maligned Customs Department. The publication had been prohibited in Australia. Very sorry.

But worse embarrassments of simpler causation have been very common. In a mad mood we included Bram Stoker's *Dracula* in a list of titles for the very young child, and bestowed on this celebrated chiller the virtues of being 'an enchanting bedtime story that will delight the heart of any five-year-old'.

Improbable as it might seem, no fewer than fifty people took this blurb at its face value and sent in the appropriate money.

The worst trouble of all was stirred up by a paperback of long repute, G. Lombard Kelly's marital manual, *Sexual Feeling in Married Men and Women*.

We elongated this title the weeniest bit and advertised it as *Sexual Feeling in Married Men and Women and Galahs*.

We received about a hundred orders and supplied Mr Kelly's classic of the bedroom arts in all good faith.

But did we get roasted alive! Literally dozens of people, clearly of defined ornithological interests, returned the book and wrote furious letters that the book contained no reference whatever to the fornicatory conventions of Australia's noblest parrot.

We lost clients right and left and there was nothing we

could do about it. You can't write and tell people who know a lot more about ornithology than you do that married galahs are uncommon; in fact unknown.

As you might imagine there were thousands of Mary Martin book-listers waiting for us to make our first false move to even the score. The moment came when we made an arrogant demand of our 8000 book-listers.

We suggested that they should each send us little gifties, expressive of the appreciation they felt for our services, and these gifties should in some way 'reflect the character of that part of Australia where they lived'.

Some of the responses were pure enchantment. One client sent a post-card which exposes the town of Albury as perpetrating a dastardly confidence trick on the rest of Australia.

The card read 'Welcome to Beautiful Albury', the print being super-imposed on a hugely endowed Scandinavian blonde with a surfboard, behind her the breakers crashing down on to the golden sands of what presumably would be Albury beach.

How crooked can a town get! The breakers would have to crash an awful long way to wash up to Albury.

Other responses were more diabolical.

Envelope after envelope that we opened proved to contain a fine red bull dust which floated everywhere, settling on books, and increasing the shop cleaning bill by a weekly fortune.

More sinister types from the Territory deposited bloody great gibbers, gift-wrapped, into the hands of TAA. Freight forward.

Our ultimate panic came with a telegram from a bloke on the Roper River, 'Sending you crated live crocodile air-freight forward. Cheers.'

For three days we waited in an agony of suspense, jittering every time an inwards consignment turned up. What could we possibly do with a live crocodile in a bookshop?

The giftie we liked best, however, came from the Alice. It was a simple toothpick stuck into a Johnny Walker whisky cork.

With meticulous care a customer had burned abstract patterns into it.

It came with a neatly printed card which read 'Genuine Antique Arunta Tribal Aboriginal Toothpick'.

The image of the Aruntas delicately and fastidiously cleaning their teeth after a meal of half-raw snake with tribal toothpicks was quite diverting.

We thought our clients might like to share the joke, so we added a $10 price tag and placed it among the Aboriginal artefacts from Yirrkala (all good bookshops sell tea and arte-facts, of course). You obviously know what's coming. And it genuinely did happen.

An authentic example of a little old lady turned up at the cash desk and before I knew what was what I had $10 and the toothpick in my hand and a request to have it gift-wrapped.

All right you mob, you're pretty smart. How do you get out of that one without hurting the feelings of the little old lady on the one hand, or ripping $10 off her for a tooth-pick on the other? You tell me.

# THE
# LIBEL CASE
# THAT
# NEARLY WAS

I promised, I think, to recount how our small struggling bookshop was threatened with a libel suit from the then Prime Minister of Australia, Sir Robert Menzies.

I don't know how long it is since a Prime Minister sued a simple private citizen for saying rude things—it must go back to William Pitt or someone like that. Until some knowledgeable historian puts the fact of this matter to rights, we have proudly assured ourselves of a weeny niche in the qualnter regions of social history.

As always with Mary Martin's mail order book-list, the kerfuffle stemmed from one of the weaker jokes. On this occasion it concerned a paperback edition of Pepys' Diary. Our blurb, if I recall it down the fading years, exclaimed 'Pepys' Diary, 60c, Elek Bestseller Library. This famous book deals with the early love life of Robert Gordon Menzies. Very searing.'

As I said before, and I say it again, it's not much of a joke, but even Blind Freddy would recognise its intention to be such. You'd also be hard put to imagine the comment to be open to any kind of literal interpretation. For if Samuel Pepys had been confiding his observations on Sir Robert to his diary, then this would make Sir Robert now about 300 years old. Our beloved ex-leader may be long in the tooth, but he's certainly not in the Methuselah class.

However that may be, to my eternal amazement and startlement I received a lawyer's letter headed with a list of luminous names such as Wilson, Wilson, Genders, Wilson, Wilson, Wilson and Gray. The senior partner of the firm was Mr K. C. Wilson, a former Cabinet Minister in the Menzies Government. To summarise, the letter, couched in terms of the highest moral indignation and outrage expostulated that the Prime Minister, while considering that his political activities could be the subject of free criticism, did not feel that libellous and defamatory remarks on his private life should be allowed. An apology must be forthcoming—or else.

Just imagine, dear readers, how tempted I was to bring about the 'or else' situation. Australia was in a critical social and economic plight and there was the prospect of the Prime Minister of the country taking a few weeks off to buzz down to Adelaide and muck around with a libel action against the mimeographed sales sheets of a back-street bookseller. I'd have been in the history books! There might even have been a Harris bust in Westminster Abbey next to Adam Lindsay Gordon!

And the libel case wouldn't have cost me a brass nickel in legal fees. In a small town like Adelaide news travels fast, and all of a sudden all the lawyers about the place decided they needed a book. While I'm the first to concede the dignity and seemliness of the legal profession, it remains true that lawyers are human. But who wouldn't want to play Perry Mason in such an outstanding court-room drama? I found I possessed for the first time in my life a great retinue of back-slapping, legal buddy-buddies. Alas, these sudden friendships disappeared when the news spread that my legal business had gone to a noted constitutional lawyer and a long-time sparring partner of Sir Robert.

Alas, too, the spectacular possibilities disappeared with a telephonic puff of wind. It is my guess, at the present stance of time, that Sir Robert hadn't really the slightest notion of what it was all about. He'd probably received some garbled telephone call and responded: 'Have a belt. Frighten a year's growth out of the creep.'

With later knowledge he'd probably become aware of the insignificance and total lack of malice or defamatory import in it all. Anyway, it was with bitter sorrow that my legal defender received a telephone call from Sir Robert's lawyers saying that it was all off.

'But surely you'd like an apology?' he pleaded.

'No apology. On no account an apology' was the response.

But a man of tender conscience is not so easily dissuaded. Deeply appalled at having promoted the unreasonable notion of Sir Robert as a rake-hell in the days of Mistress Gwynne, I insisted on tendering my abject regrets. They were composed by my heartened lawyer and are considered to this day to be his literary masterpiece.

The giant mimeograph presses of the Mary Martin Bookshop rolled, and the newspapers of Australia followed suit. They very kindly published my public apology free of charge.

Sir Robert and I had made our peace. Long may it remain so.

# GEMS
# IN THE MAIL
# THAT
# BRING A WARM GLOW

I have just received a letter addressed to me, Mr Harris, personally, from the Reader's Digest. It has me reeling with admiration at the elephantine memory and enduring sense of warm human gratitude that organisation possesses.

The last time I saw a copy of Reader's Digest was in a dentist's waiting room some nineteen years ago. How they found out about this I can't imagine. It must have been from one of the other patients who saw me cackling inanely in my chair.

Anyway, it has all culminated in a letter addressed to me, Mr Harris, personally, which reads: 'As a friend of the Reader's Digest in the Kensington Park area we would like you to be among the first to see one of the most exciting and truly helpful books that Reader's Digest has ever published.' Isn't that nice?

Do you know what they did. They presumably phoned or wrote from Sydney to Graham Nancarrow at the Griffin Press and said, 'Look, Graham, since Max Harris has been such a mighty friend of the Digest in the Kensington Park area would you hold for him copy number 197,761 of our new Atlas?'

This must be the case. Reader's Digest tycoons don't tell lies, and the letter reads: 'We have asked our printers at Adelaide's Griffin Press to hold an atlas in your name for free examination.'

So, lucky me, I can now examine it in my own home entirely free of obligation, and I pay only the special first edition price for copy number 197,761.

I guess I deserve the special privilege. I'm always button-holing people at the local delicatessen and saying: 'Look here, Herbert, you're looking a bit peaky, tired, debilitated, lacking in energy; your virility not what it used to be. You're clearly suffering from backache, kidney pains, neuralgia and costiveness. Why don't you take a twelve months' Reader's Digest course?'

I've done my bit for friendship's sake in the Kensington Park district, all right.

So I'm going to take up this offer because the Reader's Digest Complete Atlas of Australia is 'dramatically presented in a magnificent colourama'. Since most atlases I possess present Australia merely in living vibrant colour, I just have to see our proud nation 'in a magnificent colourama'.

It must be a revolutionary printing process because it's able to do what no other set of maps has ever been able to do for me. I'm going to be 'amazed by the intriguing profile of New Guinea and the struggle of primitive peoples for reconciliation with the fast-changing world'. All from a colourama map!

Also, by turning to Antarctica, I'm going to 'discover how Australia finds a national identity at the South Pole'. It's a hell of a place to have to find your national identity, especially since we've mistakenly tried to find it in Australia for two centuries.

However, from the letter I absorb a faint fear that our national identity will prove to be American. Reader's Digest, I imagine, is an American property. I've met the boss-cocky of the Digest, a delightful man, even ridden in his chauffeured Mercedes, but he's certainly American to the deepest recesses of his pocket book.

And when I'm informed that 'it tells us the whole astounding story of our remarkable continent' I worry about what is meant by the use of the possessive adjective 'our'. Does it mean theirs? American? If so, the Reader's Digest has jumped the gun a bit in this process of taking over Australia for Uncle Sam.

I've run up the old Australian flag over my gentleman's residence and we're manning the barricades in Kensington Park. The Reader's Digest has just lost a good friend in the district.

# A NICE
# WALLOW
# IN THE
# STATISTICAL SWAMP

I cannot conceal the fact that I am president of the SDDDPM—otherwise called the Society for the Demolition and Destruction of all Data Processing Machinery. In consequence what I have to say will contain as much heat as light.

We neo-luddites do not base our movement on redundancy and employment factors. There is no suggestion that we pin Che Guevara badges on our urban smocks and march on IBM.

Our movement is based on two facts. First, that data processing machinery constitutes the ultimate climactic of Parkinson's Law of Inefficiency. The amount of paper bumf, programming, processing, and debugging involves possibly 87,921 blokes in Australia doing work that previously occupied 411 blokes sitting on high stools with crossed nibs and a bottle of blue-black ink.

The second fact is that technocracy is nobly contributing to the language the nastiest vocabulary of hideous, linguistic jargon since mankind ceased to communicate by means of mutual grunts.

In the short space of less than ten years it is as if Sir Ernest Gowers had never lived. Indeed, I rather imagine that if you used the principles of Plain Words in such a technomanic organisation as, say, the Commonwealth Bureau of Census and Statistics, you just wouldn't be understood.

Let us take the first accusation first, gearing it to an impeccable example of a computerised organisation—the burgeoning, bloated, ubiquitous and irritant Bureau of Census and Statistics. Is the work of this toad-swollen department important? I don't know. Maybe it is. I do know it's costly.

Its most recent effort is a revised picture of business activities and it requires to know how many businesses you have and how many people you employ. In the dark pre-Gower days you'd have written a little letter of reply saying: 'I own two businesses, one, employing two people, makes bubbles for putting in spirit levels. The other has five people and the work concerns taking the bend out of bananas. Yours faithfully, J. Edgar Woolworth.'

The new, computerised dispensation I have before me has five pages of instructions, and a quarter of a pound of best Burnie offset (excellent paper that it is) on which I am proposing to write 'yes' twice and 'no' once. In short, one could probably purchase two rotten computers for the extra amount of paper the ignoble machine demands for 'statistical coding' purposes.

The other factor to consider is the matter of man-hours now demanded from the business population. Supposing you run one of Australia's 128,529 delicatessens. You've worked an exhausting twelve-hour day at the beef slicer, and now the law compels you to turn off the 198th re-run of the ABC's new peak-viewing programme, and you have to spend a good three hours interpreting the 2000-word set of instructions from the likely lads of the Statistics Department. This, mark you, is in addition to the regular statistical compilations demanded of you at such ludicrous length at least four times a year.

Now I'm as big a nit as the next man when it comes to official jargon. And the following occupied me twenty minutes. I imagine it would occupy at least the same amount of viewing time for the really hard-working blokes down at the local deli.

'Column Five, Separate Accounts. This question is designed to ascertain for each individual company whether complete and separate operating accounts for management, etc., purposes, not merely minimum records required for taxation and company registration purposes, are maintained. Enter "yes" if separate operating accounts for management purposes are kept for the company and "no" if no such separate operating accounts are maintained. For every "no" answer please specify in column seven the names of the company or companies, if any, with which its operating accounts are merged.'

As a Mensa member (ha ha!) I translated this in less than 20 minutes as 'If you have two delicatessens, do they have completely separate sets of business records?'

In all this compendious mass of verbal garbage, there's bound to be at least one fun question, and the fun question for all little business people in Australia is the pofaced demand of the Commonwealth Statistician to provide 'details in order of importance of principal commodities produced or sold'.

Important to whom, may one ask?

It's one hell of a task Mr K. M. Archer has imposed. It is legally binding on a delicatessen owner to specify the percentage of trade represented by chewie, fritz, fags, paperbacks, bubble-gum, deep frozen haddock, Eskimo Pies and so on. To conform properly to the unquestioned legal rights of the department, the deli owner would have to employ a bloke with a pencil and paper classifying every sale.

With its own burgeoning activity, the Department of Census and Statistics is creating a mass of new jobs checking the figures supplied by well-meaning nongs like myself, and also creating tens of thousands of new paperwork jobs filling out statistics questionnaires in industry and business.

But does all this lovely new desk work created by the technomaniacs contribute to the national productivity? Now there's a statistic I'd dearly like to encounter. But I'm certain I wouldn't find it in Mr Archer's computerised archives of useless facts and figures.

# ROMANCE
# AND AGONY
# ON
## THE DANUBE

The mini-skirts go by. The beautifully groomed females walk their poodles in the late afternoon as if the Danube were a rich man's version of the Seine.

Fathers push the elegant baby-carriages without a trace of self-consciousness.

The terrace cafes burst with life from noon until night.

Budapest has style, and knows it. After the brutal terrors of the Racos' regime and the ultimate agonies of '56, the Hungarians have come to terms with a slowly but surely liberalising system.

Next year the economic reforms will be even more radically directed towards the Tito model.

So the Budapestians live beyond their modest incomes in order to look and feel as if their incomparably beautiful city represented the very acme of a graceful and cultured way of life.

This surface and Parisian culture goes deeper than a straightforward preoccupation with personal style. The Hungarians are powerfully aware that style is the undervalued component in the creative process.

My greeting in Budapest was, of all things, an exhibition of Australian books at the headquarters of the PEN club.

It was opened by Mr Otto Lengyeu, one of the great European book designers.

He seemed to think that our books possess clarity, a faithful sense of tradition from the English prototypes, but no recognisable stylishness.

If he hadn't been so kind I'd have suspected that he was saying we are still in a phase of Japanese imitativeness. In short, our books lack their own innate style.

The compliment is dubious but the interest is generous and genuine.

There is a rich and uncorrupted humanist vein in the Hungarian temperament which cannot easily be changed by any sort of political system.

The Hungarians think of themselves as romantic, sensuous, and cynical. There in any amount of confirmation of the first two attributes in the spring streets of Budapest where the young are clutching, kissing, and hand-holding with a disarming abandon.

One feels that only a Hungarian could produce a book like *In Praise of Older Women*.

This observation leads me to a momentary digression. I happily read Vizinczey's little masterpiece in Budapest and Vienna while my compatriots at home are protected by a paternalistic government from reading this most sensitive, cool, and ironic of sexual odysseys.

At this distance Australia's tired and ugly censorship obsessions appear pitiful and ludicrous.

In Europe people discuss our bannings with tolerant interest. Their diagnosis is naively political.

'Here,' they say, 'we have corrupt politicians, nepotistic politicians, ideological dogmatists; you, apparently, are ruled by ignorant and poorly educated men.' From where they stand it's a fair comment, but it still makes my flesh crawl.

So back to Budapest to examine the cynicism.

Hungary is a nation that has won a few battles but never won a war.

Pride in a country of such a tragic history is a matter of intellectual self-respect.

This is the quality that makes the Hungarians such a delightful and impressively gifted people.

The exuberant patriotism of Barbara Kery, our guide was irresistible. She scooped up our enthusiastic responses and clutched them to her bosom.

But when the question was stupid, such as 'What are those peasants doing in the field?' there was the instant flash of dry cynicism, 'Why, working, of course.'

Duly punished for our touristic sin we were whipped off to her home to try her Hungarian white wine and cheese.

While one senses the present affluence, stylishness, wit and intellectual energy of the new Hungarians, one doesn't have to dig deep to discover the most pervasive national frustration.

They have come to terms with the system. They have a firm and selective appreciation of Western cultural imagination.

The theatre and cinema programmes are quite dominantly of Western origin.

It is the finest thing on earth to live in Budapest. If only you could travel.

Impoverished for hard currency, the most intellectually curious people in Europe are chained to the Danube.

Their art historians, their writers, their translators, their academics are bitterly aware that Western travel is not a matter of tourism but intellectual professionalism.

How can Budapest produce the world's finest art books unless the texts are by skilled historians who have been to Florence or to Delphi?

Looking down on the Danube from the Gellert, 1956, seems a long time ago. But the Budapestians have not forgotten and they are anything but reluctant to talk about it.

They say that the Budapest of today would not have been possible but for those who made the desperate gestures of 1956.

They are frankly grateful to the Hungarians who fled to Canada, Australia and the United States of America.

Have the Hungarians who went to Australia found a measure of success and happiness, they asked me?

I am not quite sure of the answer; but I hope so.

# GUESS WHAT BAT
# IS BIG
# IN OLD VIENNA
**THESE DAYS!** Way back in the early 1940s the first wave of European refugees, mostly from Vienna, poured into Australia and found it bleak, provincial, and completely lacking in any vital cultural life.

I remember very well how sorry we felt for these people and how shamefaced about our cultural uncouthness.

Well, it's more than twenty years later and I've just been in Vienna, and it's time for our compatriots of Viennese origin to return the gesture.

As a simple boy from the South-East Asian bush I expected Vienna to be a city of glittering sophistication, intellectual adventure, and episodic European grandeur.

To breathe in this mood we even chose to doss at a pub called the Sacher.

Imagine, then one's astonishment to find that Vienna is the most provincial city in Europe.

If you can envisage the women of Sydney and Melbourne all wearing modified versions of the Digger hat, the Elizabethan Theatre Trust putting on endless versions of Dad and Dave, and the boozers at the suburban clubs and pubs linking arms and singing Waltzing Matilda with ponderous zeal, then you have a fair idea of how Vienna lives it up.

It certainly is the most appallingly unstylish and matriarchal city of your dreams, what with all those women with Tyrolean feathered hats sitting on top of their lollies, the endless coffee shops filled with said matriarchs scoffing cups of cream with a bit of coffee at the bottom.

Only the occasional poodle and the occasional Viennese male break the visual monotony of this coffee shop scene.

And guess who's big in Vienna? Johann Strauss.

And guess what everyone urged us to see? Die Lustige Witwe (The Merry Widow to you, you linguistic ignoramus).

Unable to face the prospect of going out to Grinzing, drinking young wine and singing 'Ach, du lieber Augustin', we opted for a drive through the Vienna woods to Mayerling.

So did 50,000 other Viennese. That was all right by us. They're perfectly entitled to enjoy their own woods.

So all over these vast ranges we saw burly Viennese blokes getting out of their Mercedes all togged up with plus fours, big woolly socks, and stout walking boots, and bent up double with massive haversacks.

It looked as if about 20,000 Austrian heroes were about to climb the Matterhorn.

But instead they lurched off about a mile from their cars, fell flat on their Viennese backs and commenced to knock back the flagons of delicious white plonk.

A very reasonable programme for a balmy spring Sunday.

But why, dear ex-Viennese readers, the fancy dress?

All my bluffable life I've been persuaded that Vienna is the core of a sophisticated and adventurous international culture.

There's been some substance to the persuasion, too.

Musica Viva, the most valuable music society perhaps in Australian history, owed not a little of its origins to what we so charmingly were used to describe as the 'reffos'.

I'm still open to argument. Perhaps people kept pointing me in the wrong direction when it came to the cultural bit.

Even so, if any Australian city became addicted to a provincial self-consciousness equivalent to that of Vienna, it would be pilloried mercilessly by the rest of the nation.

As it appeared to my touristic eyes, Vienna is about as sophisticated as Walgett compared with Sydney.

Eleven thousand miles to see The Merry Widow! They must be out of their tiny Viennese minds!

# AN
# IMPENITENT CAPITALIST
# IN

**EAST BERLIN** I was in Paris reading the New York *Herald-Tribune* (European edition).

Under a West Berlin byline there was a report that May Day was celebrated in East Berlin with a military march-past and a barrage of anti-Kiesinger slogans, in a mood quite alien to the traditional workers' holiday. In West Berlin Herr Kiesinger addressed a crowd of 200,000 on the need for . . .

In due course this has provoked me into the profound observation that you can't believe all you read in the papers.

If the New York *Herald-Tribune* correspondent and all the guys with binoculars on the West Berlin observation stand had the ability to see around corners actually to observe the East Berlin May Day procession they would have come upon a sight that would have made their eyes pop.

Among the 250,000 marchers they would have been able to identify an affluent and stately gent wielding a silver-topped cane and with him a gentle-lady of most un-proletarian bearing; Mr Max Harris, incurable capitalist, non-communist, non-liberal, non-joiner, was actually in the massive May Day march, and so too was the heroic Mrs Max Harris.

It was an historic event for the communists as well as for the abovementioned characteristic products of the affluent society.

It came about this way.

In the course of talking and drinking with the Berlin writers the subject of May Day had come up. If we cared to watch the march, positions could be found for us on the official dais. Of course, we must be warned that it was a rather long occasion and might mean sitting for three or four hours and it wasn't all that much fun.

Why can't we be down marching with the boys, asked the simple-minded colonial? The East German writers took a long swig at their West German brandies, gulped a little, and said why not?

In fairness I pointed out that we were impenitent capitalists, great lovers of the profit motive, and generally decadent. The East Germans were more pleased than shocked. We've never had any capitalists in the May Day march, they said. This will make history.

It was then my turn to produce a reservation. Having had a taste of militarism in Greece and a lifelong ability to be instantly bored by military exhibitionism, I enquired: 'How much dreary hardware makes its way into this parade?' The answer was comforting. The military types have to be given a guernsey along with the rest of the population, but they are disposed of at the crack of dawn as it were, and they'll have dispersed into thin air by the time the rest of us get going.

And so it happened.

At 10 a.m. we all gathered off Unter den Linden in an atmosphere more of a Back-to-Wagga reunion than of any grand demonstration.

Eventually we set off, preceded by great long lines of huge red flags and followed by a rather frustrated oom-pah-pah band and more lines of red flags.

Brother, what a shambles! People ambled along smoking pipes, having arguments, looking at babies. There were few spectators because everyone seemed to be in the march. The decadent capitalist with the silver cane added to the general confusion because he kept stopping to look at things, consequently being run over by the following line of red-flag bearers.

The march only lasted a chaotic half-mile, and it seemed to give some pleasure to all except the poor character who kept shouting patriotic slogans over the amplifiers.

Not a soul took the slightest notice. It was little to be wondered. Communist psychology at its most Soviet orthodox is peculiarly unsubtle and self-defeating. In the GDR every building in every town seems to be so be-plastered with inspiring messages that the propaganda no longer registers. The visitor is aware of it. The local has become oblivious to it.

After the march I asked why it had been such a rare and undisciplined old shambles. This is deliberate, I was told. The East Germans have known enough about militarism and discipline in the Nazi past not to want any part of that psychology in the present.

One of the big debates occurred on the issue of school clothing. It was debated that school uniforms look neater, and work out less expensively than other clothing. This proposition was soundly defeated on the grounds that East Germans don't want their kids to wear uniforms of any kind.

This attitude has, of course, great propaganda value as being in contrast with the West German psychology, and the not-unexpected reversion to type of the neo-Nazi movement.

The half-mile procession broke up and people scurried in all directions. We went to the Karl Marx Allee and there I found the source of all the fearsome noise that had presumably deluded all those expert observers on the far side of Checkpoint Charlie.

The Germans are besotted with an appalling form of sport called, I think, go-karting, in which innumerable noisome and repulsive little machines race round and round in circles.

The local lads were being invited up to the boxing ring in the street to have a go. People were preparing to perform decadent dances like the foxtrot and the quickstep in the street. The Writers' Union boys were off to raffle autographed editions to the suckers. The biggest crowds gathered around the publicans' booths.

In fact, the streets of Berlin took me back to an innocent boyhood and the Mount Gambier Agricultural Show. What's so hair-raising about penetrating that little old Iron Curtain?

I subdued my disappointment and rambled off for a beer. After all, I had been the first capitalist to march down Unter den Linden on May Day.

# A
# MAN
# ALONE
This nation didn't indulge in any conspicuous mourning on the death of Dr H. V. Evatt! The obituaries were kindly. And patronising.

Dr Evatt, they seemed to say, was a man of principle and a distinguished intellect; but, of course, we all knew how wayward, wrong-headed and destructively myopic he could be. Ashes to ashes. Here today, gone tomorrow.

Now, in seemly retrospect, Herbert Vere Evatt will be studied by the biographers and historians. The first biography was to be *Evatt—the Enigma* by Alan Dalziel

Australia, unlike Britain, is the very source of the anti-hero mythology. It has always, from the nature of its environment and the character of its people, responded to the concept of heroic failure, the flawed saint, or inversely the triumphant no-hoper.

Leichhardt, the obsessed and isolate romantic, survives in the Australian legend, but who now celebrates Giles, the virtuoso explorer?

Burke combined courage with an absence of any real bush sense. His shambles of an expedition lives on. But how many of us know anything about the deeds of the complacent and envious Sir Thomas Mitchell?

The search for the mythic anti-hero is little understood by, say, the English, who believe it is an unamiable Australian quality to want to cut down the tallest poppies out of some grizzly need to reduce everyone and everything to a common mediocrity.

The truth is less simple and nasty than this. It is more that our image of the heroic is embodied in the battler, the worthwhile failure against the odds, rather than the larger-than-life victor.

The Australian political legend has been extremely thin, and this is why I believe posterity will still contemplate the flawed and complex greatness of Herbert Vere Evatt when Chifley's sanity and Sir Robert Menzies' rare political cunning have become abstract references in history text books.

That there was a greatness about Dr Evatt I think few will deny. He was a complete humanitarian, and this led to a set of social and moral principles he would never compromise for shallow political expediency, or even in the service of his undoubted ambition.

This rigid belief that right should triumph over wrong,

justice over injustice, led him into destructive and tragic situations.

His great intellectual flaw was that he could not believe in the squalid realities of human mind and motivation. He refused to believe that his own social ideals could not be made self-evident to those around him.

The inevitable consequences followed. He was deemed stubborn, domineering and an intellectual bully. He was a 'difficult' man to work with.

A man for no season, he was outmatched by Cassius Menzies, by the agile party-political footwork, and Menzies' pragmatic belief that body-blows were fair in politics no matter where they landed, or no matter what damage they did.

And it all made Evatt possibly the loneliest man I ever knew, both intellectually and socially.

To me there was no enigma about Evatt. There was tragedy, certainly. From him I learned that it is bad for a man to believe too deeply in his own truths.

I hope Mr Dalziel's book is a work of sensitivity and sensibility rather than a political retrospect. Herbert Vere Evatt was like no other politician Australia has known. He deserves a biography that comes from the heart as well as the head.

# IN
# SEARCH OF
# KIWI

**CULTURE** It is a commonplace that the average New Yorker firmly believes kangaroos hop up and down Pitt Street, and that the top end of Collins Street is a sanctuary for cuddly koalas.

By the same token, Australians affect a similar kind of ignorance about little Fred New Zealand, our nearest neighbour to the left. The New Zealand image of Australia isn't much richer, being largely formed by quick, panic-stricken trots through Sydney and the squalid stubby cliches of its holiday attractions.

In the interest of mutual self-enlightenment I have 'done' cultural New Zealand on your behalf, and there will be some panting trans-Tasman messages from old Garcia on this theme.

One must perforce start off on the urban conspectus of our dour little neighbour, since few of us know where is where and certainly not why.

Christchurch is in the South Island. It's windy, bleak, late Edwardian, paranoiac, and bitterly self-absorbed. For these reasons it is, or certainly will become, the cultural capital of New Zealand.

When two people hiccup together they instantly form one more choral society. The radio programmes testify hourly to the appalling community passion for brass bands. Christchurch, or CH-CH as it is publicly abbreviated on civic signs, has a substantive cultural grass-roots solidity based on the gallopers, the famous All Purple Ping-Pong Players (or whatever the national sport is) and a safari-mania which will certainly lead to volunteer suicide squads of citizens when all the deer and wild pigs have been shot out by such heroes as the film star, Lee Marvin.

New Zealand officialdom is fascinated by the idea of attracting the muscle-headed gun maniacs to its shores, and most of the tourist propaganda is currently devoted to this end. The sport is, one gathers, being radically updated. You shoot your deer, or maori schoolchildren, from helicopters with semi-automatic weapons! Vive le sport!

If you consider there is some exaggeration in the idea that New Zealand completely outstrips our own fair land in compulsive, muscle-headed sports mania, consider the following. Can you imagine Sydney, with its 2½ million population, issuing a 64-page newspaper on Saturday evening devoted only to the gallopers, football, and a sprinkling of other minor sports? Christchurch, with its modest population, sustains just such a massive newspaper, the Christchurch *Star Sports*, which deals only with sports results. And makes an impressive profit.

Yet for all its tweedy Edwardianism, Christchurch breathes just that heady mixture of frustration and defiance from which unexpected creative acts materialise. Christchurch may be national headquarters of the more dim-witted performing arts, but from here (and metropolitan Auckland) one feels a New Zealand creative style will develop.

It is an old and city-slicker error to imagine grass-roots schools emerge necessarily from the larger urban aggregations. Prague produced Kafka, Weifel and Brod when the world's literary thinking was pretty tired. American litera ture in the forties is surely headquartered in Faulkner country.

There is just this faint edge of creative anger about Christchurch. (In the rest of the country conservation is alive and well and purveying that well-known psychological bleach—unflappability.)

Let us move north, across to the other island, to Wellington. Wellington is Wagga Wagga with metropolitan pretensions. It is all civil service, bureaucracy, and small town business bustle. It has a short-back-and-sides campus, and the air of a midget unpeopled Sydney. This impression is mitigated at least by an intimate theatre, the Down-stage which is semi-professional in the fashion of Hayes Gordon's Ensemble, but which has about it an infectious youthful brio normally lacking in the Australian attack.

The provincial centres north of Wellington appear to have been sanitised for the visitor's convenience. Palmerston North and Hamilton are as studiedly anonymous as a motel bedroom. The landscape between them is profusely dotted with all the rural symbols of cholesterol. But there is a ready friendliness and a traditional hotel hospitality, which has long since disappeared from the Australian rural convention.

Palmerston North is blessed with Massey University, the most hideous campus in ye olde southern hemisphere. (Adolf Hitler is alive and well, living in New Zealand as a government architect.) The style is Buchenwald Brutalism, a building form which the government Adolfs have extended to the new university crematoria buildings at Christchurch. A natty piece of social foresight on these erections is the omnipresence of tin fire-watch shelters on the campus roofs. The canny New Zealanders aren't going to be caught napping if the little yellow men come south again.

To be fair, one has to set against these governmental horrors, the proliferation of splendid civic libraries, a frighteningly efficient and decentralised Country Lending Service, and a remarkable integration between the council bigwigs and the educated citizenry. With a few brave exceptions (Mildura), Australia languishes in the concepts of provincial civic culture.

Mention must be made of Rotorua, the sulphurous New Zealand Las Vegas, a shrieking nightmare of one-night-stand motels. Yet the locals have been thoroughly contaminated by the insouciance of the itinerant population, and Rotorua is surely the fun capital, in the very best sense, of New Zealand. It is only here that you discover that the utter drabbery of the nation's public cuisine is not compulsory, and that the world's finest primary produce can be turned to epicurean effect (hot smoked ham).

All this brings the cultural commercial traveller to Auckland, the nation's authentic intellectual capital. Sydney unvulgarised, zestful, young, self-aware; Auckland goes its way defining the state of the nation, analysing the Maori role, grappling with the slippery assimilation problem posed by a large migrant intake of island people, and leading a life of impertinent affluence. (A local citizen spent hours trying to find a slum area for us in Auckland.)

This geographic prologemena has been offered only as the setting for next week's exercise—an attempt to establish the national and cultural identity of New Zealanders. The New Zealanders are a highly individualistic and widely intelligent people, a fact they are at great pains to conceal for fear they will be mimicking Australia's formidable egocentricism.

And my investigating has shown that this distaste for the Australian human climate has been created by our own inability to realise that, with New Zealanders, we are dealing with a people more cultivated, progressive, and politically humane than ourselves.

# BUGGED
# BY THE
# POSTAL
**PESTS** Herewith copy of a letter I've written to one of the endless postal pests:

My Dear Circulation Manager,

My sincerest thanks for your letter suggesting that I subscribe to your weekly news magazine. Before I give you my decision on this matter I'd like to discuss a few points raised in your letter.

You wrote, and I quote: 'You and just a few others—chosen from a list of people far above average in education and the need to be well-informed—are being invited to try ... for as many weeks as you like at 12c a week.'

Firstly, I'm worried about how you found out that I'm all that far above average in education. I have a sort of university degree, yes. It's Honours Bachelor of Arts Economics Failed. I'm not at all sure this qualifies me for your offer. My university tutor, the present Vice-Chancellor of Sydney University, was wont to describe me, in despair rather than anger, as an unteachable buffoon. I've improved since then by private study and I reckon I've now reached the educational average.

But how did you find out this private information about me? I've a hideous and probably unjustified suspicion that in the go-getting American style you've introduced bugging into the Australian domestic environment. 'By golly,' say the snoops of the ... magazine Bureau of Investigation as they sit in their stake-out in the house across the road, 'that fellow Harris is far above average in education. It's about time Robert J. Moore wrote to him.' Now this I don't like. It's un-Australian, and you American big-shots should respect the traditions of the local peasants.

Furthermore, I'm considerably worried by what appears to be your idea of scale and above-average education. I did a random statistical experiment myself in the Sturt Arcade Hotel and found that four out of five blokes interviewed belonged to the category of me and 'just a few others'. On this statistical ratio it would seem that the 'few others' adds up to nine million Australians. It's nice to think that practically the entire nation is 'far above average in education', but isn't this a logical contradiction?

Talking of chop-logic, if I'm all that smart and educated, aren't I well-informed already? Surely the need to be well-informed is more relevant to those of (ugh!) average education. I can't see the moral or social reasons why a brilliant chap like myself should be given your magazine for 12c a week while the battler, the average character, the trier, should be slugged 21c a week. You're living in a democracy, digger, not in Plato's dictatorship of intellect.

Now I must get to the crux of the matter and tell you why I can't accept your offer of a discriminatory price offer as a tribute to my braininess.

It's just impossible, mate. I'm not as bright as most of the blokes I mix with. Just suppose I turned up with your magazine under my arm. I'd lose caste immediately. 'Poor old Harris,' they'd say, 'isn't he a pathetic intellectual snob. He's carrying . . . magazine just to show he belongs to the select few far above average in education.' 'Poor old Harris,' they'd say, 'he's fallen for the most transparent and simple-minded sales line based on an appeal to intellectual snobbery. He must be pretty dim to have fallen for that kind of spiel. Only a bloke far below-average education would respond to such a repulsive and corny status come-on. Let us pretend we don't see him.'

You see, Mr Moore, Mr Circulation Director, I'd actually love to read your weekly news magazine, but I can't for fear that my friends will laugh at my snobbish mind as well as my puny muscles. You've made it totally impossible.

I'll just have to continue carrying around my Australian newspapers, news magazines, and journals of opinion. Of course, I won't be well-informed. Only American journalism can produce that desirable state of enlightenment. But I'd rather be ignorant than be considered dumb enough to respond to the most blatant exercise in snobbery ever to be pumped into the Australian postal system.

# A NOBEL EFFORT—
# WITH SOME APOLOGIES
# TO

**MORRIS WHITE** This is Speed Harris, latterday E-type model of Clark Kent and the lost noble tribe of fearless reporters, bringing you a flash of cultural news from faraway Sweden. Land of the Clearasil breed of blonde youth, suicidal sex, and . . . the Nobel Prize.

It has been widely enough reported that our very own Patrick White was on a long short list of nominations for the 1969 Nobel Prize for Literature.

As an outside bet, the Swedish odds on Patrick W. shortened a point or two just before the litterateurs left the barrier. This resulted from a hot stable tip received by the newspaper, *Dagens Nyheter*. I quote:

'Australia never got a prize, and in later years it seems as if the Academy have taken a good look on the global map,' the newspaper reported knowingly.

Well, that seems as round a flat reason as any; but, in the event, we all know now that the favourite, and intellectual heavyweight of the field, Sam Beckett, won at a canter.

One's views on prizes, awards and intellectual honours are reasonably well-known. If now I'm taking an inconsistent interest in the famous Swedish event, it is simply because the Scandinavians are not dim, provincial, snobbish, nor ill-informed like us pitiful barbarians out on the edge of nowhere. They take an accurate and educated interest in civilised cultural phenomena throughout the global village.

Take, for instance, the wise reflections of *Dagens Nyheter*, 'unofficially' translated and emanating from a distinguished Australian source in Sweden.

Who will win? asks the snowy-haired newspaper. Halfway down the list of possibles, they speculate as follows:

'Or an Australian—Australia never got a prize: Patrick White, who wrote *The Fisherman's Shoes*—all be it in fearsome "cinema-memory".

'Not only geographical reasons lie behind Australian Patrick White's candidature—he is resident in Sydney nowadays, but with long spells in England and Italy behind him. His novels, often with a catolic element, have been sufficient to give him international reputation, and his *The Fisherman's Shoes* is a good bit better than ever the film version of it.'

Not all the Swedish newspapers expressed such a detailed knowledge of the work of Patrick West—sorry, I mean Morris White, of course. According to my translated handout, the *Expressen* expressed remorseful ignorance under the heading, 'Who is Patrick White?'

'I can now only say that *The Solid Mandala* is both an ensuring and a worrying discovery. The controversial impressions comes from a double-dealing in the book which slowly gets clearer and its explanation does not appear until the last pages.'

Now I ask you—that's not a nice thing to say about our local lad! Double-dealing? Straight as a die is our Morris (sorry, Patrick), and I may only be a sunburnt four-foot-two, but if those bloody Swede giants want an old-fashioned punch-up, they don't have to ask twice.

My patriotic wrath, however, diminished rapidly as I read through the long interpretation of *The Solid Mandala* in the *Expressen*. The parents of the odd protagonists in *The Solid Mandala* came to Australia because 'they wanted to be tolerant and enlightened but despite all they brought with them the inability to break the conventions, to experience classic education as a reality, to believe in physical contact without the fear of syphilis.' This doesn't flatter our moral standards. Sounds like you'll drop dead if you shake hands with an Aussie sheila. However, 'on the final pages Arthur kills Waldo followed by the author's sympathies and the love of the surrounding world.'

From syphilis to the sympathies of the surrounding world in 400 glorious pages is some achievement, and the *Expressen* critic, Bengt Soderbergh, might well be nominated on Australia's short list for the George Moore 1970 award for literary criticism.

However, the hot favourite for the Moore Critical Award is another Swedish critic, Stig Bjorkman, who really does his homework and loves his home-cooking.

*Expressen:* 'The *Tree of Man* and *Voss* seem to be written by a man with dirt under his nails, by somebody able to handle farmer's tools and a typewriter with the same naturalness.'

It's all very well for old Stig to declare these 'central works are two of the "great" epic prose poems from the twentieth century,' but no decent Australian will tolerate that crack about Patrick's fingernails, especially when Stig put on the nosebag in Patrick's very own home 'which is exquisitely and formally done up'. Patrick 'serves his own dishes himself dressed in a grilling apron' (Joke: Why doesn't Mr White employ a char?)

To summarise the Swedish view of Australia as it appears to them through the pages of Patrick White, here we have Stig sounding off for the last time:

'To live in Australia is a rather ironical challenge to a

conscious person. (But it's one hell of a greater challenge to an unconscious person: interpolation by M.H.) Australia is, despite its promises for the future, a society in the past tense only pretending to be with the times, and which is characterised by a both political, cultural and moral isolation. White talks a lot about this isolation and the almost total indifference towards art, which is the attitudes of the leaders ... White is the only author with real stature in this culturally hostile climate.'

This brings us to the Christmas crux of the matter. I don't care really whether our national author has Poseidon nickel samples under his fingernails—this bit about lonely, anti-artistic Australia is a load of whiskery rubbish. The thesis is relevant only if one conceives Morris White and Patrick West to be a pair of old codgers contemporaneous with Steele Rudd and Billy Hughes. Most Australians have managed to progress beyond the wail that the country's a cultural vacuum.

# THE
# DEATH
# OF
# CHRISTMAS

What day in November was it that we had to stand up for a silence of one minute in memory of the war dead? I think I have almost forgotten. Was it November 11? Guy Fawkes' Day no longer exists. Do you go back to the days when they used to have Arbor Day at the primary schools? Someone gave us a half-holiday after a bit of tree-planting.

Do you think Australia Day will ever get off the ground as a public holiday to which certain symbolically meaningful ceremonies have been added? Not a hope in hell. It is just one more statutory non-working day. Have you ever attended the ceremonial opening of a Parliament? In your whole life? I'll bet you haven't.

The attrition and disappearance of feasts and ceremonies in national life is a plain fact. On the one hand we have perhaps an intensification of the awareness of ourselves as a nation-State in the political and economic sense. On the other we have discarded most tribal rituals as irrelevancies. Anzac Day and the Melbourne Cup are the only two events that still carry a sense of occasion about them. And even Anzac Day has ceased to have other than a pretty perfunctory ritual significance for an ever-shrinking minority.

What is the most remarkable of all is the impending death of Christmas. Once it was a specific Christian feast, and even atheists came to the orgy because it would be too churlish not to participate in the fun and frolics. But give history a little more time and Christmas Day will be no more than an abstract Consumer Day.

Certain practices are headed for oblivion at a precipitate speed.

The Christmas card, for example, is a fading tradition. Eliminate the business Christmas card, which is a public relations gesture, and I think you will find that the habit of sending Nativity cards at the Christmas season will soon be deady-bones. Yet the Christmas card should logically be a dramatic growth industry. With ever-increasing mobility of population, friends and relatives are more likely to be geographically remote.

Whether or not the Christmas card was a senseless act of conspicuous consumption I'll not argue. At its present state of survival I am confident that people are resisting the tradition, the card itself is becoming predominantly secular in theme, and there is a widespread shift of a shrinking market to charity products like Unicef and Save The Children.

In my own geographical neck of the woods, public and retail investment in support of both the Christian feast and the seasonal mythology is becoming perfunctory and parsimonious. Civic decorations are minimal displays of ancient materials. And not one bothers to criticise the lack-lustre civic aesthetics. Even the department stores concentrate on the hard seasonal sell, reducing overheads by expending less on spectacular store decoration.

Christmas won't disappear as a consumer orgy. For compulsive consumption is built into the psychic reflexes of industrial man. What will happen is that traditional motivations, derived from the quasi-Christian principles of sentiment, simple goodwill and affection, will change. And are changing.

The advertising industry is the perfect barometer for this prediction. There is an intensification of hard-sell seasonal promotion for the practical and functional goodies of industrial life—the tool kits, the kitchen gadgetry, the mechanical aids for recreation.

The frippery departments, which purport to relate and enlarge the personal involvements of both giver and receiver, are having a thinner time of it. In consequence advertising agencies are inventing new and functional motivations for the more personal products.

For the first time in my memory the French perfumers are promoting their products as sex aids this Christmas. The fornicatory innuendo in the recent Pierre Cardin advertising campaign is unmistakable. You don't have to have a dirty mind to get the message. The male after-shave lotion for last season was quite enchantingly and undisguisedly packaged in the shape of the phallus. The text departs totally from the before and after shaving theme. We are told it is 'For the man with a woman who knows what it is all about. A new international experience to share. An excitement for before and after . . . everything! After all, giving is receiving.'

In short, cologne has become by virtue of this pretty transparent innuendo, an aphrodisiac.

By the same token Carven makes a pretty confused appeal to the Germaine Greer disciples who are prepared to prowl and hunt down the male to ensure they attain the Kinsey copulatory average. The promotion declares: 'You're liberated. You meet a man. You decide to call him. You wear Ma Griffe. He calls first.' Carven follows this up with the following incomprehensible disclaimer: 'Ma Griffe apologises for unliberating the liberated woman.'

I am a bit fuzzed by all this, but I suspect our elegant French trading friends are having two bob each-way in the Australian sex-aid market.

However one interprets such seasonal sales messages, they certainly do not involve the simplistic idea of a personal gesture between a giver and a receiver.

These luxury products are now endowed with as definable a practicality of purpose as a bottle-opener.

The secularisation of Christmas, its impending disappearance as a pagan-Christian feast, with mythic components and religious implications, may or may not be a good thing. Agnostics may simply define it as a social change from the feast of unreason to a feast of reason; may find it all indicative that the grass-roots of Christianity as the official religion are withering away. That Christianity is surviving in industrial society only as a minority moral pressure group, and not at all as a living force in the life of the communal imagination.

Christians may see the death of Christmas as a ceremonial festivity as a good thing. If religion is to survive it must survive as a living ethical system. As such the primitive ceremonies and sentiments are so much dross, confusing and degrading the central intentions of the spiritual life. Evolved Christians will probably be only too happy to shed the rituals that once gave colour to the grinding subsistence life-style of earlier Christian communities.

Yet—with Christmas dead, and all other community occasions merely one more paid holiday in the annual calendar, what forces are there left to work for the coherence of Australians as a national community.

Easter in Greece is a vivid participatory occasion. In Athens the Easter pilgrimage up to Lycebettus a visual glory that never declines in meaning. The Indonesian calendar is packed with festivals. The political parade is (or was) the civilised glory of Chile. In Bolivia . . . and so on.

The question arises whether a nation which knows its own identity only in terms of abstraction is a nation at all. The communists know this. In East Berlin the total holiday spectacle of May Day is exploited any number of times per year to ensure that East Germany is saturated with the notion of community identity.

It may well be a good thing, politically and internationally, if we behave with only a feeble awareness of our Australianness.

I am not sure. The era of national insularities may be overdue for extinction. We may work more effectively as citizens in the world, if not citizens of the world.

Should it be that we become a livelier community by virtue of an occasional sense of belonging through national occasions that inflame the imagination, then one hell of a lot is going to depend on one ridiculous horse race each 365 days.

# ON
# COLD
**WAR**   Sir.—My recent article in *The Australian* on the experiences and reactions of Australian writers in East Germany received a rather critical reception in the correspondence columns.

Most of the letters were kind enough to credit me with honesty of mind, but disagreed vigorously with my view of contemporary communist societies in Europe.

One letter suggested that beneath my occasional humourous posing as a boy from the bush is concealed a genuine boy from the bush.

Having postulated a genuine naivete about my thinking processes, it went on to impugn my political impressions as tricky, disingenuous, and tendentious.

I hope the writer is wrong.

I hope there are two propositions that men of goodwill find worth considering at this curious and climactic moment of history. The first is that convulsive changes are taking place in the cold war perspectives and alignments during the mid-sixties.

The second proposition is that many of us, particularly here in the remote vastness of antipodean Australia, refuse to admit that the communist countries are changing in character, for the simple reason that we are hoodwinked and blinkered by our own propaganda.

Certainly the denizens of European communist societies are even more cunningly and systematically duped about the West through official propaganda than we are through unofficial propaganda. Even so, the responsibility lies the heavier on us as free and enquiring spirits not to view the world through yesterday's distorting mirror.

In a general way Australians view European communism in an abnormally crude way largely because most of us take only the most perfunctory interest in the subject. The people who are articulate about it in this country are predominantly those New Australian migrants who have at some stage or other been victims of communist oppression.

They, naturally enough, as victims and expatriates tell us about a rigid and unchanging set of totalitarian societies. But this New Australian view, authentically as it may reflect the cruelties of the regimes they left behind them ten or twenty years ago, presupposes that nothing has changed or can change.

At Weimar I attended a meeting of film-makers dominated

by the brilliant young Poles, Czechs, and Hungarians, who have created a tradition of subtle and non-ideological film-making which has won the admiration of the Western as well as the communist world.

In debating their role in the important mass medium of the cinema, the Poles, Czechs, and Hungarians engaged in a good-natured free-for-all, and the Russian film-makers, despite their formidable talents, were the butts of these young intellectual blades of the communist world.

Much mirth was engendered on the theme of those Russian films in which a young collective farm worker falls in love with his tractor, and so on.

The Russians laughed, a little grimly I thought.

The ruling concept of the communist cinema seemed to be the idea of social autobiography; that is, films dealing with maladjustments between typical individuals and groups and the society as a whole.

The aim of these films is to criticise the communist state framework in terms of its inflexibility in relation to the good life of the individual.

It was a marvellous bear-baiting debate, and that it was not academic is proved by the Czech, Polish and Hungarian films we have seen during this decade—some of them so openly critical as almost to be usable by the Western right-wing for anti-communist propaganda. They exhibit a pervasive hostility to the bureaucratic overload in the communist states.

This is a far cry from the brutally repressive image of European communism we are taught to carry about in our heads. The conventions of the cold war are changing, and we antipodeans have to adjust to the new situations despite the rigid and petrified beliefs of those anti-communists whose aim is European 'liberation'.

We must do this merely to keep in step with men like the late John Kennedy, Adlai Stevenson (in his last speech) and President Johnson, each of whom believed or believes that situations of mutual accommodation can emerge between the West and European communist societies as a basis for solid peace.

To anyone who has listened to the discussions of a variety of European communist intellectuals the importance of polycentrism is self-evident.

National identity is the preoccupation of the younger generation; straightforward ideological fervour is at a minimum; the development of greater liberties within each national framework is the chief activist aim of the educated mass of the people.

This experience at first-hand leads one to an endorsement

of the growing view that the United States of America and Russia are historically moving towards realistic and enduring policies of live-and-let-live despite the occasional intransigence of Russian diplomacy in certain areas.

This suggests that there must occur certain urgent changes in the colouration of Australian anti-communism, changes which have already taken place overseas but which seem hard to effect here.

Firstly the suggestion is not that anti-communism should be abandoned. Communism as a disorganising force within the Australian economy can be opposed by many of us so that a trade union movement of some integrity and an unembarrassed Australian Labor Party can supply the dynamic towards social justice.

The imperialist implications of Chinese communism should be watched, anticipated and opposed. The integrity of Malaysia in relation to Indonesian pressures and a long-range threat from China is an imperative concern.

In the polycentrist situations of South-East Asia anti-communism is and can be a positive social philosophy, even for those of us who oppose the Vietnam conflict.

But that brand of anti-communism which perpetuates the outdated idea of a monolithic cold war between East and West should be replaced by more sophisticated and historically realistic views.

Anti-communism should become complex, sophisticated and eclectic. This means we must take another look at European tensions, and ask some questions about our preconceptions.

In this context the question of West and East Germany is all-important. Most major political thinkers have agreed that short of world conflict German reunification is unrealistic. Given the emergence of West German power it may not even be desirable. The best policy is to support a tolerant and even fraternal modus vivendi between the splinter state of the German Democratic Republic and West Germany.

The fact is that the GDR is the most puritanical, repressive and dogmatic of the European communist countries. I think it knows this—after all, the other communist countries never cease criticising Ulbricht for his ideological backwardness and rigidity. And I think it would like to develop its own neo-liberalism.

The GDR side of the Wall is the greatest acting team in the world, with a talent for social satire unequalled by anything the West has produced in the way of intimate revue, for example. The GDR is busting to let the brilliant talents of the

Berliner Ensemble have their heads in freely developing a whole post-Brechtian style of pervasive social comment.

But the GDR is still at the front line of the contracting cold war battleground, and dare not come in where it is warm. This may be because it suits West Germany to mount and maintain a constant and denigratory propaganda barrage against the GDR.

West Germany may be motivated less by fraternal love of the East Germans than by considerations of political tactics. Few can doubt that West Germany is playing a European power game and that it has developed a massive anti-GDR propaganda machine.

Perhaps West Germany has bitter reasons for so doing. On the other hand, perhaps West Germany's policy of making the GDR politically and economically unviable means that West Germany has contributed to the erection of the Wall just as surely as if it had supplied the bricks.

The historical background is peculiarly complex and not overly relevant to the urgent present reality.

Now to the dilemma of the eclectic anti-communist: Should we take sides in the animus between East and West Germany, or struggle to reduce the temper of this inter-necine situation, to advocate a West German policy which would in fact lead to the liberalisation of East German communism?

I give no answers to this question. I don't think I have them. But I do think the question is one that should be asked, although I shall probably not be thanked for asking it.

MAX HARRIS,
Park Rd., Kensington Park, SA.

# WHERE OH WHERE IS THE GREAT AUSTRALIAN CRITIC?

It is urgently a matter of this present historical moment to enquire who are the Australian literary critics, and where are they?

If the question is raised it must be posed without rancour or finger pointing, either in the direction of the academics or that of the reviewers who work in terms of perceptive but immediate literary judgments in the public arena.

The last thing needful in this far-flung intellectual outpost is a mockup of the Leavis-versus-Snow situation.

It is of no interest to have the junior lecturers from Melbourne echoing the response of Dr Leavis' students and guffawing at the 'near-culture' of the BBC or the Sunday reviews.

Nor is it any great help to accuse the universities of inward-looking and imitative critical procedures.

But it is worth asking why we have no counterparts in terms of humanity, scholarship, and intellectual stature of the English-European tradition.

There may be conflict between the Englishness and insistent particularly of Leavis' evaluations, and the wide catholicity of Trilling, Edmund Wilson, and the whole tribe of French literary intellectuals.

There is conflict, but it is between forces of wholly respectable and original stature.

In Australia, however, and despite the growth of such excellent agencies as *Australian Literary Studies, Meanjin, Quadrant, Melbourne Review,* and *Southern Review,* there is no single critic of outstanding—let alone dominating—stature.

Perhaps there is one: Professor A. D. Hope.

But I feel that Professor Hope comes reluctantly to the role of critic, as an episodic professional task, rather than as a high and constant intellectual calling.

This waywardness is by no means blameworthy, for the man is after all almost totally committed to the craft of poetry and to the distillation of his highest critical faculties in that particular form.

Where, then, are the distinguished critical minds in Australia?

Their total absence can be ascribed to two factors in Australian intellectual life.

First, the critic who works from the Australian literary

heritage is working through a thin, well-famed, and spiritually insubstantial mass of material.

Here the literary critic, devoting himself to the analysis of the domestic product, finds himself very largely setting up a series of negativist propositions, and there is very little of the life-enlarging interpretative work that makes the European, or even the American, critics significant associates in the literary experience of readers.

Critics can only rise to the stature of the literature they have to interpret.

Second, the two traditions do not exist side by side in Australia: that of the textual critic and that of the large humanistic spirits for whom criticism is based on 'risks of the heart as well as brilliance of intellect'.

This latter tradition, which tends to see any given achievement in a particular culture—albeit Christopher Brennan, Judith Wright, or Patrick White—as related to the larger communication of European humanist scholarship, assessing the achievements of a regional culture in relation to larger and distant cultural achievements, just doesn't exist.

The embracing mind which could assess the scale of our regional work still remains unfashionable.

Australia remains a country of wilful intellectual insularity, just as it was in the 1940's when the *Angry Penguins* were stamped to death in the holy name of 'anti-modernism' because they wished to relate the preoccupations of Kafka, Rilke, Thomas, Eliot and Pound to the creative processes of writers in their own ill-defined environment.

(For example, Peter Mather's *Trap* was discussed as an exercise in anti-Melbournian malaise rather than in relation to the influential efforts of Gunther Grass to use the German language as an explosive agency. *Trap* was never properly discussed because no one discussed its intentions except in terms of its Australian reference).

This problem will increase in scale because it is my guess that Australian writing will direct itself more and more towards exploring a new framework of language to express the fragmenting social and moral fabric of society.

Criticism will therefore need to be based on far more extensive knowledge and understanding of the languages of literature rather than the surface themes of literature.

Reviewers will continue to make their groping assessments with all due sincerity. But who will interpret these new works in depth in the way, for example, that George Steiner (*Death of Tragedy* and now *Language and Silence*) interprets the contemporary European cultural tradition?

In returning to this favourite theme of mine, there is no

wish to draw blood or disturb the amour propre of any academic literary buffs.

It is more an invitation, a gesture of support, for the emergence of more inspiring and more skilled literary intellectuals than we have at present.

The Australian-European intellectual will certainly have to show up from among the young.

The present literary establishment is too tainted with political and ideological commitments, too full of certitudes, too unready for that kind of skilled receptivity.

They rejected Kafka a long time ago. They are not likely to accept a Peter Mather tomorrow. It took them ten years and paroxysms of misery to get round to accepting Patrick White.

Wherever I shall one day look, it won't be in the direction of my own peers, contemporaries and superiors.

# On Being Thrown to the Literary Lions

# JONATHAN
# LIVINGSTON
# SEA

**GHOUL**   Jonathan Livingston Seagull is not your ordinary talking animal. He's not like the commonplace talking dogs, horses, and crocodiles that totter into front bars and ask for a beer. He doesn't even belong to that inevitably lewd race of talking birds which give forth obscene utterances to little old ladies in pet shops.

Jonathan is a veritable Reverend Lance Shilton (new Dean of Sydney) among birds. He is a spiritual bird, of whom one in the hand is worth two Rogers in the Bush.

He is a poetic bird, more familiar with the Profits ($4 million paperback rights) than the Laws.

He is a bird of such anthropomorphistic endowments that he makes his avian compatriot, Jemima Puddleduck, look like the late Adolf Hitler. Jonathan Livingston Seagull pants, puffs, trembles, smiles and even makes the frequent 'scree of delight' while in mid-flight.

This latter capacity, which the Oxford dictionary interprets as the ability to assemble a vast quantity of pebbles in mid-air, must be an amiable example of the post-biblical miracle. Although why Jonathan should want to make delightful screes, as against pie in the sky, is beyond me.

The anthropomorphistic faculties of Jonathan and the whole rotten seagull community may be excruciating, but the one human endowment the author should have deprived him of is the capacity to talk. Christ, can that bird talk. And talk. And talk. He talks when he's flying. He doesn't stop talking when he's got a barracuda stuffed halfway down his throat.

You see, Jonathan Livingston Seagull is seeking perfection through flight. He's not like the other nong seagulls who materialistically go off to the beach footy and buy a sardine pie and a can of fermented sea-water.

The climax comes in this quest for ultimate spirituality when Jonathan meets up with an old Chink seagull called Chiang (I kid you not—it's all in the book, page fifty-eight). With a sagacity beyond the wildest dreams of Chairman Mao, Chiang declares: 'To fly as fast as thought, to anywhere that is, you must begin by knowing that you have already arrived.'

Try working out that bit of logic, poor Ronnie and Rita Reader!

But Jonathan Seagull clues up on the instant.

'The trick was to know that his true nature lived, as perfect as an unwritten number, everywhere across space and time.'

Well, even I can now grasp the philosophy. It's pretty close to the Wordsworth-Coleridge notions of pantheism which even Wordsworth and Coleridge tended to know was a lot of useful high-flown metaphysical garbage.

It's the perfection of the unwritten number which has me whacked. What's more perfect about an unwritten number than an unwritten letter? And why is a number perfect when it's unwritten, and buggered up presumably when it's written?

It's the sociological phenomenon of Richard Bach's *Jonathan Livingston Seagull* which is the truest of the mysteries.

We have an essay of a few thousand words, an intellectually insulting, untalented, feeble fantasy, larded with gobbledlygook mystic utterance. The ninety pages are padded out with dozens of indifferent seagull photographs. It costs you five dollars to spend half an hour in Waffle-land.

Yet this is the freakish best-seller of all time. It's probably the hottest literary property of all time. There has been nothing like it since the *Poetic Gems* of Ella Wheeler Wilcox, or Warwick Deeping's *Sorrell and Son*. It has Harold Robbins inwardly groaning with pain, because *Seagull* has earned at about the rate of a thousand dollars a word, whereas the astute Harold is obligated to write a lot of words in order to make a lot of money.

It's the book of the century for a multi-million collection of people who don't read books.

The fundamental question is the old hen and the egg bit. Did the media make Richard Bach's message, or did Richard Bach's message make it on the media?

One wonders whether the book acquired an underground misty reputation since it was published in 1970 and thereby forced the media to sit up and take notice. In which case it testifies to the enormous attraction of unreason and pseudo-mysticism at the grass-roots of the community.

This in itself is revealing and terrifying (shades of Nietzsche, Wagner, and the Germany that was). Alternatively the media could have capriciously cultified the book out of a need for fresh gimmickry. The implications are equally scary.

My present querulousness doesn't derive from antipathy to mystic fantasy as such—only to meaningless mystical conmanship, vapidity dressed up as profundity.

And as teenagers, football players, be-curlered housewives, supermart managers, postgraduate hairies—as they all tumble into bookshops holding their hot five dollars for

*Jonathan Livingston Seagull,* I can sense there's something sick and disorderly about the Western state of mind. But I'm not quite sure what it is, and what causes it.

*JONATHAN LIVINGSTON SEAGULL, by Richard Bach; Turnstone Press.*

# THIS
## IS
## RACIAL RUBBISH,
## MR LINDSAY

'Of all the mass imbecilities which have demoralised mankind, this of racial equality between all peoples, white, black, red and yellow, is the most inane.

'Politically, it has already stirred up all the minor races into a state of belligerence and discontent which will impose minor wars on the dominant nations for years to come. But when it comes to racial integration between the white and black races, sanity has descended to the looney bin of the impossible, because the intermixture of blood between those races must degrade the white race to the level of the Negro and cannot raise the Negro to the level of the white.

'Where today we see some evidence of the effect of education on the Negro it is the white blood in him that stirs some animation in his sluggish mental faculties, but the Negro pure, as he exists in Africa, cannot be educated even up to the standard of the lowest content of the white race.

'He may learn to parrot all the political and sociological cliches of today, but unless he is buttressed by the white race, and policed by it, he must relapse back to the jungle, which is his predestined habitat.'

Forgive the extreme length of the preceding quotation. The object of the exercise is for you to guess the authorship of this vicious unscientific, untruthful racist rubbish.

The late Dr Verwoerd? No. A document from the heyday of the Third Reich? No. The words are hot from the press, and they come from the Sacred Bull of the Australian cultural scene, Mr Norman Lindsay, no less.

But this small slab from his chapter on Negroes in *The Scribblings of an Idle Mind* is nothing compared with his views on Catholics, Jews and homosexuals.

Before we examine these views let us get the literary ethics of the situation perfectly clear. Norman Lindsay is very old. It might be thought that it is a matter of good taste to let a man say what he likes in his declining years, not to take it seriously, not to attack his sunset views.

Norman Lindsay is not, however, senile. His cerebral apparatus is just as clear and lively as yours or mine. Youth or age has nothing to do with the need to confront superstitious racial bigotry. If it has to be challenged in a clever undergraduate it has also, and perhaps the more, to be challenged in a clever old man.

Negroes, according to our national Sacred Bull, are only fit for the jungle. At least they're better off than homosexuals, who don't appear to be fit for anything. In particular homosexuals can't contribute to the creative arts because 'of the destructive effect homosexuality has on the creative faculty'.

For Norman Lindsay, the artistic uselessness of homosexuals is demonstrated by the seventh-rate work of Leonardo da Vinci and Michelangelo. Well, that just about writes off homosexuals by critical definition, doesn't it? (Norman Lindsay is not a homosexual. He is not a Negro).

How about Roman Catholics? Well they've 'had it' since the Renaissance:

> 'Since the Reformation all great achievement in the arts has come from the Protestant peoples, while the creative urge has become moribund in all peoples still dominated by the Catholic Church.'

That disposes of Roman Catholics. (Norman Lindsay isn't a Catholic.)

Jews? Well, according to Lindsay, only the Jew Freud could have invented anything as nasty as psycho-analysis. (Norman Lindsay isn't Jewish.)

How about modernists? In art Lindsay reserves his spleen for the post-impressionists of long ago. Van Gogh and Cezanne are disposed of as 'witless asses'. I'd hate to hear his views on artists who have followed these great figures in the evolution of modern art forms!

The point is that Norman Lindsay's unholy ramblings are not the splenetic views of an elderly man negating everything except his own little areas of activities.

They are the views of a fiercely individualistic young man in the Sydney of the 1920's. In fact over the last forty-five years Norman Lindsay has never changed, altered a view, nor assimilated new values into his painting. And this is his own creative tragedy.

There is no potential disputation over the merits of his long life's work. His painting began as a schoolboy eroticism in a Nietzschian disguise, and it's never got much further.

As a cultural theorist he propounded a wild mixture of provocative views which had some influence among the golden boys of the 1920's, but as men like Kenneth Slessor developed they left Lindsay theories way behind.

Lindsay's contributions to the Australian scene have been incidental and almost accidental. *The Magic Pudding* is his masterpiece. He added some amiable and witty light novels to the fictional scene.

Let him be praised for these achievements.

# PORTER UPSTAGED BY BLUFF HAL

I must confess that I admire Hal Porter—for the reason that he is the most completely private man I've come across in the writing world. The authentically faceless man.

In *The Paper Chase* he assumes stance, pose, and gesture with a fearful thespianism that diverts the reader in the same way a modern audience is diverted by the itinerant performances of an old trouper of the Beerbohm Tree persuasion.

We have Hal the bluff, Hal the conservative, Hal the anti-intellectual, Hal the wag, Hal the perpetual upper-former, but never for a moment do we sense that he has looked into his morning mirror and told us what he really sees there.

Does he see anything there? Perhaps he is merely the sum total of his various roles; perhaps a very complex and private person. I do know that I understand his refusal to be other than a conglomerate of contradictory public personalities. Porter will be an entertainer, a professional eccentric, but not a public sacrifice.

But this doesn't help greatly with *The Paper Chase*, a pure run-of-the-mill autobiography in which there is only one coherent and evolving character, Hal himself.

It is a quite different work from *Watcher on the Cast Iron Balcony* and of unquestionably lower stature.

The *Watcher* was an exercise in affection and evocation, and it was written with flawless literary skill. It didn't matter one solitary gumleaf whether the 'watcher' was Porter himself in knickerbockers or a fictional identity. Porter the writer stood outside the material and produced a beautiful and enduring work.

With *The Paper Chase*, Porter strode centre-stage and it's all a bit of a bore. Porter in all his roles is a bit of a bore, despite the exhilaration of his literary style when he hits his metaphoric straps with brilliant quippery, flashes of imagery, and a wit that is often both violent and deadly. The reader can't really become involved in a man without qualities, and the affectations become a little dismaying when both author and reader are perfectly aware of their transparency.

Hal Porter has produced something of a dilemma for himself. He has become a novelist of great ability. Certainly there is only one writer in this country who produces greater short story writing. Is he to continue in autobiographical vein or return to the harder disciplines of his craft? I would certainly advise him to move back into the anonymity of the writer proper, despite the financial seductions of popular autobiography.

It is of archival interest to diagnose Porter's dilemma a little deeper than is customary in a critical notice.

If, as Porter himself says in *The Paper Chase*, his life is a desperate effort 'not to escape others but to escape oneself,' then this Keatsian self-annihilation is motivated by a single fierce dedication—the will to BECOME a writer.

The business of writing, which is more a part of the human experience of such an individual as Porter than the roysterings of mateships, is dealt with less than candidly in *The Paper Chase*. It is dealt with in terms of passing reference, casual irony, as a minor incidental.

The fact is that Hal Porter had a long, grim, lonely, and unfashionable apprenticeship in the craft of writing. For this end result, of not being but becoming a complete writer, Porter has created the rigid Byzantine identity that underlies the public odd-ball. But the ikon splinters, authentic passion erupts, when criticism is directed at Porter's writing rather than at Porter himself. He finds criticism intolerable, perhaps more intolerable the more perceptive it is.

Added to the decades of neglect and unfashionability is the problem of the kind of writer Porter is. He is admittedly anti-intellectual for the evident and admitted reason that he is a man of limited intellectual interest or capacities. Nor is he a man of great complexity, either spiritually or emotionally. He has hauled himself into the position of being a significant and skilful writer by his own bootstraps.

However, a writer with such limited natural endowments tends to produce work on a hit-or-miss basis. *The Professor* is an embarrassingly bad piece of playwriting, and Porter screamed back 'boo-sucks' to the critics when they said so.

I can understand this splenetic vulnerability. Porter has lived too long in a climate of critical indifference and even overt Philistinism, from both avante and derriere garde, to endure praise or attack on his brainchildren with indifference. I'm all on his side.

But is it not odd that the central passion of Porter's life receives such cavalier treatment in *The Paper Chase*? Why does Porter's notable photographic memory black out entirely when the human contexts of his writing life are involved? The reason—sheer vulnerability—leads to an absurd lack of candour and to a preoccupation with the trifling as a substitute for the real stuff of his experience.

I shall be exact about this and refer to the era when I was, according to Mr Porter's generous fantasy, 'slender and handsome as Flecker's Hassan or a Syrian sweetmeats-vendor'. His Adelaide memoirs consist largely of a soggy and sentimental reminisce about Russel Ward's father, then headmaster of Prince Alfred's College.

But surely the modest relationship between headmaster and English-master had not the huge and exciting formative implications of Porter's bosom friendship with the late Arthur Davies, a fellow-teacher, and an eccentric, loveable literary genius of the rarest kind.

In Adelaide we remember Davies-and-Porter, two interacting and inseparable imaginations. But Davies is blacked out of Hal's impeccable memory. There remains only the dull yarns with Boxer Ward. Is Porter afraid to analyse the qualities of that—to us—inspiring relationship?

Porter refers to my publishing one of his 'already published short stores'. Here again there is less than candour. In Adelaide Porter published his own stories in an edition of about one hundred copies, perhaps the rarest piece of Australiana of that period. This was a deeply traumatic moment for Porter—a lonely, timid venture into publication. This event is completely suppressed in favour of a lot of cliche raconteuring about the pranks of local medical students.

Good heavens, even with my limited knowledge of the man I could tell a tale of the vulnerability, the dedication, the meaningful gaiety of Porter during his Adelaide period. He could tell it better himself, but has wished not to do so. Why?

His answer—that he has only essayed a piece of surface entertainment so that he can live from writing—is not good enough.

From Porter we expect a work of art. After all, wasn't that what he too wanted as the outcome of those chilling years of literary apprenticeship?

# MING
# THE
# MIRTHFUL?  I am disposed to think that Australia is one of

the most humourless countries on earth. There exists, of course, the dry leg-pulling humour of the Australian proletariat, of which Frank Hardy is the arch-priest. But there the matter ends.

When the pubs are emptied and the barrackers have dispersed from the Hill, the Australian language reverts to a grey verbal solemnity.

This stems, I think, from the calibre of the articulate and educated section of the community. Australia possesses a basic layer of proletarian humour, but no superstructure of educated wit.

Why?

After all, from the Augustans and Sam Johnson to Shaw, wit and stylishness were part of the necessary apparatus of the articulate man. But how many Australian books, from fiction to lit crit, are expressed in witty and elegant style; how many newspapers employ the sharp edge of wit in preference to thundering solemnity; how many critics examine the world with the eye of a Meredith, or a Wilde, of a Shaw, or a youthful A. D. Hope?

The reason is that wit always implies criticism, usually social criticism, and the operations of wit can be more devastating and dangerous than the most carefully wrought diatribe. Academics in Australia are a notoriously insecure tribe, hence the inevitable solemn parade of erudition instead of the diagnostics of style.

The Australian Broadcasting Commission is an impeccable example of the national jelly-legged condition. Through sheer policy attitudes it has created a sacred cow solemnity about all themes from the weekly price of peas to the activities of ratbag religions.

In short, wit has no part in the life of frightened people, and the corollary to this thesis is surely that Australia is peopled with conformist minds to an abnormal degree.

This gloomy theory leads to our literary theme of the week: the revival of interest in the role of wit and humour in public life and human communication.

Some time ago we had a book called *A Pope Laughs*, a collection of quotations which exemplify the effervescing humanity of the late Pope John. More recently controversy erupted all over Britain in connection with a slender book on the wit of the Duke of Edinburgh.

The argument has been that what is put forward as magnificently witty coming from the Duke would be deemed vulgar badinage coming from Joe Blow.

I am inclined to disagree with the deadpan British critics who made this observation, on the grounds that wit is often contextual rather than intrinsic. There is a delicious and devastating comeuppance involved when a royal personage instructs a solemn conclave to remove the collective finger which is not involved when Ron Barassi instructs his forward line to do the same thing.

The Duke of Edinburgh has a real wit which allows him to dispose of the pompous circumstances in which he is in fact involved. Admirable, surely.

The next book to be published in this vein is one which will interest us all. It is called *The Wit of Sir Robert Menzies*. Being a fearful and largely humourless people we have not much questioned this aspect of the Prime Minister's public character. Is Sir Robert a real wit?

My guess is that he could be if he had room and proper occasion to apply it. His introduction to Slasher Mackay's book on cricket, for example, displays a pretty sense of the comic and even the primitive beginnings of an ability to send himself up.

But I have grave doubts about the merit of his proclaimed political wit. This, to me, usually consists of a debased form of legal wit, the ready scoring off an opponent by virtue of quick, destructive, and yet not necessarily meaningful repartee.

To me, hustling humour and legal wit belong to an order lower than the pun. The speaker has all the tricks in his hand, the demolition of the opponent is carried out without real intellectual work or penetration. It is all a bit too facile and tricksy to relate to the high peaks of wit.

# YEVTUSHENKO
## WITH
## ALL
## THE STOPS OUT

The Regent Cinema was packed to the roof: there had been nothing quite like it in living Adelaide memory, that so many people should foregather for a recital of poetry and by a Russian patriotic poet at that!

Yevtushenko lived up to his popular reputation and to the expectations of the amazingly enthusiastic audience.

He declaimed from his earlier work, from the long poem-sequence *To the Bratsk Station*, and from his very recent collection *The City of Yes and The City of No*. Yevtushenko's own Russian performances were preceded by readings in English translation by Dame Edith Anderson, and Peter O'Shaughnessy, and this procedure enabled the audience to experience to the full the vast difference between Slavonic and Anglo-Saxon poetic conventions.

Indeed, the unobtrusive and yet exact artistry of Peter O'Shaughnessy provided both a foil for Yevtushenko's crackling histrionics and also a confrontation of opposing verse-speaking techniques.

Yevtushenko's poetry is essentially a simple poetry in terms of content. Even without understanding Russian one can sense how emphatic and repetitive the rhymes are, how rhetorical the use of assonance, the moral convictions, the general reliance on impressionistic imagery.

It is a lyrical and spirited poetry, but it differs from lyrical poetry as we expect to encounter it because it is obviously written to be heard more than to be read (no poet writing in English would use the rhetorical device of invocation with such naive insistence as Yevtushenko).

As Yevtushenko declaims it, it is poetry with every emotional stop out. Its purpose is to make the heart beat faster, passions stir, sentiment to melt into gentleness, excitement to burst into the shout of joy or pain. Yevtushenko's willowy body works to the passions and intensities of the poetry.

His gestures are very Russian, very public, reminiscent of Lenin, of street orators, but they often modulate to the quiet nuances of a Turgeniev conversation piece.

But the public style of Yevtushenko himself and the non-intellectual impressionism of his verse do not make him a shallow poet when studied on the printed page. This is verse from a different convention, that is all. The critic who could find the writing of Yevtushenko dull is merely a man cocooned within a set of preconceptions about poetic form:

this kind of critic in his cloistered study wouldn't enjoy Byron's *Don Juan* or Pushkin's *Onegin* any better.

Yet it is possible to see that Yevtushenko's superb histrionics have their limitations, for very often the portentous vocal delivery is too much of a burden for the verse to bear.

Very often one felt that diminuendo led crescendo, and crescendo to diminuendo, just for the sake of working up a froth of verbal excitement.

There is something to be said for interpreting poetry in the O'Shaughnessy style, even Yevtushenko's poetry. O'Shaughnessy speaks poetry with any amount of vocal colour: he is not of the late T. S. Eliot's plain-chant school of persuasion. But he allows the imagery to do its work through the hearer's imagination. This is a subtler and more delicate technique of communicating the sounds of poetry.

It really boils down to the fact that Yevtushenko addresses himself to a different audience, a vast, simple, but willing audience for whom the poet is a man who speaks directly to their emotions. This illumination, that Yevtushenko writes his poetry for all manner of men, of all levels of education, gives one a startling apprehension of how different are the functions of art in the Slavonic socialist countries.

Yevtushenko's recital brought all these considerations to life, and there is little doubt that he will have a disturbing effect on the sedate values of Australian poetry during his tour of this country.

No poet could watch Yevtushenko at work, humanising and animating a sea of petrified Adelaide faces, without feeling that our forms of poetic activity have become a mite dry, specialised, and unwholesomely detached from any robust participation in common experience.

For the ordinary citizen a visit to a Yevtushenko performance will dispel for ever the notion that a poetry recital is an occasion for long-hairs to bore each other to distraction.

# IN
# PURSUIT
# OF
# NON-FREEDOM

One of Kafka's aphorisms simply reads, 'A bird went in search of a cage.' I suppose by this he meant that humanity finds the myth of personal freedom intolerable when it becomes a partial reality.

This is the theme of V. S. Naipaul's *In a Free State* (Andre Deutsch); certainly the most magnificent achievement over the past years in the English language novel.

When circumstances change, and individuals find themselves in a free state, rather like certain elements in the physical universe of science, they can be destroyed, spiritually annihilated by that very condition which has been ideally projected as the ultimate goal of a human life.

For Naipaul the free state may occur among a group of people on a derelict ship plying between Piraeus and Alexandria; on a long and dangerous ribbon of African road between a city in flames and the secure womb of a distant European enclave. It can be the disastrous freedom of a low-caste Indian servant emerging from poverty and servility into the libertarian environs of Washington; or a West Indian dreaming of property and dignity in Notting Hill Gate.

It is to be expected that Naipaul would be the writer to produce a minor classic on the theme of human beings propelled into the nightmare no-man's-land of a free state. A Caribbean citizen of Indian parenthood and resident in England, Naipaul himself has long symbolised the supranational writer, the eye freed from attachments, the heart that can seek out no group affections of kinship or cultural bonding.

From *The Mystic Masseur* to *The Mimic Men* and now *In a Free State*, Naipaul has come to deal with the fierce corrosive destruction which attends the human spirit that inhabits a floating universe.

There is nothing, therefore, surprising about the thematic preoccupations of Naipaul. What surprises me is that there have been so few critical observations on the fact that the agony of freedom, the hunt itself for the poisonous grail, has been the substance of most major achievement in the novel over the past decade.

There is nothing esoteric about the idea of the individual in a free and unbelonging condition. We each can define it within the terms of some personal experience, this being in a free state.

Personally, I recall those insomniac hours in the transit

lounges of international airports, when the aircraft disgorges its disoriented human cargo to mill around in a sort of surrealist limbo land. Each individual feels suspended forever between one set of acceptable realities, and the next. Each individual is an isolated element, completely alone within himself. Observe when the flight is called back on board the aircraft how eagerly the mob embrace the discomforts, tensions and longeurs of that communal womb!

People who have been dangerously ill or who are dying know all about what it's like to be in a free state. The 'important' things of life in the social cage become stupefying and irritating irrelevancies. The psychological minutiae of everyday living assume their real non-importance, and the experience is terrifying.

The sick or dying person has perforce moved from the swim of healthy day-to-day activity; to be alone, and able to assess the values of ordinary life, affection, interest, ambition, with a terrible and destructive clarity.

The dying person knows no other human being. Has no one to cling to. He has become a free and different creature, living in another element. He can't escape his clear relentless perception of the valueless values of the human group of which he, too, was once a part. Life by definition is making things matter that don't matter.

This is the leit-motif of one of the world's least read great novels—Rainer Maria Rilke's *The Notebooks of Malte Laurids Brigge*. The dying patriarch in that masterpiece will have none of your Christian passivity and acceptance of the process of dying. He roars like an infuriated bull, enraged not by the fact of death, but by the callousness of a God who would remove him prematurely from a comforting participation in the human condition. To put a man in a free state is the last gratuitous indignity imposed on the individual by a merciless Creator.

I suspect Keats expressed experience of a similar yet gentler order in the perpetual presence of his own dying; always in the context of living most richly, yet suddenly seeing into the 'core of an eternal fierce destruction'; or being invariably 'annihilated in the presence of a child'.

As we get more dissatisfied with our caged and urban condition, the message of the novel in the 1960's has surely been that the individual spirit can only survive in the search for the wires and bars of organised human order. The pursuit of freedom or of progress is the full Gadarene catastrophe. *Zorba the Greek* is a diabolical fairy tale, the last great delusion of vitalism.

I think of Saul Bellow's Mr Sammler, unable to effect his escape from the attachments and commitments of a gothic

New York into the planet he imagines he would like to in-habit. Of Barry England's strange *Figures in a Landscape* in which two lone escapees, totally alien in temperament and cultural compatibility, fuse into a hideous cunning comple-mentarity. The two individuals become one functioning entity, separable only by violent death.

I think of Vonnegut's *Slaughterhouse Five* which says that man's voyaging is not inter-stellar but back to those few moments when he has felt most completely embedded in the common human condition.

I might also mention the novel that should assuredly prove the most disturbing literary experience of the forth-coming publishing year, E. L. Doctorow's *The Book of Daniel*. This is an agonised fictional reconstruction from the cold-war era of the 1950's when the Rosenbergs were exe-cuted in America as spies for Russia. The novel fictionally re-creates the upbringing of their two children, beings doomed to live to death in a free state, never reconciled to or at one with the society which killed their parents many past and amnesed years ago. It is a work of frightening, lonely dream-like wisdom.

As I assess the cartography of the novel over the past decade, a couple of curious considerations occur. We live now in a time of important novels, but not of important novelists.

In a way the novel has become a form of cri de coeur, and not a vehicle of trained social observation and inter-pretation. One no longer looks forward to the next major works by the major creative novelists. By its nature a cri de coeur occurs only once. Like men arrested and allowed one telephone call, writers are permitted one desperate com-munication to their fellow men from the lower depths they are inhabiting.

The other thought concerns the regional improvement of our own creative output. After Patrick White who? And saying what? Between the irrelevant skills of the elderly practitioners and the dim-witted youth myth of utopian free-doms, we are producing a nothing-literature, not even a toy literature. Well, at best a play literature.

Why should this be so? After all, like Shylock, we Aus-tralians are capable of bleeding.

But are we? We may not be the richest, most powerful, most anything nation on earth. Yet we may well have produced the most comprehensive cage-system of any cultural or national group.

The historic literary works of the modern mind have come from men who have experienced the desolation of the free state, the limbo of freedom, and who are seeking for lost modes of belonging, for tolerable forms of corporate existence.

We have our young, and they are of no help. They are off on an orgy of romantic utopianism, the waffling literary anarchy of the middle-class comfortables. Ideological idealism, unrelated to any real experience of desolation, is a cerebral luxury equivalent to the E-type Jag or the weekend speed-boat.

The common quality of major writing in the 1960's and early 70's is that it comes from ecologically disturbed human beings in disturbed cultures. Kafka's birds are in search of their cage.

But we Australians are all right, Jack. That's not our scene. Remember after all that our national glory is the budgerigar.

We are the cage-bred species par excellence. How should we paint or sing or write of the cruelty of the free state who have never known it.

# MOSES!
# IT'S A
# BURNING
## BUSH
I feel I must be pretty close to being Mr Average Australia; Community Standards Incorporate in one frail bodily frame as it were.

My very utter top poet is John Laws. Delicious shudders. And I approbate the action of Qantas culture-makers in selecting John Laws, of all the Australian writers living or dead, from H. Lawson to P. White, as the only great poet to be selected for their taped entertainment on the jumbo jets. (It's true. I kid you not.)

And top lodger in my theological mind is the Reverend Roger Bush. No one more effective in lifting the nightie of my spiritual darkness. Number one on my ecclesiastical hit parade for 292 weeks (it's his third gold hassock).

Little wonder, then, at my wrath that there has been so much kefuffle about *The Little Red Schoolbook* and so little acclamation for Roger's, *Little White Schoolbook*. When I finished reading it I was choked with emotion. Quite choked.

Bushie bursts into flames over the subject of sex as it should be understood by his supposedly pre-pubescent readers. Unwilling as I am to criticise my brilliant theologian, I must make a teeny comment on his view of sex as expounded in *The Little White Schoolbook*.

Nobody has got any organs. Not none. Anywhere. I'm post-pubescent, and over the years have developed a fairly clear idea of what you do with what. But a frank moral manual for ten-year-olds that doesn't locate the procreative zones must be considered inadequate.

Take, for instance, this brilliant passage which clarifies sundry matters very simply for our school kiddies:

'The late D. Unwin in his great work *Sex and Culture* (1934) confirms his findings that productive social energy is proportionate to the sexual discipline exercised by the two previous generations. He surveyed eighty primitive peoples, sixteen civilisations, and covered 4000 years of history.'

Now that information will have the tinies rocking back and forth in their high chairs and scattering Weetbix all over the lino. But how much productive social energy will be engendered for society by this forceful Bush logic if the youngies in all innocence start exercising sexual discipline over their navels or their knee-knuckles?

No, you can't have a straight talk on sexual morals without identifying little boys' dinkies or little girls' twiddles. It can't be done.

For all its wholesomeness *The Little White Schoolbook* can be accused of ambiguous passages conducive to un-natural behaviour and to attitudes of genetic racialism. I proceed to adduce the evidence.

Roger Bush says, and I quote: 'Sex is falling in love with your Sunday School teacher or Physical Education Mistress.' I don't like the sound of this.

At the Mount Gambier Baptist Church Sunday School we went through some fourteen different male teachers over the years. At least four of them were as camp as a row of army tents. And my physical education instructor at Saints was much given to flagellation, dribbling profusely as he wielded a cane on the pubescent bots of us aristocratic scholars.

If sex is falling in love with your Sunday School teachers, then I got it all wrong.

I was, if I remember correctly, unduly heated by the pre-sence of Dahlia Hickinbotham who sat next to me. I thought the Sunday School teachers were a mob of coy creeps. I was no doubt a backward child.

In any case, on page fifty-eight, Roger asserts that the church doesn't approve of homosexual conduct, and he doesn't set an age limit on this disapprobation. Contradic-tory fellow, old Bushie.

Now to the problem of genetic racialism—a serious accu-sation in all faith. I quote:

'Sex is two people, old and white-haired, sitting quietly on the verandah, holding hands, watching the sun set in the Western sky.'

There's a nasty implication in this erotic vision of the Rev Rog. It's the teenage hair syndrome of our age mani-festing itself in a man of mature and clerical responsibility.

Why can't sex be two people, old and bald-headed, sitting noisily on the verandah shaking hands and all that? It's not all of us who will share Roger's great good fortune to age into silver-haired patriarchs having vicarious sex on the geriatric verandah. The baldies are just as entitled to their sunset thrills.

And why a capital W for Western? Since when did we WASP'S take over proprietorship of the sky, or any part thereof? Unconscious bloody imperialism if you ask me.

As you see, my moral standards are getting pretty confused. It could well be worse for nine-year-olds. So I'll turn to the simpler issue of drugs.

The Rev Rog describes the symptoms of pot-smoking in colourful terms—'drowsiness, a dry mouth, laughter, talkativeness, anxiety, feelings of unreality and bloodshot eyes.'

You could have fooled me. Sounds ghastly. But then, what are the symptoms of the drug alcohol?

Let us turn to the two paragraphs which are all the subject apparently calls for, on page 120.

What, no symptoms? No warning adjectivals? Nary a word that alcohol shows up in symptoms of bleariness, vomiting, staggering, bellicosity, uncontrolled sexual rapacity, and excessive micturition? Nary a word.

POT IS DISASTROUS, PERIOD. But only 'misuse of alcohol' leads to broken homes and road fatalities. Our author suggests that the 750,000 school children of Australia arrange a school visit to 'one of the alcoholic clinics in your city', which is one way of dodging the issue. Ask the head at your local primary school to take you on a half-day junket to an 'alcoholic clinic' and see how far you'll get.

No, alas, I really do fear that the courageous author of *The Little White Schoolbook* is dodging the booze issue.

I really must apologise. I truly am capable of constructive criticism.

A schoolbook is a schoolbook is a schoolbook. Ipso facto. By definition. Spelling is part of the syllabus. And a high moral tone should be accompanied by unquestionable spelling standards. Because literacy is what education and schoolbooks are all about.

I worried slightly about this matter when the author appeared on ABC television (May 11, videotape available for verification) and said he didn't object to kids demonstrating as long as they were fully 'convicted' about what they were doing and didn't take refuge in 'anomity'.

So a moment ago I just flicked through a couple of pages of *The Little White Schoolbook* at random. For homework tonight, Roger must check his essay from beginning to end —and write out the correct spelling of 'concensus' and 'scott-free' one hundred times.

Last class of the day. Mathematics. On my estimate the printing cost of *The Little White Schoolbook* would be about twenty-three cents. It retails at $1.50. It's selling like a bomb. It may well make the proverbial packet.

Might I suggest that the profits go towards fighting the true immorality and obscenity of our age. Mr Justice Howard Zelling declared in his famous judgment that a whole generation thinks of obscenity not in terms of linguistics, but as poverty in the midst of affluence, social injustice, ecological destruction, war.

I agree. These are the real obscenities. And the young are right to think of them thus.

I feel sure the Reverend Bush also agrees with a whole heart, although these subjects didn't rate a mention in his 150 pages of moral homilectics.

I suggest that the profits accrued from *The Little White Schoolbook* be devoted to a crusade against those immoralists who exploit poverty and human misfortune in our society. I'll join with the Rev Roger in his Sydney home town, and we'll fight the slum landlords, the rackrent exploiters of poverty.

If the evidence provided by the Press, and recently by ABC television, is at all credible, there's no trouble in pinpointing the major slum landlords of Sydney.

Come on, Roger, let's go get 'em.

# THE
# ADELAIDE ORGY
# OF
# THE ANTI-POETS

It was Voznesensky, the Russian poet, who gave the game away.

In Russia, he declared, poets are treated like film stars, adulated, performing before vast, emotionally-roused audiences. This shows the Russians have a great natural love of beaut poetry.

The logic of this could well be flawed. The phenomenon might well demonstrate the paucity of film stars as much as the popularity of poets.

One might also enquire whether a susceptibility to the rhetorical word, albeit charged with the emotions of the poet or the calculated emotions of the cunning demagogue, evidences a semi-literate and underdeveloped grass-roots structure of civilisation.

After all, the prose-poetry of Adolf Hitler roused the simple-witted German populace to an ugly Wagnerian tumult of murderous emotionalism.

I would prefer to think, along with the late-lamented Ern Malley with his famous misquotation from Lenin that 'The emotions are not skilled workers'.

There is an opposing view, not popular among the contemporary young, that poetry has to do with communicating beautifully what you think about what you feel; even what you think about what you think.

Poetry differentiated itself long ago from song and from oral entertainment when it became associated with the written word and the act of reading. This was not essentially a retrograde development in human culture, to have an art form which calls for private contemplation and enjoyment from the individual. Poetry at its best is the act of I and Thou in Martin Buber's sense. The sensibility of the poet communicates with the sensibility of the reader in a private and reflective relationship.

But we now have the poet as film star; and poetry as a form of theatrical entertainment.

The greatest achievement of the Adelaide Festival of Arts in its entire history has been to summon together the most remarkable gathering of the literary theatricalists in one place and at one time.

I don't know anywhere else in the world where a pride of theatrical literary lions has foregathered such as Voznesensky, Allen Ginsberg, Lawrence Ferlinghetti, and as a maverick ring-in, Rod McKuen.

Thereby it has been possible to examine the weird Russian-American youth conception of poetry as a branch of the performing arts, and to make better-informed judgments about the whole business.

At both the performing level and the personal level there is, alas, no difference between the excessive egotism of the litterateur and the actor. Voznesensky writes poems about Ginsberg; Ferlinghetti writes poems about Voznesensky; Ginsberg namedrops mercilessly—'this is a number I recorded a short time ago with Bob Dylan, etc'.

The psychopathology of coteries is unmistakable. They can't quite get over the fact that they're mates together on the celebrity circuit.

All very bad for poetry at the creative centre—especially when, like Ginsberg, you are affecting the stance of a Hindu-Buddhist guru who has transcended the destructive self-aggrandisement of the ego. A bit of a contradiction keeps showing up, like Banquo's ghost, among all the beads and the bells.

So, in Adelaide we had a literary line-up that equates with Frank Sinatra, Dean Martin, and the well-known cinematic 'rat-pack', as they described themselves.

Did the entertainment of these literary performers match up with their egotism? My word it did.
Voznesensky attracted only 400 people. This is no sorry reflection on the literary philistinism of the festival audience. Yevtushenko familiarised Australians with what Ferlinghetti described, and gently satirised, as 'the Russian heroic style'. Voznesensky is an even more explosively emotional exponent of the spoken word than Yevtushenko. He is also the better poet.

But I think audiences are rightly entitled to be suspicious of heroic emotional ham. As I mentioned before, a cunning politician can rouse an audience to greater excitement with bad prose expressing villainous values than a poet can stir valid feelings with valid poetry. The public literary heroics of the Russians are as shallow as a paddle pool. And the genuine admirers of Voznesensky's poetry will prefer to read Voznesensky's poetry.

Lawrence Ferlinghetti packed in a near full-house at the Adelaide Town Hall, and in a sense he was the most satisfying of the anti-poets from verbal outer space. That is, as an entertainer at an acceptable level of subtlety.

He is a simple sort of bloke, as indeed they were all intellectually very simple indeed; and occasional Ferlinghetti lines are possessed of an innocent funniness. He seems nice, uncorrupted, and wholesome. One feels that a substantial poet of some subtlety would have emerged at some other place at some other time.

But stripped of occasional wit and accidental verbal felicity, Ferlinghetti suffers from an untreated gastroenteritic condition of the mind. He is hopelessly addicted to free associative 'catalogue' techniques. A major poem takes Vosznesensky for a ride down the main street of Las Vegas (yes, they have both been there). Inventive verbal imagery takes in all the visual vulgarities of that urban scene in one long atmospheric catalogue. End of poem. Big deal.

Ferlinghetti has a natural linguistic energy, untempered by any complex ability to interpret or distil his surface sensory experiences except in terms of a set of acceptable rhetorical disconting cliches

His poetry, alas, is pinheaded. At a public reading, however, verbal impressionism is about all you can take in given the pace required of the spoken word. So Ferlinghetti is good value as an entertainer-poet.

Ginsberg is not only good value. He's a theatrical genius.

And like all good professional performers he gives of himself unstintingly. He adores his vast huge hairy audience and he'll work for them until the dawn comes up like thunder. His message is simplicity itself. The world is a beautiful and holy place. Except when it's ugly and awful and brutalised by those who don't love the beautiful people. The evangelical ethos is remarkably akin to the special salvation preached by Jehovah's Witnesses.

What a superlative witness Ginsberg is! He is the master of the accidental happening on purpose. He plays his harmonium amidst a confusion of guitars and sitars, bouncing on his behind with the resilience of a port wine and cannabis jelly. He sings poems by William Blake, and in a cunning progressive graduation from mantra to country and western.

Ours not to be querulous that William Blake doesn't need the country and western tune-making of Allen Ginsberg. Everything is innocent, loving and community sing-song. One would be a proper purist idiot to act the literary nark.

Ginsberg is the lapsed kantor from the synagogues of New York. Who cares that he now redirects this Jewish talent through the musical paraphernalia of the West Coast gurus, the endless spurious maharishis spawned in oddball America since way back when Christopher Isherwood was a pup?

Ginsberg has happily found that he has barrel-chested chanting virtues; and surprise, surprise, that true poetic forms are most properly to be derived from the natural breathing patterns of the human organism.

Ginsberg is at the Town Hall to create surface joy and surface agony, to make us feel we've had a nice night's transcendental entertainment. He does it well, willingly, fervently, in full charge of his audience.

I am sure no one else but this loveable propagator of unthinking emotional reflexology could have got away with hauling three tribal Aboriginal song-men on to the Town Hall stage to provide one-third of the evening's festivities.

It probably didn't occur to dear old Ginsie that it might be patronising in the extreme to suggest to Australians that they take notice of Aboriginal mythology after an experience of this country which had been going on for all of seventy-two hours.

I doubt if Ginsie discussed with anyone whether it is the practice in Australia to exploit the Aboriginal as either a sideshow attraction or to submit his pristine tribal song conventions to the alien and corrupting influences of a white man's Town Hall Saturday night entertainment. I know I wouldn't introduce a Balinese troupe of Ramayana dancers into a Denpasar night club! I just wouldn't have the elan to get away with it.

On the other hand Ginsberg had everyone happy, including the Aboriginals who unfortunately revelled in the attention. True enough, that great Aboriginal musicologist, Dr Catherine Ellis, looked faintly discomforted up on the crowded stage, as did the anthropologist accompanying the song-men. But how could any harm come from it all when everyone is loving everyone else so abandonedly? Tush! And pish!

Let's not be churlish. Ginsberg is the true Jesus freak of dissident youth, and his theatre craft deserves plaudits as much in its own right as Sir Laurence Olivier's does in his.

As for Ginsberg's actual poetry? Not to worry. It disappeared in the balding, blinding rays of Ginsberg's midnight sun long ago.

It was there. So was Ginsberg. And Ginsberg won hands down.

# REGRADING
# THE
# SENIORS

In the 1940's there was a remarkable degree of cross-fertilisation in the arts in Australia. The now celebrated myth-making of Nolan, Boyd, Tucker and Percival was almost certainly absorbed from the Angry Penguin poets. The painters took over a set of aesthetic intentions to which they subsequently adhered firmly; and although in some cases it has taken two decades for these intentions to come good in the works of art (e.g., Albert Tucker), Australian modern painting is now mature and meaningful.

Australian poetry has had no such history. The dominant poetic convention has come to be descriptive verse of a slight and purely incidental kind, distinguished by jolly proficient craftsmanship and felicitous verbal decoration. But these descriptive landscapes illuminate nothing beyond themselves; the reader senses a faint trace of anthropomorphism and nothing more.

Any literary editor will inform you how Australia's Muse is domiciled at Birdsville. Each day's post is loaded with poems celebrating the behaviour pattern of our indigenous feathered friends. One literary magazine has banned all poems on dicky-birds for the space of one year, unless the poem be an epic from A. D. Hope on the mug galah.

Bird-watching is a poor substitute for the contemplation of the human condition. While endemic among the younger poets, and proving a fatal hobby for Douglas Stewart and Judith Wright, it is only a 'dominant poetic convention'. For James McAuley, A. D. Hope, Vincent Buckley, and the Catholic intellectual poets, birds are essentially for the table, roasted. Their insistence that poetry should be masculine, muscular, and geared to some set of intellectual or ethical values is a useful counterbalance to the thin convention of delicate, natural observation.

The only argument with the poets named is that their ratiocinative processes often fail to achieve embodiment in memorable language. They write verse rather than poetry (to assume a difference by definition).

In this kind of situation it seems irresistible to me to accord R. D. FitzGerald the stature of the most substantial living poet in Australia (Slessor having virtually retired permanently). *South-most Five*, FitzGerald's first book in eleven years, contains poetry, real poetry, mind-and-heart poetry, the poetry of sustained and ordered sensibility. The technical framework for each statement is usually sketchy, because FitzGerald is unwilling to relax his grip on the essence of what is to be said to indulge even one phrase of irrelevant adornment. It is meditative poetry, but not the expression of what is generally understood to be the mood of meditation—Wordsworth's tranquil recollection. Meditation for FitzGerald amounts to taking time off to wrestle with the angels.

It is interesting that he is not more honoured in the Australian literary sense. In this volume there are works of even greater strength than the famous 'Wing At Your Door'. The collection suggests to me, at least, that there is not a poet in Australia who can come near him for making simple language serve to communicate complex experience. With FitzGerald the process is always one of having something to say and finding the most perfect forms in which to say it. Too often, as with A. D. Hope, the preoccupation is to set out an exercise in poetic form and hope that somewhere along the line content will emerge fortuitously.

FitzGerald's content is often thought of as tortuous and convoluted. On the contrary, it is indicative of his completeness as a poet that he can at times make the most obvious observation and most beautifully establish its human significance. 'We shouldn't allow ourselves to develop fixed ideas as we get older:' this is all that the dedicatory poem 'The Tempered Chill' has to say. But observe the way the language converts this into an exposition of the intellectual temper of the whole man:

> 'Though here is evidence
> that years burr as they go
> the edge-tool of sense,
> I will not have it so.
> And surely that is enough
> to preserve the tempered chill,
> softening or wearing rough
> being failure of will.'

Although it would be more attractive to turn to the superlative imagery and agony of a major poem like 'Bog and Candle', it is an instructive exercise to see what happens when FitzGerald indulges his descriptive capacities, and compare the result with the poetry of the latter-day Douglas Stewart.

In the third of his Roadside Compositions, FitzGerald produces landscape description that excels in quiet exactitude even what such poets as Campbell or Stewart achieved in their most exalted moments.

> 'and having said
> the grass is good this year, but shows a rut
> developing here and there and looking red
> along worn sides of hills: that as I walked
> kicking up dust and powdered dung of sheep,
> a hare came loping towards me, saw me, baulked,
> crouched—then lost his nerve and fled with a leap.'

In the last stanza FitzGerald turns on the idea of this landscape-in-itself and rejects it.

> 'having said this much I know and regret my loss,
> whose eye falls short of my love for just this land,
> too turned within for the small flower in the moss
> and birds my father all but brought to his hand.'

There is nothing really to acclaim in this. But how it contrasts with the insipid and obvious preoccupations of Douglas Stewart and Judith Wright in their recent companion publications. The arch and appalling bird simplicities of the present Douglas Stewart do not seem to come from the same man who published 'The Birdsville Track'. 'Lyrebird' it would seem, was created for the Ballarat recitations, a romantic effusion which begins

> 'And cannot always—pick, pick, pick—be fluting
> And floating—pick—down there with fall and fern.'

and finishes—

> 'So round the emerald cliff and out of sight
> And filled the gully twice with silver light.'

In between, the verse is all unredeemed Tennyson. And so it is with 'Kookaburras', 'Three White Herons', 'Firetail Finches' and all the rest of the feathery creation. What was once in Stewart an authentic compulsion towards significant detail in the natural landscape has become an affectation, a studied simple-mindedness. The compulsion is gone, the proficient versifier remains. The composer of the book's blurb is convincing only himself when he claims that underlying 'their charm as Nature poems, they are explorations of the nature of man and the universe'. If only this were so!

I rather think Douglas Stewart is himself aware that he has entered a phase of dog-days of habit rather than the high summer of compulsion, from the way he has consciously and laboriously tackled the modern atomic theme in 'Rutherford', a big heroic poem. In earlier writings his chosen mythic heroes, Ned Kelly and Scott, were able to stand up to the romanticism and old-fashioned rhetoric of Stewart's style with all the stops out. The atomic scientist doesn't lend himself as a type to rhapsodic surrounds and lyrical sentiment. Stewart's 'Rutherford' rings false all the way through —much of the poetry comes through to the reader as unconsciously comic, not many distances removed from that of such Victorians as Darwin with his 'Botanic Gardens'. This is not to say that a poem could not be concerned with interpreting a man like Rutherford, but that Stewart is not the one to write it; these days he appears to lack the versatility and adaptability to find an apt language to deal with such a theme. One day Douglas Stewart may again find themes and insistent values within himself, and then we'll have poetry from him once more. But this volume is purely for the birds.

R. D. FITZGERALD: *Southmost Five*. Angus and Robertson.
DOUGLAS STEWART: *Rutherford*. Angus and Robertson.

## PATRICK WHITE'S CHARIOT

After the intense mysticism of *Voss*, Patrick White has neither lowered his sights nor plunged onwards into remoter depths of abstraction. *Riders In The Chariot* is less opaque than the previous novel; the narrative line is firmly, and sometimes excitingly, maintained so that the book may be described as easy reading in the sense that Tolstoy, Katzantzakis or Faulkner compel the reader forward. It should be said at once that this is a novel of impressive intellectual power. It is a brooding metaphysical work, large in scale and style, striking in its insights. At its best it has a crystalline beauty that one had forgotten could exist within the conventions of the novel. The total book is a brilliant conception in the technical sense—In the Interweaving of characters and the bringing together of narrative elements. White continues to probe the nuances of human feeling and to uncover concealed meanings and layers of motivation. But when a novelist allows himself no facile devices and sets down his material with the exact spiritual intensity of the poet, the chances for perfection are remote. *Riders In The Chariot* is not without its minor flaws and major breakdowns, aberrations of style and occasional failures to sustain the inner life and logic of the characters. It is as if Patrick White occasionally endured moments of exhaustion when the writing broke loose from his control. Critics may indicate failures in the novel with considerable self-satisfaction, but only by isolating the lamer conceptions and passing affectations of style from the nobility and power of the whole. From another aspect the creative stature of White shows up in relief against the occasions when control slips from his hands.

His story follows the destinies of a group of people living in the town of Sarsparilla (a locality that one inevitably associates with Castle Hill).

The characters come together geographically and spiritually as if by a mysterious ordination of events, for each of them is responding to a compulsion to find some form of self-redemption. The climax of the novel comes with the mock crucifixion at Easter of Himmelfarb by a drunken group of factory workers, and with Himmelfarb's subsequent death. Superficially the idea of an Australian crucifixion invites comparison with Katzantzakis' handling of the same theme. But despite the agonising realism and ingenuity with which White handles the whole extended crucifixion analogy, I feel that this moment is more a coda than the central incident. The search is more important than the Grail, and White's characters, brought together by the common symbolism of the Chariot, are defined by their manner of searching rather than by what they find. Personally I regret the necessity of the crucifixion analogy to give the book its final sense of 'consummatum est'.

A bare outline of this kind does faint justice to the range of White's observation. The novel is full of magnificently realised characters. While the mood of the book is typical of White, the author gives freer play than before to his social instincts. The story opens in a mood of Meredithian wit, lightened further by patches of superb comedy. The Australian years since *Voss* was written have sharpened White's already acute sense of irony, and there is even an unambiguous and relentless hatred poured out on the blunted self-satisfactions of Australia's texture-brick subtopias.

Having noted the stature of this exciting work, one is at liberty to express reservations, and there certainly are reservations to be made. It is a serious accusation that the device of a crucifixion weakens the integrity of the dominant theme. This might be a too severe impression that comes from a single reading of an exacting work, but certain stylistic devices call for less ambiguous criticism. Occasionally White becomes literary and affected, resorting to undisciplined, pretentious writing:

'The tram was easing through the city which knives had sliced open to serve up with all the juices running—red, and green, and purple. All the syrups of the sundaes oozing into the streets to sweeten.
'The blue-haired grannies had purpled from the roots of their hair down to the ankles of their pants, not from shame, but neon, as their breasts chafed to escape, from shammy-leather, back to youth, or roundly asserted themselves, like chamber pots in concrete.'

Such prestidigitatory cleverness is unworthy of a fine stylist. This is also a peculiarly Patrick White device, which one can classify as 'the paragraphic addendum'. This idiosyncrasy is frequently most effective and highly faithful to perceptual thinking modes.

'Alone is not the same,' Mrs Flack would usually reply. And smile.
'It is very comfortable,' she said. But did falter slightly.
'That makes it more frightening,' she cried. And burst suddenly into tears.

The device has become part of White's conventional language. His ear has become unconscious of it and the reader is required to become similarly unaware. But this is easier said than done. The over-exploitation makes it irritating; not because it is idiosyncratic but because it is used whether or not the passage calls for little explosions of afterthought. It is there even when a limpid fluency of prose is demanded by the content of the moment. One suspects it is a bad habit, a literary nose-picking, tolerable but not desirable. *Riders In The Chariot* wears a number of such blemishes. Privately, and for no small-minded reason, one is rather glad that it does.

# MEMOIRS OF A SAINTLY MAN

I have steered clear of educational theory in the course of my thunderings. This is not because of any animadversion to education on my part, but the subject is so grossly over-written that I've avoided it like the plague.

Confessionals, however, I am prone to.

The autobiographical treat in store for you was inspired by a rhapsodic piece by Dany Humphreys on the open class-room.

It seems that at Geelong Grammar they have had an open classroom for six years. In this open environment the angelic progeny of the Victorian gentry begin the day by organising their school-work by themselves and in accord with their own inclinations. Boys are scattered through the house. Some read by the fire. Some, cop this, are researching in the library. Some play chess. 'Lorraine,' and I quote, 'is hearing Joe read, and there are two in the linen press hearing each other spelling.' Gawd, how naive can pedagogues get!

The theory behind this splendid arrangement is that 'children are naturally curious and want to find things out'. I'll certainly not dispute this fact with my columnist colleague, but by what contortion of mind does she conclude that natural curiosity includes algebra, geography and spelling?

No doubt Dany Humphreys has irrefutable evidence that through natural curiosity the little darlings of Geelong Grammar Prep School programme themselves diurnally to sweat through algebraic equations and or 'Little Nell', etc.

My own evidence is autobiographical, and is argumentative only in that it promulgates that hoary old canard about juvenile human nature being much the same from generation to generation.

I have become in the ripeness of time, a saintly man. Ask anyone—from the Reverend Roger Bush to Phillip Adams, to name but a few thousand.

On reflection I realise that I have become a man for all Australian seasons not through educational indulgence of my natural curiosity as a child, but through the rigid disciplinarian learnings to which I was subjected greatly against my will and in distinct defiance of my natural lack of curiosity about certain subjects.

Take Scripture for example. At the Mount Gambier Baptist Sunday School my natural curiosity was much directed towards the invisible sexual equipment of Chrissie Ireland,

Dahlia Von Stanke, and I seem to recall a latterday Bellbird lady, Carmel Millhouse. Given the open schoolroom approach I would have educated myself enthusiastically in this area of human knowledge, and had this learning instinct been indulged you might well at this moment be reading the words of a pioneering child sex maniac!

As it was, I was subject to a relentless biblical and cathechistic disciplinarianism.

This frustration of natural sexual prurience in favour of the Bible led to latterday school glories which I don't regret even to this day.

I went on to become the first atheist to top the Collegiate School of Saint Peter in the Scripture examinations, and with a mark of 100 out of 100. It was a matter of some distress to the school governors; taken as a personal punishment from the deity by the quiverful of clerical chalkies who instructed us in the subject; and it influenced certain naive lads of my own age that atheism must surely be the path splendid to Christian salvation.

On the other hand we did have a sort of open classroom libertarianism in mathematics. We sort of programmed ourselves. Perversely perhaps, my natural curiosity directed itself towards the mathematics of betting on the gallopers. A natural curiosity, surely, for a child who came from a gambling family, and therefore perfectly in accord with the Dany Humphreys' theory.

I became the St Peter's College bookmaker, and since this was the year that Wotan won the Melbourne Cup at unheard-of outside odds, I really made a killing. This, no doubt, laid the grounds for later and idealistic belief in economic reformism.

But I think most of all of the maths results. A maths master, depraved enough to tamper with the immortal words of Dryden, wrote on my annual report: 'Some boys to some faint meaning make pretence, but this fool Harris never deviates into sense.'

I suffered, of course, for the self-educative pleasures of the open classroom in later years. At university it cost five years, and the nervous collapse of some half-dozen tutors before I accidentally got a pass figure for first-year pure mathematics.

But I think most of all of the disciplinarian virtues when I contemplate compulsory organised sport. No open classroom approach on the playing fields of our Eton. You played Aussie football in winter or you got thumped. You missed practice, and you got thumped.

I possessed no child-like, wide-eyed curiosity about football. Didn't fit Dany Humphreys' concept one little bit. Besides, I was small, light, but fortunately fast.

For the sake of sheer self-preservation I became a champion little rover, with a strong left-foot kick and remarkable cunning around the packs. I compensated for size by becoming a dirty little rover, expert in the trip the umpire couldn't spot, sharking from my own, not the opposition's rucks, and brilliant in the melodramatics of staging a free kick. My style was greatly admired.

From this coercive education in football I learned most of the things which have made me the fully-rounded Renaissance Australian man I'm acknowledged to be today. It's all very well to be other-worldly, a poet, a Goethe, a sensitive plant, but to combine these reflective qualities with all the Vance Packard techniques to scramble up the social pyramid, there you have consolidated all the qualities of greatness and modern saintliness.

From the sports master who thumped kids and the moral qualities of our national game, I learned all the cunnings which pass as virtue, dynamism, acumen, and ambition in the industrial Australia of today. I can write poetry. I can also give a business competitor a slight push in the back when he's under the economic ball, ready to take a mark. God bless the disciplinarians of yesteryear!

We now totter on to the university as an open classroom, as it has become in the tutorial system of today. The students shamble out of the open classroom at school to the open situation of the university, intellectually pinheaded, but radically convinced of their egalitarian cerebral endowment. University staff bow to this pressure of the times, and effect a tutorial atmosphere of equal endowment and expertise. Malformed embryonic viewpoints and ideologies are received with servile respect and solemn seriousness.

No-one is to blame for this nullification of learning as the prime purpose of the operation. If a lecturer were to come the raw prawn over the egotism of student ignorance, it would be salutory in terms of intellectual process, in terms of challenge and confrontation. But the result would be the occupation of the administration block, ferocious SRC meetings, and a resounding demand for participating student democracy. After the sacking of the lecturer, that is.

In my day, says he geriatrically, I came under the mentorship of the Oxford don, J. I. M. Stewart (who is also the novelist, Michael Innes). It was his wont to contemplate a tutorial group of students as if a tin of stagnant worms had been placed beneath his aristocratic nostrils. It was his pleasure to carve us up one by one for every loose theory, generalisation or romantic exaggeration.

This nasty academic disciplinarianism has gone the way of all non-flesh.

But, as I recall, it was our savage pleasure to try to take this shrill and gaily-plumaged rooster and decapitate him. To find an illiteracy in a Michael Innes novel and throw it back at him. To insist on quoting Kafka when Kafka was unknown. To slurp an eminent foreign linctus called Canadiol to distract his thought in mid-flight.

We worms were forever turning. And this, I think, had something profoundly to do with the creative processes of education.

Alas, the open-classroom exponents from Geelong Grammar can easily dispose of this antique belief as a load of old cobblers.

Education is not nowadays conceived to create saintly Renaissance fellows like myself. You don't walk through flames, undergo the trials of the Spartans, battle away to forge an identity. Thereby becoming adept in the ways of the world and with ideals for a better world.

You just waddle off to the Geelong Grammar linen press with Lorraine and hear her spelling.

Look, somebody's got to be joking about this open classroom. I don't want to hear about it from Dany Humphreys.

I may be saintly, but I'm also cynical. I'd just like to hear from Lorraine to find out exactly how her spelling is getting along in that little old cosy linen closet.

# A
# WORLD
# WE MUST ENDURE

**TILL WE DIE** The literary merits of Kurt Vonnegut's *Slaughterhouse Five* are insufficient to explain the adulatory Vonnegut cult that has swept through the campuses of America and through the older liberal humanist communities on both sides of the Atlantic.

The memorability, the absolute rightness of *Slaughterhouse Five*, doesn't derive from qualities that the bamboozled literary critics can properly analyse. It's a novel. Of a kind. It's an anti-war book. Sort of. It's a sort of creative masterpiece. In one sense of the word. The British reviewers have handled it with tongs and gloves—holding it at a respectable, almost myopic, distance.

It is perhaps the temper of Vonnegut's mind that has triumphed over the generation gap. If he has written an anti-war book, it is unlike any other anti-war book. It is possessed of a wry fatalism, a gallows-humour, and it is devastatingly deficient in either statements of anger or self-pity. Billy Pilgrim, the tattered hero of the work, looks like a Coca-Cola bottle, endures violence, tolerates death, moves with uncomprehending simplicity through a disordered world.

But, ultimately, he is incorruptible. He is the distillation of that unconquerable passivity which in the end is the only thing which can defeat the endless brutalism of humanity. So it goes.

Vonnegut himself, who has grown old over a slow typewriter, lived for seventeen years in his one suburbia, raised the kids, measured his life in cigarette packets, would be wildly diverted by the suggestion that he is himself a kind of existential Mahatma Gandhi, a high priest of the simple philosophy that the world has to be endured.

The paradox, of course, is how a book of this kind, no anti-war book at all in the obvious sense of the word, can suddenly become a Bible for a generation of desperate young political activists. And for the enlightened among their parental generation.

Richard Aldington's formative anti-war epic, *Death of a Hero*, worked from a bitter and relentless anger. Hasek invented Schweik to demonstrate the vast and mechanical stupidity of the military apparatus. *Catch-22* defines war as a surreal farce which the individual can destroy by refusing to believe in it. These classic works served their own times and contexts.

Vonnegut's is the only recent work which really sub-
serves the disoriented agony of the contemporary young,
and the passive frustrations of the old.

Vonnegut was present at the most senseless and appalling massacre of modern warfare—the destruction of
Dresden. But he was down below, not above; an American
POW who survived the fire storms because he and his
fellow-prisoners were locked in a slaughterhouse. He has
been non-writing this incredible experience for twenty-five
years. 'Write an anti-war book? One might just as well write
an anti-glacier book.'

In the interim, his careering imagination established a
name for him in the science fiction field. SF addicts place
*Player Piano* among the few masterpieces the genre has
produced. The beginnings of Vonnegut's unaffected and
disturbingly casual fatalism were discerned by some readers
and critics in his delightful but neglected *God Bless You,
Mr Rosewater*.

When the time for *Slaughterhouse* finally arrived, it refused to assume the proper shape for a novel, the integrated themes for a manifesto. Partly personal memoirs of
the Dresden inferno, overtly the progress of an unbelieving
pilgrim; launching off sporadically into the outer spaces of
lunar satire, it mysteriously turned out in the end to have
the perfect shape for a contemporary readership.

Which brings us back to readership and the Vonnegut
cults, particularly among students both radical and square.

Revolutionary romanticism directed against the corporate
State is not of the stuff that endures. It colours and heightens
undergraduate life, provides a form of expression for simplistic idealism, and it justifies emotionalism at a post-
pubescent age when the young haven't the time, nor the
inclination, to submit themselves to the slow acquiring of
ordered intellectual positions.

But it's not all a time of wine, roses and slogans. Both
romantic radicalism and, even more importantly, rational
and responsible student political dissent bring the young
very close to the world's hostility and brutalism. Remember
Kent. They come to discover the blind and ruthless forces
of society which are operating through the paranoic
American psyche in Vietnam, through the Russian brand of
cold-blooded cynicism in the Middle East.

As daredevil and hellbent as the young might seem, they
don't shrug off this manifest hostility of an outside world
that makes war, not love. They are afraid of it. They don't
know how to deal with it as a human phenomenon. They
have no philosophy to guide their desperate ideology of

confrontation. There's no answer to this personal dilemma to be found in Guevara, Fanon, or Marcuse.

One was beginning to be proud of the Australian sense of order and tolerance over the moratorium, but, at the last minute, the sibilants of hatred, the aspirants of Red-baiting came pouring uselessly from Government politicians.

These gentry destroyed the climate of the civilised condition simply to indulge in an explosion of animus.

But hatred in the end always seems to be the most dearly loved of the emotions.

And this is the world that *Slaughterhouse Five* is concerned with. It has to be endured. Until you die. So it goes.

This wry message has got through to the young. It is the sort of sad humanistic message they have been wanting to hear. What Vonnegut learned sitting helplessly over his typewriter for twenty-five years after Dresden is that all of us Billy Pilgrims, young and old, are afraid of humanity. The great communicatory triumph of *Slaughterhouse Five* as a literary work is that it helps us to live with that fear.

Until we die. So it goes.

# WALLOWING
# IN A
# DISMAL
**TROUGH**   The time has surely come for sharp dialogues and
fairly ferocious confrontations.

The critical boys are broken-spined with bending over
backwards. Let's put the thesis without equivocation.

Most current art is affectation, posturing. It is non-com-
munication based on minimal talent, nugatory sensibility,
and the preening conviction that an idiot ideology is sufficient to bluff the gallery directors, the critics and the public,
into submission.

In consequence, critics, like Allan McCulloch and Laurie
Thomas, who don't want to be deemed fuddy-duddies, do
more evasive fancy footwork than a Cassius Clay.

Most of the poetry coming from the young is undisciplined emotional regurgitation, an outlet for subjective
romanticism, a splendid therapy but desperately gauche
when enshrined in all the solemnity of print.

I wouldn't know about current music.

Most creative cinematic expression at the experimental
level partakes of the egocentric emotional and aesthetic
indulgences of the poets and the artists in equal measure.

These intemperate and wide-ranging reflections were trig-
gered by a heroic project undertaken by Channel Nine in
South Australia. The station is showing some thirty experimental, non-professional films, and offering a $1000 prize
for the best. The judging panel is headed by Kym Bonython
and a collection of terrifyingly naive but passionate film
buffs.

Of the first three films put to air, the children of the fifth
form at Sydney Boys' High School shot to a commanding
lead because of their direct wit, honest trying with the
camera, and the elementary lucidity of their spoof.

Against this Homicide-inspired piece of schoolboy fun,
there was set the inevitable abstract brief piece devoted to
those wearily over-exploited shapes of the Sydney Opera
House. Music perforce by Bach.

Then an incredible feature called Bucke Shotte by some
ex-Commonwealth Film Unit character called Peter Weir.
For extravagant boredom, infantile surrealism and disjointed
continuity, this simplistic creation will take a lot of stacking
in the twenty-seven self-expressive films that threaten to
follow on our late-night telly box.

The fact of the matter is surely that we are in the dismal
trough of an arty-crafty age, a period of creativity for crea-

tivity's sake, being subjected to acts of self-expression which call for few organised talents or intellectual skills. To say is enough. To have something to say is an irrelevancy.

Poetry is the easiest theme to discuss because it is the least corrupted.

These days, the grass-roots lust for bad poetry is forgiveable. The young pop addicts acquire the saccharine lofty thoughts of Rod McKuen's *Listen to the Warm* and *Stanyan Street* with a great deal more enthusiasm than their grandparents purchased giftlet editions of the pearls of Ella Wheeler Wilcox. The McKuen cult is cheering in that it shows pop-addiction does not require the total extinction of verbal response!

At the other end of the spectrum, the outpourings of Leonard Cohen inspire the sophisticates and drop-out-minded young with an idiom that is entirely unexamined emotional indulgence.

Those more seriously committed to poetry of the moment, having rejected the decibel level of Ginsberg and Ferling-hetti, are thumbing through *Children of Albion—Poetry of the Underground*, a collation of the more recognised of the unrecognised young verse writers and speakers. Australia has, by comparison and for its population size, an impressive range of 'underground' talents, explosive young free expressionists who are sweeping the ageing poetic establishment to one side. They have a mature champion and most respected mentor in Thomas Shapcott, who carried out the impeccable compilation for *Sun Australian Poetry Now*.

This necessary young movement is not without talent. Young poets are emerging at a moment when we are all coming to realise that the established names in Australian poetry have become boring, insistent, repetitive and irrelevant. Only in A. D. Hope can the voice of the late Yeats be heard in the land.

Queensland University Press has sensed the new situation, and its poetry paperback series is doing for the Australian dissenting poetic tradition what Cape Goliard is doing overseas.

For all these positives, there remains the hard-core fact that young poets are rushing like Gadarene swine towards their great, muddy, emotional wallow. And there is no critical apparatus, no ideology, no set of views about the properties of words, to keep the mass of meandering, formless, post-pubescent meditations out of print.

What's worse, we all have to pretend that it's beaut or that it has its place.

Otherwise, we are Philistine hangovers from the birdies-and-beasties era of formal, modern Australian verse. With a gloriously inaccurate historical instinct, James McAuley had only to produce a book called *The End of Modernity* and one knew that a new generation would instantly heave the whole load of anathema overboard. A. D. Hope had only to produce his impeccable essay on free verse as non-poetry for the pleasure of his ageing readers, and the age of free verse would be upon us. And out of all this academic dogmatism Australia's only international reputation had come to be one of freakish and unique poetic dreardom.

How in this sorry context can one now attack the play-poetry, word-waffle, and urky underlying sentimentalism of the contemporary output?

One can only insist, at risk of abuse or scorn, that poetry must be both effective and significant communication, irrespective of form, and that it is the word 'significant' that has to be thrashed out definitionally by the young poets; between us and the young poets.

Even so, poetry suffers less air pollution than almost any of the arts.

The murk lies thickest around the activity of the current artists. It is here the polemic should be fiercest.

Some weeks ago, Sidney Nolan and I wandered around the international kinetic exhibition at the South Bank Heyward Galleries in London, a display that cost $60,000 to mount in terms of electronic gear. We threw nails at random on to a magnetised sheet, made a plastic jelly wobble through an electric foot control, went through all the sideshows of an electronic fun fair. I kept thinking that art, as I am prepared to define it, is a piece of space haunted by a human presence.

This enormous display could be satisfactory only to the untutored young, for whom pure surface sensory effects are big deal all on their own.

I also kept thinking what do Laurie T. and Allan McC. say when they come up against this ingenious load of old electronic cobblers. The art world is one great spurious mess.

It is possibly the moment for the backlash effect, to abandon the fancy footwork, to stand up and punch it out. If not, a cunningly materialistic society will eliminate that dangerously effective saboteur in its midst, the creative mind, and instead everyone can be his own artist or poet or filmmaker, producing psychological placebos to cure minor conformist disorders.

# POLITICS
# MUST
# BE
# TABOO HERE!

I should like to raise my tiny voice over a literary matter that has had some publicity but which is certainly not familiar material in any far-flung outpost of the Australian empire.

It appears that the Russians have published a substantial anthology of the Australian poets in Russian translation and that James McAuley's work has been excluded 'for civic and political considerations'.

This pronunciamento was made in the Soviet News Bulletin put out by the Russian Embassy in Canberra.

McAuley has written savagely about this astonishing way of conducting literary affairs in the current issue of *Quadrant*, but I think the matter merits a wider airing in the public Press.

I rather fancy that my own work has been excluded from the massive Russian anthology, but probably this has been motivated by an antipathy to 'modernism' which the Russians and James McAuley share in equal measure. Fair enough.

But I agree with James McAuley that the exclusion of a poet on non-literary grounds is about as frightening an exercise in what McAuley calls 'the politicisation of literature' as one could possibly imagine.

The most frightening thing about it is that it is so stupid a gesture, devised to defeat by virtue of one rigid bone-headed editorial piece of corruption, whatever goodwill the Russian interest in Australian literature could have created.

It reveals appallingly how little the Russians in Russia or in Canberra know of the literary process in the Western world, whether the literary individual is of left, right, centre or no political persuasion.

The only two communist writers I know are Frank Hardy and Judah Waten, and I don't imagine that either of these blokes, committed as they are, would take up any challenge to justify the pronouncement in the Soviet News Bulletin.

It is so much a rule of thumb in our literary world that the inherent literary merit of any piece of creative writing is the critical determinant, that the inclusion or exclusion of an individual's work because of his views and activities outside literature is a thought that wouldn't enter any editor's head.

I edited this year's *Australian Poetry* for Angus and Robertson. It is a fact that some of the best poetry is being written by individuals who are possessed of a fierce hatred for my brand of liberal humanism.

It is also a fact that some poetry which I sincerely deemed to be of an indifferent calibre came from poets I like very much as human beings. These factors were of the most complete irrelevance.

This principle of total and automatic critical fidelity to the work presented went, I found, even further.

One has to move right outside the limitations of one's own special prejudices and predilections about poetic form and content, and to assess fairly an unsympathetic poetic form or genre as a creative achievement within its specific set of intentions.

One does not adopt an automatic critical reflex of negativism when a poem is in free verse or Augustan pastiche because one happens not to be attuned to that particular form.

The point is, that I cannot imagine any editor or anthologist doing otherwise.

I would be perfectly content to have my work assessed editorially by James McAuley. I don't think he would be unduly worried by my performing the editorial role.

The Russians, I think, have been thoroughly misled by what some of the more unsophisticated of our literateurs refer to as Australia's literary gang-warfare.

They don't realise the parry-and-thrust on ideological and critical issues goes so deep and no deeper.

When members of our literary community look as if they are wielding stone age clubs on each other, it is not clear to outsiders that matters of judgment are involved, and not matters of creative integrity.

The Russians have obviously assumed the various divisions of the Australian literary community go all the way, and that 'the deliberate exclusion of James McAuley for civic and political considerations' will win approbation in some quarters.

They have notably failed to realise that despite the hubbub of literary politics in this country, they will not find one voice, even among extreme leftists, to support their appalling idea that you can cast aside your literary and intellectual integrity, and leave out a good poet because of his political stance.

If there is one such voice I should be fascinated to hear it.

# OUR
# MOST
# SUCCESSFUL
# FAILURE?
Australia has produced a goodly crop of anti-heroes.

Our whole national mythology is based on the anti-heroic event, the deeds of battlers at Gallipoli, Tobruk, Eureka, deeds that call for neither caps, bells, nor celebration, but rather the satisfaction that one more set of battlers has given it a go.

The myth of our egalitarian Australianism is dying a rapid death, but the folk legends of a young people die harder.

In fact, why should the Australian legend die at all? The more we fit the common cloth of an international modernity the more we may be disposed to contemplate the dour and yet strangely inspiring existentialism of our sparse collection of hero-figures.

And who better fits this idealised mirror-image of the Australian as he-who-succeeds-out-of-failure than Henry Lawson, whose centenary we are celebrating in a modest fashion?

When Peter Larsen met Louisa Albury at the Pipeclay diggings near Mudgee in the 1860's, the scene was already set for a grim tale. The father who was content with a migratory bush life, and the deeply resentful Louisa who had urgent visions of a life less gross than survival housekeeping in the Australian bush in 1867, led to the nervous uncertainties of the small boy who went out bush carpentering with his father.

These were not diminished by a severe deafness which struck him at the age of fourteen and remained with him for the rest of his life.

Drought, poverty and his mother's deep-seated hatred of bush life created both recessive and imaginative tendencies in the young Henry. When his mother parted from his father and rented a small cottage in Phillip Street, the environmental surrounds were not altered that much for an impressionable adolescent.

The urban misery of Sydney was not concealed beneath any veneer of prosperity and everything suggested that failure is the common outcome of human aspiration as Henry followed his mother through socialism, suffrage, radical republicanism, to the pitiful escape worlds of spiritualism.

Young Lawson must have looked and sounded as much a no-hoper as he felt. Showing little aptitude for intellectual processes he groped from one casual job to another. From the little packing-case room he had built himself at the back of the house he sent off his first verses to *The Bulletin*, and they were accepted with some enthusiasm.

The success story began after the grim bush apprenticeship?

Hardly!

Henry was trying to fight his way out of deaf-shyness and into the company of men up in the Blue Mountains, and he found a way of a sort. Booze.

However, his literary break-through eventually led him, not perhaps out of poverty, but out of his ambivalent relationship with bush life into the simpler squalors of radical journalism and into contact with hard-hitting editors like Archibald. In his knockabout battle for a crust up to 1895 there was a new dimension in being one of the battlers.

He was also a writer, one of the lucky ones who could distil the bitterness of daily experience into social communication.

A writer who is read is never alone.

He married Bertha Bredt, a trainee nurse, and Henry led her his usual grim peripatetic dance from Sydney to Perth to New Zealand and back to Sydney; and then in 1900 off with borrowed money to try his growing literary luck in England.

Two years brought him a modicum of major publication, but also an increasing alcoholic intake, a splintering marriage and the usual nostalgia.

At thirty-six Lawson found himself back in Sydney, separated from his wife, emptied of ambition and application, bankrupt and a sporadic alcoholic. The pristine spirit had gone out of his writing. He drifted around the *Bulletin* offices to cadge a few bob for booze.

The noble and the loyal in the literary scene rallied over the surviving years and made all manner of efforts to rehabilitate the cynical, unhappy, yet charming hobo of letters. But Lawson had carved his destiny too precisely. At fifty-five he was found dead in a backyard.

Fortunately the unalleviated gloom of Lawson's life is not the basis of the Lawson legend.

It is rather the work itself.

And in the critical examination of Lawson's output lies a problem for the more sophisticated readers in this centenary year.

Was Lawson really a great writer? Or was he a regional innovator whose work struck a responsive chord at a time when the Australians were struggling to assert and believe in a national identity? Through a great deal of his writing there is facility, sentimentality and complete intellectual slightness, but Lawson often saves the situation with his sense of the ironic, the flash of humour and the enchanting credibility of his characterisations.

But this is not enough in a writer whose very name symbolises the highest historical achievements in an 'Australian' literature. This is only to say really that his writings were not actually bad.

It is also a failure to understand the processes of writing and what happens to writers who are creative and who must also produce an endless commercial output in order to live. These days the writer can be spare of output, disciplining, controlling and setting his own standards of achievement.

Bitter, twisting poverty is never a real element in the writer's human situation.

In consequence there is a tendency to judge a writer by all that he has written rather than by the best that he has written.

In her usual scrupulous way, Judith Wright summed up our feelings in 1967: 'In the thirty or forty sketches and tales by which he is remembered he did touch greatness and it is of a wholly individual kind.'

The 'touching of greatness' is exactly what one feels about Lawson. The outsider or the formal critic can dispose of Lawson's verse as almost wholly lacking that interpretative process by which significant experience is perfectly formulated. As he lacked hearing so he seems to have lacked some unspecific dimension of poetic sensibility. He possessed sincerity, sensibility and a facility in versifying. But he was not a great poet as the world understands greatness in poetry.

In his prose pieces, however, there were occasions when everything clicked into place, when style, themes and technique were wholly integrated, and the result is a perfect and satisfying interpretation of a specific Australian, and human situation.

These accidental meetings with perfection are, to me, enough.

There is the touching of greatness, and this is rewarding. For Lawson was also a battler as a writer, as well as a battler as a social human being.

There is nothing wayward or provincial in paying tribute to achievement which lacks consistency or scale. Marcus Clark's journalism does not detract whatever merit subsists in his one major novel. In fact, if we are to cling to the national legend there is something peculiarly generous and truthful in the Australian situation that we pay tribute to a talent that fought its way to the edge of genius in thirty or forty stories.

This kind of assessment may be cold comfort to those fine editors, Dr Colin Roderick and Mr Cecil Mann, and, in passing, to those fine publishers, Angus and Robertson, who have sponsored and sustained the necessary industry which even now is still bringing all of Lawson's work together.

Dr Roderick may well argue, and he does so persuasively, that Lawson's greatness lies in the comprehensive humanism of his writing. Dr Roderick may well be right and I rather think he is.

But a completely humanistic temperament is an achievement of the person and not of the writer as an exponent of creative perfection. If Lawson was a sentimentalist as a writer he was a wholesome sentimentalist, but that same motivation destroyed occasionally the truth of what he attempted to depict.

Where and how Lawson 'touched the edges' in complete literary achievement is not finally determined. We have to know the whole conspectus of his literary output, and it was in Lawson's centenary year that Dr Roderick's first volume of the definitive verse appeared. Cecil Mann's three-volume collected short stories had already been published.

Australia's celebrations may not be all that spectacular apart from the modest Lawson festival. But the Lawson scholars have done the old battler proud on our behalf. The present set of publications is worth any amount of public clap-clap-clap.

Whether in all honesty some of us can accord Lawson the literary stature Dr Roderick would wish for him, nonetheless we are endlessly grateful to the editors and publishers who have brought together a definitive Lawson, each volume of which has borne the stamp of modest yet authoritative scholarship.

# AN EDITOR COMPLETE WITH A CONSCIENCE

Editors were big fish in the days of Stephens of *The Bulletin*; in more recent years there's been a constant arboriferation of journals; editors come and go.

Only Clem Christesen and Stephen Murray-Smith have endured, providing the only constant guidelines to the evolution of Australian writing through their respective journals. Each has in his own way been important to the establishment of new literary reputations and to the climate of intellectual life.

Yet the age is too competitive for either of them to be other than shadowy figures outside established literary circles. Their sphere of influence is contracting as intellectual life is fragmented into splinter groups.

*Meanjin's* long and solid contribution to Australian literature is the better known. Stephen Murray-Smith and *Overland* are known in the public area, but the long-range contribution of both the man and his journal are greatly under-appreciated.

Stephen Murray-Smith is that fine and rare thing in Australia—the complete man of conscience. Add to this the fact that he is the warmest, most enthusiastic and most generous personality who ever stood centre position in any Australian situation, and you have just about got the complete picture of the man. He never plays literary lions, he never editorialises to his contributors, he is naturally predisposed to the act of responding to the written word. In short, he's the perfect audience.

This makes him sound a paragon of editors, which he nearly is. Enthusiasm, curiosity, and an eagerness to find gold in any soil is the prerequisite of the good editor, and Murray-Smith has all these virtues in abundance.

Murray-Smith was one of that band of rebels which Geelong Grammar produced and which included Russell Drysdale, Geoffrey Dutton and John Manifold. Unlike these more deliberate rebels, he was genuinely never at ease in the context of the establishment and, unlike them, he retains not even a residual tolerance for the social pretenders.

Murray-Smith developed a love affair with the Australian Left and *Overland* was produced out of this commitment. It owed its initial success to bulk trade union purchases, but Murray-Smith's love of the Australian Left was never very easy, even in its enthusiastic heyday.

The man of conscience, and an intellectual into the bargain, never fits the pattern comfortably, and the unease of it all is evident in the long, inflammable, love-hate relationship between Murray-Smith and the ebullient but orthodox Judah Waten. Murray-Smith's great crisis of conscience came with Hungary, and produced a new but rather lost liberal Left, with Dr Ian Turner as the fulcrum.

But, even before Hungary, I could sense in Murray-Smith a different and non-political conflict. His passion was for writing and writers. His backward search was and is for an inspirational Australian dream. He found it most of all in *Such is Life*. He surrounded *Overland* with a coterie of writers, to whom he gave personal loyalties that seemed to transcend his political commitments. This group was politically nondescript, vaguely and fuzzily to the Left. They were appallingly individualistic—Turner, David Martin, Laurence Collinson, Dorothy Hewitt, on and on.

It was clear that if it ever came to a crisis of conscience, Murray-Smith would never be cast into any kind of wilderness. He would never fight on from a new position. The god that failed Murray-Smith was not the god that failed Koestler. *Overland* continued to flourish after Hungary, and Murray-Smith was able to concentrate on a larger and more inclusive view of his editorial role.

He was, and is, fortunate in his domestic relationships. He and his wife, Nita, complement each other in their eagerness not only to recognise but to embrace the unknown writer and his modest manuscript. All other literary journals of reputation have concentrated on holding that reputation by an obsession with 'names'.

It is argued that name-obsession is a necessary survival technique for little magazines in the context of Australia's small circulations. *Overland* was too modestly framed to have to be overly concerned with pursuing celebrated contributors. It has proved, in the reasonably long run, that this modesty of purpose was the best survival tactic of all. *Overland* still survives with Stephen Murray-Smith at the helm.

But now Murray-Smith is in his mellow years, allowing himself only the occasional sensation of letting rip publicly with the four-letter word in the Melbourne Town Hall. He developed late, academically, in the area of education theory and now wears a doctorate, albeit very sloppily. He also discovered late the critic buried in the enthusiast, and in recent years has become one of the sharpest and least bluffable of the critical evaluators.

Even so, after discovering his public feet after stumbling through two decades of Australian Left history, it is Murray-Smith as the private individual who will perhaps best survive in the records of Australian writing. One inevitably thinks of him as the editor scurrying from occasion to occasion, meeting to meeting, seminar to seminar.

There is, he'll surely forgive me for remarking, a comic and ant-like freneticism about the busy scurry of his life. He'll have a ready answer. The proof of the foraging is in the publishing. *Overland* has just published Dorothy Hewitt's *Windmill Country*, a verse collection that's been acclaimed widely and which has proved a sell-out. There weren't many editors who recognised the makings of a significant talent over the years in Dorothy Hewitt. But there was one. Guess who?

# LONDON
# INSULTS
# OUR

**BEST**   Some years ago the balloon went up with a vengeance
on the conflict which had long been marked by antipathy
and indignation between Australian writers and the London
literary coteries.

The occasion was a letter from the poet, Geoffrey Dutton,
to thirty of Australia's leading writers, informing them that
their collective work in the fields of poetry, short-story and
criticism had fallen below the minimum standard required
by the British Penguin organisation for a projected series of
New Writing books.

Dutton had been commissioned by Anthony Godwin,
chief editor of Penguin Books in England, to assemble an
*Australian New Writing* and he got together a pretty potent
string of contributors: A. D. Hope, Hal Porter, Patrick White,
David Campbell, Judith Wright, Randolph Stow, Charles
Higham, James McAuley, Vincent Buckley, H. P. Heseltine
and so on.

One out of every four contributions had previously been
published in *Meanjin*.

Godwin, in rejecting the collection, stated that it was of
'far too low a standard for us to publish'. He found the 'only
ones of any real standard' were those of Patrick White and
Randolph Stow (both published in Britain and both Penguin
authors) and James Murray (his first published effort).

Dutton then procured the report by Francis Hope who had
been asked by Penguins to appraise the manuscript. Francis
Hope is assistant editor of the *New Statesman* and someone
for whom Penguins say they have a high regard.

This report rubbishes most of Australia's accepted writers
and is worth quoting at some length.

After admitting that he is no expert on the Australian
literary scene and has only studied one Australian magazine
with care (*Quadrant*), Hope says:

> 'This writing combines the vices of parochialism and an
> attempted superiority about parochial society; it is like a
> school magazine in which the school's few intellectuals
> parade their dislike of the school, but betray their in-
> ability to think beyond it.
>
> 'There are, of course, a few exceptions. But half-a-dozen
> Cookaburras (Hope's spelling) don't make a summer, and
> furthermore, these redeeming contributions are mostly by
> names too well established already (White, A. D. Hope,

Stow, Judith Wright) to make any impact as "new writing".'

In addition to the above writers he excepts Robert Hughes from his general criticism and then gets down to cases.

Taking prose first, he says all the stories suffer from the fact that other people have gone a great deal further in the same direction before.

*Surprise* (Hugh Atkinson), for example, doesn't strike me as more than a clumsy attempt at Maugham . . . and Peter Mather's *A Description* says nothing that Salinger and even Ray Croshing haven't said better.

> 'It may be suffocating to live in philistine suburbia, but *Babbit* has already been written and anyone who wants to flay his own community for spiritual inertia has to reckon with the fact.
>
> 'Hal Porter (*The Letter Writer*) at least manages to inject some comic effects into his denunciation, although I think that he merely makes disgust disgusting . . . But there is some literary skill in his contribution, which there isn't in Peter Cowan (*Top Executive*) or Elizabeth Harrower (*The Beautiful Climate*).
>
> 'The supposedly sharp vision simply isn't compatible with sentences which dully mark time, like "He was a difficult man, for what reason no-one had been able to discover, least of all Hector Shaw himself", nor with pomposity like "there were the whole house and grounds for us to utilize" (why not *use*) and "we engaged in philosophical dialogue that usually left at least one participant with his brain aglow . . .?" nor with the false Biblical simplicity of "and there was that about it which he did not understand".
>
> 'This insensitive use of stale words and syntax is matched by a flat, complacent unoriginality in the situations and ideas of the stories. Even if one wishes to make the point that life is often banal (as *Top Executive*, for example, apparently sets out to do) one shouldn't use banality as a literary weapon.'

Hope finds that H. P. Heseltine's *Australian Image* is less embarrassing but suspects that almost any Australian university lecturer in English could do as well. Of Chris Wallace-Crabbe's piece on Melbourne he says:

> 'Most of the *New Statesman's* "Out of London" series have covered much more ground, and gone much deeper, in less space.

'Once again the language is tired and slack, the sort of thing that would fit very easily into a Chamber of Commerce handout: "Always a city with good restaurants, Melbourne is now profusely served with eating houses, small and large, expensive and cheap, catering for all nationalities and tastes."

'This journalistic quick response affects thought as well as style: "the city's traditionally cold heart is thus surrounded by the ebb and flow of Mediterranean life" is silly thinking as well as silly writing, since it doesn't begin to scratch the surface of the problems involved.'

Hope thinks the poetry is generally rather better but there are 'some feeble items such as David Martin's *The Poetic Prevalence of Nuns*, a joke which doesn't come off and certainly goes on too long'.

And so apparently does J. R. Rowland (*Canberra in April*) 'who has only a little to say although it is perhaps worth saying, and at half the length might make some impact'.

Geoffrey Dutton (*The Smallest Sprout*), he says, begins and ends well but produces some very prosaic lines. Douglas Stewart (*The Pea Hen*) is neat but is another one who squeezes his idea dry by writing too much.

He likes some of the work of Rosemary Dobson, Charles Higham and Bruce Dawe, but finds faults in each. Dawe's *The Last Word* he describes as 'one of those unmemorable poems that come into any literary magazine in shoals'. The same goes for Francis Webb, David Campbell, Vincent Buckley, Max Harris and R. D. FitzGerald; they have a few sharp phrases, not very much command of pace or rhythm, and leave the reader feeling 'is that all?'

Having praised the 'individual and memorable' voices of A. D. Hope, Judith Wright and James McAuley (although the latter's contribution is a little bit of froth), he concludes that the poems would make a thin anthology.

'It would hardly appeal to a wide market of ordinary readers if there's nothing, apart from Judith Wright, that begins to measure up to the standards of expatriate Australians (like Peter Porter) but it wouldn't be any sort of literary disgrace.

'I am afraid I can't say the same about the prose. Once again the expatriates (Colin McInnes, for example, or *London Magazine* critics like Charles Osborne and Alan Seymour) have done much better; but also, in this case, there are fewer contributions which reach even an acceptable mediocrity, and the cumulative effect of the bad ones is disastrous.'

So there it is. If Francis Hope is to be taken seriously—and the assistant editor of the *New Statesman* must surely be taken very seriously—all of us (excepting Judith Wright) must up and off to London WC1 to get into the quality class.

In the meantime all Australia's critics and readers have been wildly mistaken in esteeming Peter Porter as only in the average pack of poets; in adjudging Alan Seymour to be about as feeble a critical writer as they come; in not considering Charles Osborne at all, and in thinking of Colin McInnes as an English journalist pure and simple.

McInnes's facile ubiquity, it will be remembered, gave rise to the proud claim in *Private Eye* that it was the only journal in Britain never to have featured dreary articles by said McInnes.

The outcome of all this is that Geoffrey Dutton has sent the whole correspondence and the reader's report to the authors to let them know how lousy their standards are. Explosive noises can be heard from Brisbane to Hobart, from old Bob FitzGerald down to young Bruce Dawe.

And Morris West's Society of Authors has been called to action stations. There has been no mention of payment to the invited, accepted, and now rejected authors.

# THE PUBLIC SEVERITY
# AND
# PRIVATE SINCERITY
# OF PATRICK WHITE

Thirty Years! And every one of them spent with and among Australia's writers.

I am tempted to sketch in my impressions of them as people. A public engagement of the reader with the personal identity of the writer is not an exercise in voyeurism or popularism. Very often, some understanding of the writer adds a further dimension of understanding to the writings.

I must begin with the hardest bit, Patrick White, because he will thank me least and perhaps punish me longest. He is Australia's greatest writer. He is also considered the most implacably remote. It is even fashionable to describe him, from the cold areas of exclusion, as 'patrician', and thereby imagine the man has been absorbed into a single word.

Patrick White has an overt contempt for journalists, newspapers, public occasions, and the whey-faced idiot box. One has to admit there are solid grounds for this 'noli me tangere'. On those occasions in earlier years when he did offer personal communication at the level of the mass media, the experience proved more degrading than salubrious. And Patrick White doesn't forget easily.

But this doesn't make him 'patrician' any more than the piercing severity of his eyes, his slowness to speak, his considered but throw-away side comments prove he has adopted a wilful theory of Brechtian 'distancing' between himself and other people.

At first meeting, he has the appearance of a person who is making his judgments about you and who gives no hint of what those judgments are likely to be. This judicial and cynical public face is nothing more than wariness, insecurity, uncertainty about the intentions of people and an assessment of the potential mutual gain that may emanate from establishing some human relationship.

Patrick White doesn't suffer fools and phonies gladly. He takes some pains to avoid them. If this is patrician behaviour, then it is of a reasoned, considered and humane order.

Within his domestic context, Patrick White is anything but stand-offish. He has a real passion for people and a clearly evident delight in social intercourse. He cooks superbly, entertains with an unaffected natural warmth, and is a clear believer in the graces of good conversation of the social as against the over-intellectualised order.

It is impossible to categorise his circle. He is not disposed to concentrate his relationships among those who share his literary profession, although he does not eschew writers, painters or musicians.

If anything, the writer is reflected in the man in his delight in women of defined and liberated personality—the exuberant and uninhibited Zoe Caldwell is an immediate example that springs to mind. Few writers anywhere have created characters reflecting a vital, rounded female identity better than Patrick White, from Mrs. Lusty in *The Ham Funeral* onwards.

But White does not draw on his acquaintances in any way whatsoever to delineate his fictional characters.

This, I think, stems from a remarkable facet of White's intellectual equipment, the only piece of literary equipment he shares with Hal Porter; and that is an all-embracing and yet remarkable idiosyncratic memory recall. Years later, after a single night as a guest in someone's house, he is able to recall names, poodles, objects, clothes, occasions, gestures.

White's personal genius possibly lies in his ability to command a vast area of experimental details that are lost to most of us. In consequence, he is able, when he writes, to establish a wholly credible and yet completely 'created' world of characters and spiritual undertones. White is lucky enough not to need to pinch from his own autobiography. It is for this reason he is not a 'researcher'.

This fact has led to some hilarious gaucheries on the part of academic critics who have, at appalling risk, played the game of 'spot the influences'. A solemn journal study was devoted to the influence of certain T. S. Eliot ideas on Patrick White. It was a matter of fact and historic chance that Patrick had never quite got round to taking a look at T. S. Eliot's poetry.

I could scarcely believe that of the Leichhardt literature, including the source material. In fact, the one and only 'trigger' for *Voss* was, I think, Chisholm's *Strange New World*.

Over coffee and brandy, conversation does not turn on any analysis of White's past creations, nor gratuitous details of his present projects. There is no literary egotism about the man, although he will freely discuss the trials and tribulations of the writing profession. But the hellishness of the writing process itself is rigidly demarcated from the relaxation of normal civilised social intercourse.

Patrick White sweats his novels out, and he sweats them out under the additional burden of uncertain health; he suffers chronic and recurrent bouts of asthma. I have never known him to talk over the immediate substance of his literary preoccupations, to articulate about the pessimistic, often wayward, and yet ultimately humane vision of human affairs which provides the nucleonic centre of everything he writes.

Patrick White, on the surface of life, is the ordinary man—admirable, civilised, likeable, testy, angry, acid, clear and high-minded in his critical judgments, but not predictable in those judgments. He finds his own opal patch wherever he finds it.

His Achilles heel is the hypersensitivity which is common to most intensively creative people. Ignorant, misinformed, inferior criticism from people with inferior critical resources gnaws at his vitals.

But there is an unusual quality to White's vulnerability to philistinism, offrontery, and intellectual barbarism. Again, his sensitivity is a side product of his being a man for whom creative writing achievement, his own or anyone else's, can't be a matter for the snap judgments of any Joe Blow who cares to assume the critical stance.

Patrick White accepts, in all good humour, that I have made my own public judgments on the relative merits of his own plays. But he reacted violently to the review of a Christina Stead novel in *Australian Book Review*, held me editorially responsible for choosing a reviewer who was out of sympathy with Christina Stead's literary intentions, and cancelled his subscription.

The prevalence of amateurishness, indifference, wrong-headedness and plain aesthetic second-rateness are at the heart of his continuing love-hate relationship with the Australian context. Fortunately for Australia, this same love-hate context occurs in almost every cultural environment in which he finds himself.

The dichotomy of feeling in the man is not, as so many have claimed, a product of intolerance towards the common citizenry, towards Sarsparilla.

When he returned to Australia, he acquired an apricot-painted timber house at Castle Hill, Sydney. There he probably found the denizens of Sarsparilla, but towards them he directed a witty and affectionate glance of amusement wherever he found people who were real and individual people.

It is another, and completely positive thing, that he loathes the conformist dehumanisation of urban life. The world we have come to inhabit provides good reasons for hate and some occasions for love.